Continuous Delivery for Mobile with fastlane

Automating mobile application development and deployment for iOS and Android

Doron Katz

BIRMINGHAM - MUMBAI

Continuous Delivery for Mobile with fastlane

Content Contributor: Kyle Mew
Commissioning Editor: Kunal Chaudhari
Acquisition Editor: Isha Raval
Content Development Editor: Jason Pereira
Technical Editor: Rutuja Vaze
Copy Editor: Safis Editing
Project Coordinator: Sheejal Shah
Proofreader: Safis Editing
Indexer: Rekha Nair
Graphics: Jason Monteiro
Production Coordinator: Deepika Naik

First published: February 2018

Production reference: 1270218

Published by Packt Publishing Ltd.
Livery Place
35 Livery Street
Birmingham
B3 2PB, UK.

ISBN 978-1-78839-851-0

www.packtpub.com

To my father, Angelo, for his inspiration and direction in molding what my career has become from pursuing computer science and falling in love with programming from an early age. To my wife, Serena, for her infinite patience throughout the late nights spent writing this book, and being the candle light of my life.

– Doron Katz

`mapt.io`

Mapt is an online digital library that gives you full access to over 5,000 books and videos, as well as industry leading tools to help you plan your personal development and advance your career. For more information, please visit our website.

Why subscribe?

- Spend less time learning and more time coding with practical eBooks and Videos from over 4,000 industry professionals

- Improve your learning with Skill Plans built especially for you

- Get a free eBook or video every month

- Mapt is fully searchable

- Copy and paste, print, and bookmark content

PacktPub.com

Did you know that Packt offers eBook versions of every book published, with PDF and ePub files available? You can upgrade to the eBook version at `www.PacktPub.com` and as a print book customer, you are entitled to a discount on the eBook copy. Get in touch with us at `service@packtpub.com` for more details.

At `www.PacktPub.com`, you can also read a collection of free technical articles, sign up for a range of free newsletters, and receive exclusive discounts and offers on Packt books and eBooks.

Foreword

Being an iOS developer for the last 6 years, I have spent a lot of time dealing with code signing, preparing localized screenshots, and doing manual deployments. After working on my first Ruby on Rails application, I saw how easy the release of software could be, so I decided to build fastlane.

fastlane solves all of the problems around iOS tooling that larger mobile development teams experience as they grow—automatic building, code signing, screenshots, push certificates, and others. Before fastlane, most companies maintained their own shell scripts, resulting in breaking builds every other month due to changes in the Xcode build system.

In this book, Doron gives an introduction to fastlane, and how you can use it to optimize your mobile development process. While fastlane offers documentation online, this book is a great resource to get started with mobile app automation using fastlane. Doron did a great job going through the available fastlane features and how you can make use of them.

Felix Krause - Founder of *fastlane*

Contributors

About the author

Doron Katz, originally from Sydney, Australia, completed his bachelor's in internet science (the University of Wollongong), before pursuing a master's in management (Charles Sturt University), including a certification in Microsoft Solutions Development.

On moving to San Francisco, Doron has worked with various companies, from start-ups to larger organizations, as a software engineer and project manager. Additionally, he is a regular contributor to various distinguished technical publications and has published numerous white papers and also coauthored *Developing an iOS Edge*.

I'd like to thank my father, Angelo, for inspiring me to be my best and pursue the technical path I eventually took; my mother for being so strong and inspirational; my wife, Serena, for being a source of support for me; and finally, Felix Krause, for authoring such a great tool in fastlane, supporting me, and writing the foreword for this book. I'd also like to thank Kyle Mew for his contribution to the content of the book.

About the reviewers

Dario started his career as an iOS developer in Rome, the eternal city, when he was 20. The context he liked most and which helped him to grow was working on the instant messaging platforms context with MONK software.

After four years in Rome, he realized he needed to be surrounded by a more international environment. Almost one year ago, he joined Tictrac, a London-based start-up that helps people to take care of themselves by providing health advice.

He loves travel, rock music, pasta, and red wine.

Muhammad Ali Ejaz currently works as a software development engineer at Amazon. His experience ranges from working as a developer to cofounding a start-up, to serving in outreach organizations, to giving talks on CI/CD at various prestigious conferences. His passion for computer science is reflected in his contributions to open source projects, such as GoCD and his role as a volunteer computer science teacher for underprivileged kids.

When he is not coding, he enjoys traveling, reading, and tasting new cuisines. You can follow him on Twitter using the handle `@mdaliejaz`.

> *I want to thank my Mom and Dad, who have always been my inspiration. I'd also like to thank Ahmad and Sana, my siblings, who have been a constant source of cheerful support. A lot of what I am today is because of them.*

Amit Kothari is a full-stack developer based in Melbourne, Australia. He has more than 12 years, experience in designing and developing software systems, and has worked on a wide range of projects across various domains, including telecommunication, retail, banking, and finance.

Amit is also the coauthor of the book—*Chatbots for eCommerce: Learn how to build a virtual shopping assistant.*

Packt is searching for authors like you

If you're interested in becoming an author for Packt, please visit `authors.packtpub.com` and apply today. We have worked with thousands of developers and tech professionals, just like you, to help them share their insight with the global tech community. You can make a general application, apply for a specific hot topic that we are recruiting an author for, or submit your own idea.

Table of Contents

Preface

While working for a start-up in San Francisco, as an iOS developer, I've had the arduous recurring task of having to gather all the coding contributions from my fellow colleagues, run some tests, and package the project for the stakeholders and beta testers to test, find bugs, patch, and re-distribute.

Finally, when we get to the green-light stage, we package the application once again for publication to the App Store, update the metadata, update or add new screenshots, and so forth. Of course, with start-ups growing as rapidly as they do, so do the size of their development teams, which leaves you having to spend time on-boarding the new team members and setting up their environments with provisioning profiles and certificates.

Having your attention and focus diverted from your primary goal of feature development bug fixing in order to deal with repetitious application-delivery tasks is certainly frustrating, which is what inspired me to investigate ways to automate this process.

We already implement regression testing in an automated manner, through continuous integration, so there should be a way of being able to automate the process of packaging our apps, pushing them to TestFlight or the App Store, and dealing with provisioning our apps. Introducing *fastlane*...

Who this book is for

fastlane is a powerful Ruby-powered toolchain that empowers iOS (and Android) developers to automate the process of delivery through what is called **continuous delivery**. If your passion is for developing workflows that automate the process of building and packaging your apps for distribution, without having to deal with provisioning and other code-signing processes, this book is for you.

This book is primarily targeted at mobile developers (iOS primarily), although we will be touching on some tools that Android developers can take advantage of. This isn't a Swift or Objective-C book, and you will certainly be able to follow with just some basic mobile development skills, although we will be working a lot in the command line as well as Apple's Developer portal and iTunes Connect. Some knowledge of how apps are built, provisioned, signed, and distributed will be helpful, but we will also be introducing a lot of the basic concepts in each of the chapters.

What this book covers

Chapter 1, *Introduction to fastlane and Continuous Delivery*, is an introduction to the fastlane toolchain, and why you should adopt continuous delivery as part of your workflow.

Chapter 2, *Setting Up fastlane and Our Sample Project*, sets you up for the rest of the chapters by guiding you through setting up and installing fastlane and the sample project.

Chapter 3, *Manage Provisioning Profiles with sigh*, covers how to manage provisioning profiles manually via Xcode and how to leverage fastlane to automate the process of provisioning your apps using sigh.

Chapter 4, *Manage Code Signing Certificates with cert*, explains how to work with developer and production certificates using Xcode, and how to leverage fastlane to automate the process of certifying your apps using cert.

Chapter 5, *Sync Profiles and Certificates with match*, covers how to improve your certificate and provisioning workflows leveraging match, making it easier for you to on-board new developers and share the right code-signing credentials to get that developer started right away.

Chapter 6, *Manage Push Notification Profiles with pem*, discusses how to manage push notification profiles manually, and automate your workflow using fastlane and pem.

Chapter 7, *Creating Our iOS and Android Apps with produce and supply*, goes through how to easily create your app on iTunes Connect and the Developer portal via terminal and produce, by using fastlane, or by creating an Android app on the Google Play Store using Supply.

Chapter 8, *Build and Package Apps for the App Store with gym*, explains how to build and package your apps the traditional way using Xcode, and how to leverage gym as part of your fastlane continuous delivery workflow to automate building and packaging your apps.

Chapter 9, *Distribute to Testers with TestFlight and Crashlytics*, covers how to add continuous delivery distribution to your testers using TestFlight and Crashlytics within fastlane.

Chapter 10, *Review Your App Metadata with precheck*, explains how to automate the process of reviewing your app for red flags using precheck prior to uploading your app to the App Store for review.

Chapter 11, *Taking Localized Screenshots with snapshot*, tells you how to automatically generate screenshots of your apps for iTunes Connect using snapshot.

Chapter 12, *Put Our Screenshots inside Frames with frameit*, discusses how to prettify your screenshots by putting them inside frames using fastlane's frameit action.

Chapter 13, *Upload Screenshots and Metadata with deliver*, explains how to deliver your generated and prettified screenshots automatically to iTunes Connect, as part of your fastlane workflow, using deliver.

Chapter 14, *Automate Unit Tests with Scan*, covers how to include automated testing as part of your fastlane workflow and continuous delivery goals using scan.

Chapter 15, *Integrating Git into the fastlane Workflow*, discusses how to leverage the industry-leading Jenkins CI within your fastlane workflow in order to integrate continuous delivery with continuous integration for a completely robust, agile, end-to-end system workflow.

Chapter 16, *Creating and Using fastlane Action Plugins*, explains how to make use of some powerful Git commands within fastlane in order to build an intimate relationship between your code repository and your continuous delivery workflow.

Chapter 17, *Integrating Slack into the fastlane Workflow*, covers how to enrich and empower your fastlane continuous delivery workflow by leveraging system and third-party action plugins.

Chapter 18, *Continuous Delivery Best Practices*, explains how to leverage the popular communications platform Slack to inform your development team as part of your continuous delivery workflow.

Appendix, *Configurations, Tools, and Resources*, contains tips on how to make the most of fastlane through best practices and anti-patterns.

To get the most out of this book

You are encouraged to follow the examples sequentially, from Chapter 1, *Introduction to fastlane and Continuous Delivery*, to the final chapter, using the sample project and code.

The Chapter 2, *Setting Up fastlane and Our Sample Project*, covers setting up your environment, installing fastlane, and any other prerequisite tools.

You will also need to have an active Apple Developer account, which you can get from developer.apple.com.

Download the example code files

You can download the example code files for this book from your account at www.packtpub.com. If you purchased this book elsewhere, you can visit www.packtpub.com/support and register to have the files emailed directly to you.

You can download the code files by following these steps:

1. Log in or register at www.packtpub.com.
2. Select the **SUPPORT** tab.
3. Click on **Code Downloads & Errata**.
4. Enter the name of the book in the **Search** box and follow the onscreen instructions.

Once the file is downloaded, please make sure that you unzip or extract the folder using the latest version of:

- WinRAR/7-Zip for Windows
- Zipeg/iZip/UnRarX for Mac
- 7-Zip/PeaZip for Linux

The code bundle for the book is also hosted on GitHub at https://github.com/ PacktPublishing/Continuous-Delivery-for-Mobile-with-fastlane/tree/master. In case there's an update to the code, it will be updated on the existing GitHub repository.

We also have other code bundles from our rich catalog of books and videos available at https://github.com/PacktPublishing/. Check them out!

Conventions used

There are a number of text conventions used throughout this book.

CodeInText: Indicates code words in text, database table names, folder names, filenames, file extensions, pathnames, dummy URLs, user input, and Twitter handles. Here is an example: "Open Client.xcodeproj in Xcode, then switch to the Fennec scheme."

A block of code is set as follows:

```
export_options(
  method: "ad-hoc",
        provisioningProfiles: {
    "com.doronkatz.firefox": "Provisioning Profile Name"
  },
  manifest: {
    appURL: "https://yourapp.com/yourapp.ipa",
  },
  thinning: "<thin-for-all-variants>"
)
```

Any command-line input or output is written as follows:

```
fastlane init
```

Bold: Indicates a new term, an important word, or words that you see onscreen. For example, words in menus or dialog boxes appear in the text like this. Here is an example: "You are also able to create new signing identities from this dialog screen by selecting the **Create** button."

Warnings or important notes appear like this.

Tips and tricks appear like this.

Get in touch

Feedback from our readers is always welcome.

General feedback: Email feedback@packtpub.com and mention the book title in the subject of your message. If you have questions about any aspect of this book, please email us at questions@packtpub.com.

Errata: Although we have taken every care to ensure the accuracy of our content, mistakes do happen. If you have found a mistake in this book, we would be grateful if you would report this to us. Please visit www.packtpub.com/submit-errata, selecting your book, clicking on the Errata Submission Form link, and entering the details.

Piracy: If you come across any illegal copies of our works in any form on the Internet, we would be grateful if you would provide us with the location address or website name. Please contact us at copyright@packtpub.com with a link to the material.

If you are interested in becoming an author: If there is a topic that you have expertise in and you are interested in either writing or contributing to a book, please visit authors.packtpub.com.

Reviews

Please leave a review. Once you have read and used this book, why not leave a review on the site that you purchased it from? Potential readers can then see and use your unbiased opinion to make purchase decisions, we at Packt can understand what you think about our products, and our authors can see your feedback on their book. Thank you!

For more information about Packt, please visit packtpub.com.

1
Introduction to fastlane and Continuous Delivery

Welcome to the first chapter in *Continuous Delivery for Mobile with fastlane,* as we begin our exciting journey of making our lives as developers more efficient. Before we begin to dive deeper into all the powerful tools that make up *fastlane,* we will first talk about what *fastlane* is, giving you a high-level introduction to the suite of tools that make up this powerful toolset, and explain why you need them.

This chapter will serve a segue into the subsequent chapters of this book, offering a broad understanding of what the *fastlane* suite of tools consists of before we start setting up our project and *fastlane* environments.

Welcome to *fastlane*

As mobile developers, we constantly strive for efficiency, optimizing our code base through refactoring, proper code decoupling, intelligent code reusability, and other object-oriented best practices. These are even more pivotal when working in teams, working with tools like `Git` for collaborative code sharing, and tracking tasks using agile methodologies.

For project managers, being able to mitigate risks, reduce risks, and quantify development is pivotal to a project's success. This is what has led to the umbrella concept of Continuous Development, which encompasses the iterative methodologies of **Continuous Integration (CI)** and continuous deployment and delivery.

Development is a complicated domain in and of itself, and through rapidly introducing new code authored by different developers, the risk of introducing bugs is extremely likely. Besides the obvious errors, regression issues can many times be masked into future iterations, only to be discovered later, when technical code commitment is deeply entrenched.

Automation testing

Continuous Delivery (**CD**) and **Continuous Integration** (**CI**) have emerged as an industry standard in order to instill confidence in each iteration of code change. Tool automation relies on *automation testing*, which is broken down into several types of testing and testing categories:

- Unit testing
- Regression testing
- Integration testing
- Acceptance testing

Unit testing

Unit testing is the lowest level of testing, whereby the developer asserts a set of conditions that need to be true, as well as some that should be false and should essentially be very narrow and well-defined in scope. For instance, developers would assert what should happen when a text field has no input or when special characters are inputted, and will test various other constraints of the text field.

Regression testing

Regression testing is a type of testing that is written to address a bug and ensure that the bug will not occur again in the future. It will, therefore, be tested in future builds, and new tests will be added on top to ensure that those tests pass perpetually, providing the same outcome.

Integration testing

Integration testing is performed across various realms or containers to ensure that in a decoupled environment, a code is fit into a bigger piece with another bit of code, and to make sure the integration is successful.

Acceptance testing

Acceptable testing is not an automated test but is rather manual testing that is done by the product owner to ensure the feature is implemented correctly. The testing is not done based on code/component isolation, but as a complete use case, end-to-end, from a user's perspective.

This kind of test falls under continuous delivery, which we will be discussing later in this chapter, whereby the business/product team must assert whether a feature has been implemented correctly for it to be a candidate for production release.

CI is the practice of having developers continuously (several times a day) integrate code into a shared `Git` repository, triggering an automated build that will regressively verify the integrity of the latest code commit. We will take a look at what CI and CD are next.

Continuous Integration

CI serves to detect errors in the entire code base early on through the frequency of code integration by developers, whereas having significant gaps between integrations will result in more masked and complex errors accumulating.

CI entices developers to commit *early and frequently*, integrating the code commits into shared code repositories daily, or even hourly, instead of building features and code in isolation to integrate them when the feature is complete. Committing frequently and early adds greater transparency and the ability for other developers to access new code and catch potential issues early on. It solicits opinions, debates, and testing in a more agile manner, and reduces merge conflicts; or, at the very least, it discovers conflicts early on.

Through development strategies such as **GitFlow** (`https://www.atlassian.com/git/tutorials/comparing-workflows`), teams appoint a team member who will review code rapidly, prior to it being pushed into the main development branch where an automated test tool picks up the latest code and tests for regression issues.

Prominent CI tools widely used in the industry include **Jenkins** (`https://github.com/jenkinsci/jenkins`), **CircleCI** (`https://circleci.com/about/`), Atlassian's **Bamboo** (`https://www.atlassian.com/software/bamboo`), and **TravisCI** (`https://github.com/travis-ci/travis-ci`), which ideally perform the part of either detecting new commits as they come into a branch or working at daily/hourly intervals and performing an automated build, as well as running predefined test cases. The outcome of these tests is composed in a CI report that details the result of the build, as well as all the test cases.

The key term is *automation,* the use of tools to automate testing and delivery continuously, reducing the possibilities for developers and testers to cause errors.

In the later chapters of the book, we will demonstrate how to integrate *fastlane* into a development-CI workflow with Jenkins. Now, we will take a look at CD.

Continuous Deployment

Continuous Deployment, according to `Agile Alliance`, is the philosophy of minimizing *the time lapse between development writing one line of code and the new code being used by live users in production.* In fact, it can be considered an extension of CI.

CI reduces risk through automated bug discovery (unit testing and regression testing); Continuous Deployment reduces risk by being able to distribute the product to alpha and beta testers more frequently, to obtain feedback more quickly.

That is, teams will benefit from being able to solicit earlier feedback and test hypotheses more rapidly through Continuous Deployment, which affords practices such as A/B beta testing. Reducing lead time reduces the risk of the unknown that comes with assumptions.

To achieve Continuous Deployment, the team relies on infrastructure that automates and instruments various steps leading to deployment so that after each integration successfully meets the release criteria, the live application is updated with new code.

Instruments and processes, such as CI, which we just mentioned, provide the process and mechanism for continuously pushing code to a centralized repository branch, triggering an automated CI build to test for any regression concerns.

What is continuous delivery?

Continuous delivery is commonly mistaken with CD; however, they are distinct differences, despite sharing commonalities. CD implies that every change is deployed to production continuously, whereas continuous delivery implies that the team ensures every change can be deployed to production but may opt not to. The distinction is the ability to filter or omit a change from production. This is usually due to business reasons (release timing). Take a look at the following diagram:

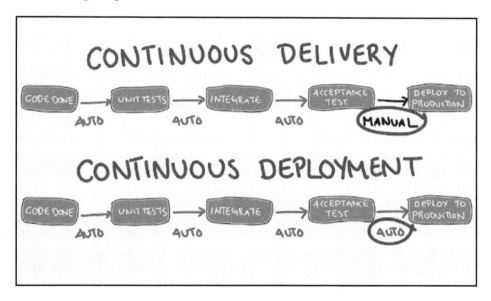

Figure 1: Family of tools that are part of *fastlane* (Source: fastlane.tools)

Like Continuous Deployment, continuous delivery focuses on automation tools in order to promote code from the shared code repository into distribution to beta testers or production. The code is picked up from a branch that should always be in a deployable state, gets built through CI, and is subsequently deployed using CD. Continuous delivery is the business choice to promote beta features into production manually.

This doesn't mean that the feature is not delivered to beta testers; in fact, it is more common that the feature makes it to the beta testers as well as a business team to decide on the timing of the release. It is also based on other factors, such as if the code been well-tested, with the decision left to the product owner.

Benefits of CI, delivery, and deployment

The benefits of CD and CI include the following:

- **Lower-risk releases**: By being able to constantly release software internally and externally, the risk of long-term and hard-to-detect errors/issues is low.
- **Quality releases**: Through automation tools, more automated testing, CD, and CI, developers gain the benefit of being less prone to errors. *Unit testing* and *regression testing* ensure that the code is more soundly built.
- **Respond to market faster:** Releasing frequent small changes, to not only testers but even production, allows for **User Experience** (**UX**) and other feature feedback to be given more continuously, allowing for the project to pivot more quickly. This reduces the cost of having to change a larger set of features through a commitment to less code prior to feedback.

This is where CD comes in, along with *fastlane,* with the ability to orchestrate code that has been tested by delivering app iterations rapidly to beta testers, and subsequently, to end users in production. Next, you will learn what *fastlane* is and how it helps to automate the tasks of packaging and distributing your app, providing greater transparency and removing barriers to deploying your app more continuously.

What is *fastlane*?

fastlane can be simply described as *the easiest way to automate building and release your iOS and Android apps,* via a suite of tools that can work either autonomously or in tandem to accomplish tasks such as:

- Automation of building and packaging iOS apps producing `.ipa` files
- Automation of taking screenshots of your app across different screen types, sizes, and languages
- Automation of uploading the screenshots and metadata and the packaged files to iTunes Connect directly, bypassing Xcode

- Automation of and management of refreshing, renewing, repairing, and managing signing certificates, provisioning profiles, and push notification profiles
- Synchronization and sharing of your certificates and profiles efficiently across to other team members
- Automation of managing and onboarding testers using your app, through TestFlight
- Automation of running tests for your app

The benefit of leveraging one or more *fastlane* actions is in your ability to save hours and even days, saving you the laborious task of having to submit, provision, and take screenshots manually, and instead allowing you to focus on what matters: that is, feature development. This is the mantra of Continuous Deployment and CD—the ability to code and release iteratively and rapidly, with minimal barriers. This is what *fastlane* is.

You also won't need to remember and call the individual *fastlane* actions individually; by using a Fastfile configuration file, you can store the actions in the sequence you want, under a grouping you can define and label, such as `alpha testing`, and call all the actions that belong to that grouping.

fastlane was the brainchild of Felix Krause (`https://krausefx.com/`), developed and open sourced on **GitHub** (`https://github.com/fastlane/fastlane`) back in 2014. After achieving a cult-like following by indie developers and eventually becoming mainstream and being used by thousands of companies, in late 2015, *fastlane* was acquired by Twitter (`https://krausefx.com/blog/fastlane-is-now-part-of-fabric`) as part of Twitter's Fabric development suite (`https://fabric.io/login?redirect_url=%2Fhome`). Just over a year later, in early 2017, Fabric itself was acquired by Google (`https://krausefx.com/blog/fastlane-is-joining-google`), as part of Google's Firebase mobile development platform (`https://firebase.google.com/`), and the author moved to Google. Despite the project moving to Twitter and then Google, it very much remains an open source and active project.

fastlane is a Ruby-powered configuration file, called a `Fastfile`, grouped by lanes to serve different purposes and needs. For instance, you have a lane for deploying to the App Store, from which you have specific tasks, called actions, that you want to accomplish, such as incrementing your build number as you build your app, running actions such as cocoapods installment, running tests, taking screenshots, and uploading your app and associative metadata to the App Store. Take a look at the following code snippet:

```
lane :beta do
# Increment build number in XCode
  increment_build_number
# Build your app
  gym
# Upload to TestFlight
  testflight
end
lane :appstore do
  increment_build_number
# Run cocoapods install
  cocoapods
# Run tests
  scan
# Take screenshots
  snapshot
# Provisioning
  sigh
# Upload app, screenshots and meta-data
  deliver
# Run your own custom script
  sh "./customScript.sh"
  ...
# Notify your contacts on Slack
  slack
end
```

As shown in the preceding Fastfile code snippet, you would have another lane for the beta, to beta test your app and run through the automated tasks (actions) you would associate with beta testing, from incrementing your build count to building your app and pushing it to TestFlight. Of course, you could plug in other third-party tools, such as pushing to Fabric instead of TestFlight, as we will demonstrate in later chapters.

The real power of *fastlane* is in its extensibility, its ability to integrate with all of your familiar existing tools; there are currently over 170 custom actions (`https://docs.fastlane.tools/actions/`), according to the official website, with the ability to integrate with all major CI systems, such as Jenkins, which we will cover in later chapters.

Why *fastlane*?

Over the years, iOS developers have come to appreciate the pain that comes with interacting with the App Store, iTunes Connect, and the Apple developer portal. The manual process of having to go into the portal in order to deal with provisions profiles and to hand a new team member access to code sign the app frustrates the best of developers.

Updating the App Store screenshots each time the app's UI changes and each time a new iPhone or iPad screen size is introduced is laborious, especially when the screens have to be done for each locality (English, German, French, for instance).

Deploying the app to testers, and subsequently out to the App Store itself, is another cumbersome set of tasks that developers will often hesitate or drag their feet at. To deploy a new app to beta testers, developers have to go through the process of having to increment the app's bundle version number, push a new version back to `Git`, code sign the app with a valid provisioning profile, generate an IPA file, and then deploy it to TestFlight.

This is what makes *fastlane* a quintessential tool for the iOS developer; it breaks down the mental and physical barriers to CD through simple commands that, when grouped into lanes, allow not only developers but even less savvy technical folks to trigger a set of actions that accomplishes all of the preceding actions with minimal fuss. Reducing the cost of ownership by allowing any developer (or non-developer), as opposed to depending on one centralized subject-matter expert, means there are fewer bottlenecks.

The *fastlane* suite of tools

fastlane consists of the following family of tools, for both iOS and Android:

Figure 2: Family of tools that are part of *fastlane* (Source: Fastlane.tools)

In brief, the *fastlane* tools accomplish the following automations:

- **gym**: Automates building and packaging of your iOS apps, generating `ipa` files
- **deliver**: Uploads screenshots and metadata, as well as `.ipa` files to iTunes Connect directly, without having to manually do so via Xcode
- **snapshot**: Automates taking screenshots of your app for different screen types/sizes, devices, and languages
- **pem**: Takes the hassle out of refreshing and renewing push notification profiles
- **sigh**: Takes the hassle out of provisioning your app and device
- **produce**: Automatically creates your iOS app on iTunes Connect and the dev portal, without the need to enter it manually on the website
- **cert**: Automatically maintains iOS code signing certificates
- **pilot**: With boarding, makes managing your TestFlight testers and builds easy, right from the Terminal
- **match**: Helps in syncing and sharing your certificates and profiles with other team members
- **scan:** Makes running automated tests on your apps a great deal more convenient

Furthermore, there are numerous custom actions that integrate with familiar tools you already have as part of your workflow, such as:

- Slack
- Cocoapods
- Gradle
- Crashlytics
- Git
- IFTTT
- Jenkins CI
- SSH

Spaceship under the hood

The suite of tools that *fastlane* provides are all due to Spaceship (https://github.com/fastlane/fastlane/tree/master/spaceship#readme), a framework that directly connects with the Apple developer center through APIs via HTTP, rather than previously *scraping* Apple's web services. This increases the speed of all the *fastlane* tools tremendously; in fact, it speeds up over 90% of actions, as it bypasses the overhead involved with loading images and other unnecessary assets not pertinent to the tasks at hand. The following is the logo of Spaceship:

The Spaceship is a Ruby library that exposes the Apple developer center and iTunes Connect API. It's superfast, well-tested, and supports all of the operations you can do via the browser.

Spaceship even handles authentication (including 2-factor authentication) with Apple's servers securely, storing the result in the user's local folder privately. You can try out Spaceship in Xcode Playgrounds by typing in `fastlane spaceship` (you will need to install `pry` first by typing in `sudo gem install pry`). Take a look at the following screenshot:

```
[5] pry(#<Spaceship::Playground>)> app = Spaceship.app.create!(bundle_id: "com.doronkatz.sampleApp", name: "Spaceship App")
=> <Spaceship::Portal::App
        app_id="3HZ5D83T9B",
        name="Spaceship App",
        platform="ios",
        prefix="UU98N6FWB5",
        bundle_id="com.doronkatz.sampleApp",
        is_wildcard=false,
        features={"push"=>true, "inAppPurchase"=>true, "gameCenter"=>true, "passbook"=>false, "dataProtection"=>"",
"homeKit"=>false, "cloudKitVersion"=>1, "iCloud"=>false, "LPLF93JG7M"=>false, "IADS3UNK2F"=>false, "V66P55NK2I"=>f
alse, "SKC3T5S89Y"=>false, "APG3427HIY"=>false, "HK421J6T7P"=>false, "WC421J6T7P"=>false},
        enable_services=["gameCenter", "inAppPurchase", "push"],
        dev_push_enabled=false,
        prod_push_enabled=false,
        app_groups_count=nil,
        cloud_containers_count=nil,
        identifiers_count=nil,
        associated_groups=nil>
[6] pry(#<Spaceship::Playground>)>
```

In the preceding playground screenshot, we created a new app called **Spaceship App**, by trying out a Spaceship command. Consult the Spaceship documentation by typing `docs` in Playground, and you can find some more recipes you can try directly on here. However, as with most, you won't need to work with Spaceship directly, as *fastlane* will appropriately facade a lot of the tasks through simpler actions, but it is useful to look a little under the hood and see how the *fastlane* engine works.

Accessing the *fastlane* documentation

Before we begin working with *fastlane,* it's important to point out where you can access the *fastlane* documentation. Make sure you bookmark **docs.fastlane.tools** (`https://docs.fastlane.tools/`) for future reference, as well as the project GitHub page at `github.com/fastlane/fastlane`, as they will both no doubt come in handy throughout this book as we work on our project. In particular, the following sub-sections will prove especially useful throughout this book:

- **docs.fastlane.tools/actions**: A list of built-in *fastlane* actions. You can also type `fastlane actions` in the Terminal to get a list of all the pre-built actions and their associated details, right in the Terminal.
- **docs.fastlane.tools/codesigning/getting-started**: A quick reminder page on how to work with provisioning profiles and certificates.
- **docs.fastlane.tools/plugins/available-plugins**: A list of all available plugins, some troubleshooting for popular plugins, and guidance on how to create your own plugins.

Additionally, you can also check out sample *fastlane* setups (`https://github.com/fastlane/examples`) from other companies, which you can refer to as you learn more about what each of the lanes and actions does and understand *fastlane* in greater detail.

Summary

In this chapter, you got an introduction to what *fastlane* is, as we mentioned the suite of tools that make up the toolchain. Additionally, we introduced you to the concepts of CI and CD and why they are quintessential to contemporary development teams.

In the next chapter, we will start to set up our environment by creating our project in Xcode and an initial setup of *fastlane*.

2
Setting Up fastlane and Our Sample Project

In the previous chapter, we got a bird's-eye view of what *fastlane* (https://docs.fastlane.tools/) is, along with all the actions that it encompasses. In the next chapter, we will begin to explore each action in isolation in greater detail, but before showing you how you can include *fastlane* as part of the toolchain, and rather than describe its abstract functionality, this chapter will explain the concepts in context through real-life scenarios.

We will project the narrative of you being in a start-up, working on a real-life app, which is in fact, a popular open source app, **Firefox for iOS** (https://github.com/mozilla-mobile/firefox-ios). We will be referring to this code base and app throughout the book to illustrate how you, as a developer, will vastly enhance your development environment and workflow through the use of *fastlane*.

The rest of this chapter will be dedicated to:

- Setting up your computer with Xcode command-line tools, and any prerequisite software
- Downloading the Firefox for iOS (https://github.com/mozilla-mobile/firefox-ios) code from the GitHub repository
- Setting up *fastlane* over the top of our project

Installing the Xcode command-line tools

The first thing we are going to do is make sure you have your Xcode command-line environment set up. You should already have Xcode installed, but we will need its associative command-line tools because of the **GCC compiler** (https://en.wikipedia.org/wiki/GNU_Compiler_Collection).

 It is assumed that you have macOS Sierra installed, but if not, it will most likely work with older versions, though this is not guaranteed.

First, make sure you have the latest version of Xcode installed, which is Xcode 8 at the time of writing, by going to the App Store and seeing if any updates are available. Next, let's see if you already have the full Xcode package installed by typing the following in a Terminal:

```
$ Xcode-select -p
```

If you get back the full path to your `Developer` folder, as follows, you are already set and have the full Xcode package installed:

```
$ /Applications/Xcode.app/Contents/Developer
```

If not, let's get the latest version of the Xcode command-line tools by typing the following in a Terminal:

```
xcode-select --install
```

You should get a prompt similar to the following:

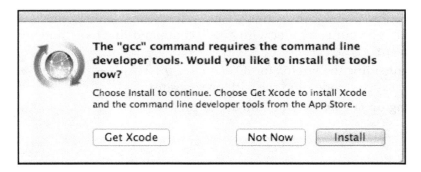

Alternatively, you could also manually download the Xcode command-line tools by going to **Xcode** | **Preferences** and then the **General** tab, and select **Downloads**.

In the **Downloads** window, you should then choose the **Components** tab and select the **Install** button:

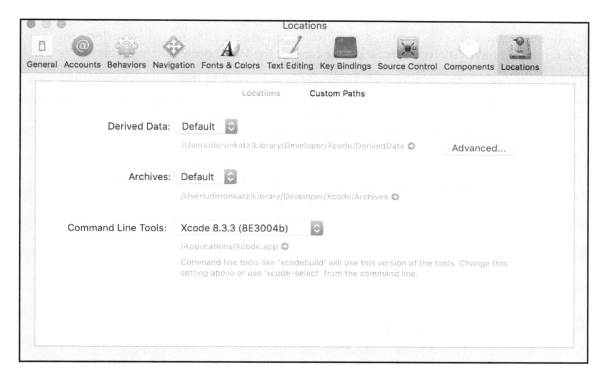

Installing Homebrew, Git, and *fastlane*

Homebrew (`https://brew.sh/`) is a powerful package manager that opens the gateway for you to install hundreds of open source tools, one of which will be Git, as well as *fastlane*. To install Homebrew, type the following on the command line:

```
/usr/bin/ruby -e "$(curl -fsSL https://raw.githubusercontent.com/
```

It should prompt you a couple of times, including entering your password to provide permissions to install on various paths. When you have finished installing Homebrew, the final line of the prompt suggests that you update your Homebrew, which is a good practice to do regularly, so go ahead and run the following:

```
next:brew doctor
```

Presuming you haven't encountered any errors, you are ready to install your first brew app, **Git**; but if you have received errors, please consult the Homebrew documentation.

If you don't already have Git installed on your system, type in the next line; otherwise, you can skip this step:

```
brew update \ brew install git
```

To confirm that Git has installed successfully, verify by typing `git --version`.

Next, we will install *fastlane*, which you can do either via Homebrew or, if you prefer, via a Ruby gem, as follows:

```
sudo gem install fastlane -NV
```

With the preferred way, via brew, you can install as follows:

```
brew cask install fastlane
```

Alternative methods of installing *fastlane*

While using **brew** is the easiest method for installing *fastlane*, there are indeed other methods as well. The first is to download the `.zip` file directly, at `https://download.fastlane.tools/`, and then run the install script in a Terminal.

You can also install *fastlane* directly via **RubyGems** (`https://rubygems.org/`), by typing the following in the Command Prompt:

```
sudo gem install fastlane -NV
```

Updating *fastlane*

In this book, we are working with *fastlane* 2.44.1. You can verify which *fastlane* you are currently on by typing:

```
fastlane --version
```

To easily update *fastlane* when a new version is available, you can enter the following command:

```
sudo gem update fastlane
```

Installing Carthage

One last thing before we start working on setting up our project is to install **Carthage** (`https://github.com/Carthage/Carthage`), a dependency manager for allowing libraries and frameworks to be added to our Xcode project. Once more through Homebrew, we will install Carthage using the following:

```
brew install carthage
```

Troubleshooting common problems

Of course, there will be times when installing won't go smoothly due to the nature of the various environments developers work on, different operating systems, and gem versions.

Setting up our project – Firefox for iOS

Before we set up *fastlane*, we will need a project to set it up over. As we will be working with others on Firefox for iOS, now that we have Git installed, let's grab the code. We will first fork the application code into our own repository; so in your browser, go to `https://github.com/mozilla-mobile/firefox-ios` and select the **Fork** button in the top-right corner.

> You will need to have your own GitHub account and be logged in to be able to fork a repository.

Once you've forked the Mozilla project into your own repo, pull the code from the master branch as follows (note—replace with your GitHub username from the forked repository):

```
git clone https://github.com/<your-user-name>/firefox-ios
```

Before we can build the app, we will need to pull in all the project dependencies, so navigate inside the project folder in the Terminal and type the following:

```
sh ./bootstrap.sh
```

Take a look at the following screenshot:

```
*** Cloning Fuzi
*** Cloning ios_sdk
*** Cloning libPhoneNumber-iOS
*** Cloning EarlGrey
*** Cloning sentry-cocoa
*** Cloning onepassword-extension
*** Checking out Deferred at "35b8927c1b94ce074e10793c57e1f80d0e2227fa"
*** Checking out Fuzi at "1.0.1"
*** Downloading EarlGrey.framework binary at "EarlGrey 1.9.0"
*** Checking out EarlGrey at "1.9.0"
*** Checking out Alamofire at "4.3.0"
*** Checking out GCDWebServer at "3.3.2"
*** Downloading ios_sdk.framework binary at "CPU family and min iOS version"
*** Checking out JSONSchema.swift at "1c052b83baa8c497e12cde6a8afca0f54574612f"
*** Checking out KIF at "v3.5.1"
*** Downloading Leanplum-iOS-SDK.framework binary at "Leanplum iOS SDK 2.0.1"
*** Checking out libPhoneNumber-iOS at "0.9.2"
*** Checking out onepassword-extension at "a614e290396346e3cb69e4951656eb8033390
*** Checking out readability at "ccc8e9bf4c5400814d9b7a3ea83c21540da4c76f"
*** Checking out SDWebImage at "3.7.4"
*** Downloading sentry-cocoa.framework binary at "3.0.3"
*** Checking out SnapKit at "3.1.2"
*** Checking out SwiftRouter at "2.0.0"
*** Checking out SwiftKeychainWrapper at "3.0.1"
*** Checking out SwiftyJSON at "3.1.4"
*** Checking out XCGLogger at "Version_4.0.0"
```

For curiosity's sake, you can take a look at the Carthage file (`Cartfile`) to see a list of frameworks this project uses at https://github.com/mozilla-Mobile/firefox-ios/blob/master/Cartfile.

For the purpose of this book, we won't be going beyond any operational instructions on Carthage, but you are encouraged to learn more about Carthage by consulting their official documentation at `https://github.com/Carthage/Carthage`.

Running Firefox for iOS

So far, we've installed the necessary tools, forked the Firefox for iOS project into our own repository, and pulled in the project dependencies. To make sure everything is set up and working in your environment, let's build and run the project by opening up the `Client.xcodeproj` project file in Xcode. Open `Client.xcodeproj` in Xcode, then switching to the Fennec scheme. The first file you will see is the `Cartfile`, which is a dependency management file used by Carthage (`https://github.com/Carthage/Carthage`). The following code refers to the various third-party libraries the project takes advantage of:

Provided there are no compiler errors, you can build and run the project, and if everything runs smoothly, you should see the following running in your simulator:

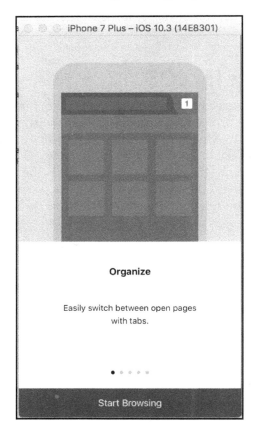

Configuring *fastlane*

Great; we now have the team's project running smoothly on our computer, and we are ready to start contributing code. Realizing that our team's workflow isn't exactly efficient, we are going to take some initiative and introduce *fastlane*. In order to convince the rest of the team that this tool will change their world, we are going to first set it up over our forked project and demonstrate rather than theorize.

To initialize *fastlane*, in your project folder, simply type in the following:

```
fastlane init
```

The prompt will ask you for your Apple ID so that you can hook into iTunes Connect seamlessly through the command line. After you've gone through all the prompt questions, *fastlane* will create a `fastlane` directory and fetch all of your app metadata from iTunes Connect.

 You will need to ensure your Apple ID has been given the correct permissions to access the app your team is working on in the Apple developer portal.

The primary file we will be concerned with throughout this book is `fastlane/Fastfile`. The `Fastfile` will contain all of the actions you will be dictating in order to distribute your app as part of the continuous deployment. In the next chapter we will start working with provisioning profiles, but for now, we will stop and commit our code and take stock of what we've accomplished. Type in the following to commit your code:

```
git commit installation of skeleton fastlane Fastfile
```

Updating *fastlane*

fastlane gets updated quite frequently, and since under the hood it relies on connecting to Apple APIs, it is generally a good idea to keep your *fastlane* updated. To update *fastlane*, in the command line, enter the following:

```
fastlane run update_fastlane
```

You should see something like this:

```
[21:34:29]: -----------------------------
[21:34:29]: --- Step: update_fastlane ---
[21:34:29]: -----------------------------
[21:34:30]: Looking for updates for fastlane...
[21:34:34]: Updating fastlane from 2.41.0 to 2.44.1...
[21:35:26]: Finished updating fastlane
[21:35:26]: Cleaning up old versions...
[21:35:37]:
[21:35:37]: Please help us test early releases of fastlane by opting into
nightly builds
[21:35:37]: Just replace your `update_fastlane` call with
[21:35:37]:
```

```
[21:35:37]: > update_fastlane(nightly: true)
[21:35:37]:
[21:35:37]: Nightly builds are reviewed and tested just like the public
releases
[21:35:37]:
[21:35:37]: fastlane.tools successfully updated! I will now restart
myself...
[21:35:38]: ----------------------------
[21:35:38]: --- Step: update_fastlane ---
[21:35:38]: ----------------------------
```

Summary

This chapter provided you with the foundations for setting up your environment, along with the sample project we will be working from, Firefox for iOS (https://github.com/mozilla-mobile/firefox-ios), cloned and running on your machine. We went through a brief explanation of some of the tools we will be using alongside *fastlane*, such as Carthage (https://github.com/Carthage/Carthage) and Homebrew (https://brew.sh/).

This is the last of the introductory chapters, as we are now well on our path toward becoming efficient continuous deployment contributors and helping our fictitious team deploy earlier, more rapidly, and more efficiently. In the next chapter, we are going start solving real-life problems and using *fastlane* to create and maintain provisioning profiles with a sigh.

3
Manage Provisioning Profiles with sigh

Introduction

With a brief introduction to *fastlane* in the first chapter, along with setting up our environment and project in the subsequent chapter, we are now ready to work on effectively contributing to the **Firefox for iOS** (`https://github.com/mozilla-mobile/firefox-ios`) project, having just joined the team.

The first thing we will need to do after getting access to a project is to make sure our provisioning profiles are set; a manual and cumbersome process to have to deal with, especially when working in teams and onboarding new members. It has no doubt caused a lot of sighs from developers, which brings us to our first lane, appropriately named **sigh** (`https://docs.fastlane.tools/actions/sigh`).

The objectives of this chapter are to work through the problems of creating, downloading, renewing, and repairing provisioning profiles (`https://developer.apple.com/library/content/documentation/IDEs/Conceptual/AppStoreDistributionTutorial/CreatingYourTeamProvisioningProfile/CreatingYourTeamProvisioningProfile.html`).

We will first briefly discuss what team provisioning profiles are, as well as how to create a team provisioning profile the traditional way.

We will then introduce you to the first lane in our toolset, sigh, and how the lane will save you time, through the Terminal, to work through the various common problems associated with provisioning profiles.

Finally, we will demonstrate how developers like you can automate these processes by integrating the lane into our `fastFile` as part of our workflow working for the Firefox for iOS mobile project.

The following skills will be learned in this chapter. We will be working with a sigh through the command line to:

- Create a new provisioning profile
- Download the provisioning profile
- Renew and repair the provisioning profile
- Integrate the lane into our project Fastfile

Development distribution overview

Before this chapter goes into what provisioning profiles are, it is important to understand how an app is distributed at a high level. The Member Center, or developer portal, as this book refers to it, is a paid developer program that developers enroll in to be able to gain the privilege to distribute apps to devices for testing, as well as for publishing to the App Store.

The following diagram illustrates the path a developer takes in three phases:

- Enroll
- Develop
- Distribute

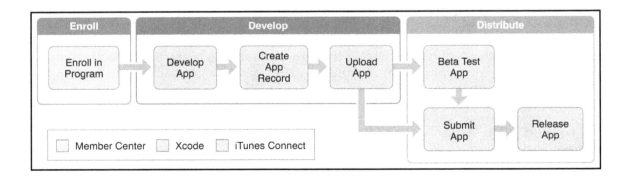

Enrollment

The first thing a developer will need to do is enroll in the **Apple Developer Program** (`https://developer.apple.com/programs/`), paying a nominal yearly fee of $99 USD. In return, Apple provides the developer with access to the developer portal and iTunes Connect. Enrolled developers also gain access to the latest beta releases of Xcode, as well as pre-release iOS operating system releases, before the public has access.

Developers have three types of memberships (`https://developer.apple.com/support/compare-memberships/`) that they can then opt for:

- Individuals
- Organizations
- Educational institutions

Individuals

As individuals, this program is suited for those who are single/sole-proprietors and will be selling apps on the App Store using their personal names.

Organizations

This falls into two sub-categories, the first of which is a standard organization that trades under a company/organizational name on the App Store and is required to provide a D-U-N-S number.

The second is the *Enterprise Program*, for apps that are proprietary and used exclusively internally within a large organization, without needing to be published in the App Store.

Educational institutions

This tier is a *free-tier*, for universities and other institutions that are looking to advocate for, and teach, iOS in classrooms. The following chart from Apple compares the various tiers and their benefits, as well as resources:

	Sign in with Apple ID	Individual	Organization	Enterprise Program
Xcode Developer Tools	●	●	●	●
Xcode Beta Releases	●	●	●	●
Developer Forums	●	●	●	●

	Sign in with Apple ID	Individual	Organization	Enterprise Program
Bug Reporter	●	●	●	●
Test on Device	●	●	●	●
Beta OS Releases		●	●	●
Advanced App Capabilities		●	●	●
App Store Distribution		●	●	
In-house App Distribution				●
Safari Extensions		●	●	
Developer ID		●	●	●
Technical Support Incidents		●	●	●
Team Management			●	●
TestFlight Beta Testing		●	●	
App Analytics		●	●	
Cost	Free	99 USD*	99 USD*	299 USD**
Requirement	13+	18+	DUNS Number	DUNS Number

Develop

Next, in the sequence, the developer will develop his or her app on Xcode. Simultaneously, the developer should create the app record on **iTunes Connect** (`https://itunesconnect.apple.com/login`), with the associated app ID that will match the bundle ID Apple will have associated to the project in Xcode. The developer will at some stage upload the app to iTunes Connect in order to distribute the app.

During the create-app record, the development provisioning profiles and associated development certificates are generated, which this chapter will discuss in greater detail.

Distribute

Finally, after uploading the app to iTunes Connect, the developer will either use his or her existing development profile and certificate to distribute the app to beta testers or will generate a production certificate and App Store provisioning profile to submit the app for review by Apple and subsequently release to the App Store.

For more information, including a checklist on the workflow described, refer to Apple's official documentation at `https://developer.apple.com/library/content/documentation/IDEs/Conceptual/AppDistributionGuide/Introduction/Introduction.html`.

This chapter will focus on provisioning profiles, with the following chapter looking at creating certificates.

What are provisioning profiles?

As a seasoned developer, you are no doubt quite familiar with provisioning profiles. When you create a new app through Xcode, entering the various project information, Xcode will create the signed team provisioning profiles that will give you the ability to run the app on your devices, as opposed to just on the Xcode simulator.

The anatomy of a provisioning profile is composed of:

- App ID (such as `com.packt.yourapp`)
- Your signing certificate, which was issued by Apple (more on this in the following chapters)
- List of device UDIDs that are sanctioned to run your app
- Special entitlements, such as CloudKit, Push Notifications, and HealthKit

Take a look at the following screenshot:

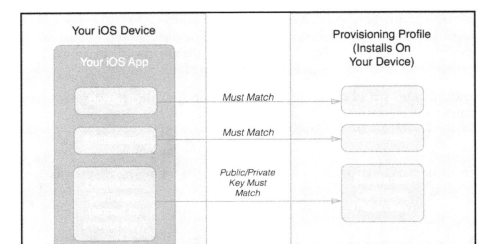

Think of provisioning profiles as a special *hall pass*, or permission, that Apple grants you to run your apps on your physical iOS devices for development testing purposes; and not just on your device, but distributing your .ipa file across to other testers. Without provisioning profiles, developers are restricted to conducting their testing and debugging solely through the Xcode simulator.

Provisioning one's app is essentially associating (or provisioning) the devices that can run the app, along with the aforementioned entitlements, resulting in a provisioned profile that is subsequently downloaded from the developer's developer portal account and installed on the developer's device. It is then signed upon the app being compiled by a private key contained within the developer's certificate, ensuring integrity through matching the private and public keys. Take a look at the following diagram:

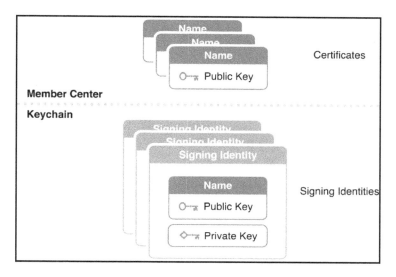

When Xcode compiles and builds the app, it seeks the development certificate which contains the associative public key from the developer account (**Member Center**), and then matches it with the signing identity certificate which contains both the private and public keys from the developer's keychain.

Apple places great importance on code signing apps to ensure that they are not tampered with, from the developer's account to the end users' devices, so if the information that was signed doesn't match, the app will not be able to be installed by the end user for security reasons. That is, it provides assurances that:

- The app is from a known source
- It has not been modified since it was last signed

While the certificate is used for code signing, which will be covered in the next chapter, essentially, certificates use the provisioning profiles to deliver code signing for different types of app distributions, which we are going to discuss next.

About Bundle IDs

Specified in Xcode when creating a new project, the Bundle ID is the single identifier of that app, used for provisioning devices and associating services such as CloudKit with that app, and is written in reverse-DNS formats, like `com.packt.firefox`. The **Bundle ID** identifies your app in various places besides Xcode, such as in **iTunes Connect**, to match the **App ID** registered in the developer portal and in certain services such as **iCloud container ID**, or to prefix in-app purchasing identifiers. Refer to the following diagram:

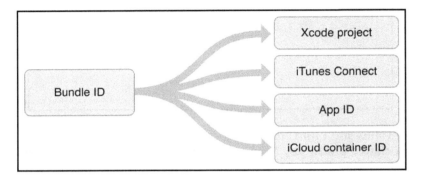

Types of provisioning profiles

There are four types of provisioning profiles that developers need to be aware of:

- The development team provisioning profile
- The ad hoc provisioning profile
- The App Store provisioning profile
- The Enterprise provisioning profile

The development team provisioning profile

The most straightforward way to create a provisioning profile is, in fact, done automatically. Xcode creates and manages a type of development provisioning profile called a team provisioning profile, which affords all team members the ability to sign and run an associated app, with Xcode taking care of all the configuration steps to add the intended entitlements and services that are required for the app. Under the hood, Xcode will still create the certificates and developer provisioning profiles in the developer's development account. Take a look at the following diagram:

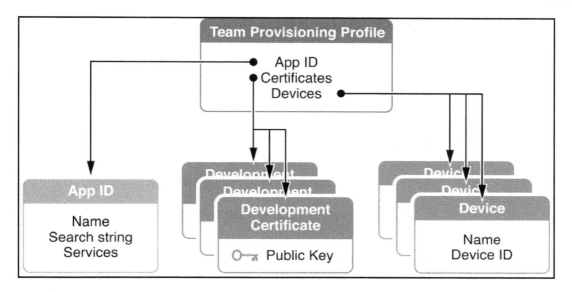

In the preceding diagram, the team provisioning profile matches the App ID, the associative development certificate that each team member possesses, and the list of devices provisioned, as we discussed earlier.

Ad hoc provisioning profile

Similar to the development provisioning profile, ad hoc profiles can be distributed to beta testers but can only be created with a production certificate, not a developer certificate. The distinguishable differences are in how you test your app.

With the previous provisioning profile, you would test with test entitlements, such as the Development Push Notification Certificate, whereas with the production-signed ad hoc provisioning profile, you would test your app using production entitlements.

App Store provisioning profile

Unlike other platforms such as Android, and short of jailbreaking one's iOS device, Apple ensures that all apps are appropriately signed prior to being distributed to test end users during the beta or publishing to the App Store. It's a strict policy that Apple enforces and all developers adhere to.

When, as a developer, you have tested your app using the development (and perhaps ad hoc) provisioning profiles, you are ready to publish your app to the App Store. This profile does not require any test UDID* devices, but rather, through the submission process, has Apple re-sign your app using their own signing certificate. App Store provisioning is used instead to verify the originator of the app, which is you, prior to Apple approving.

Enterprise provisioning profiles

There is one other provisioning profile: the Enterprise provisioning profile. Similar to ad hoc in nature, apps don't eventually get distributed to the App Store, but rather, through the **Enterprise channel** (https://developer.apple.com/programs/enterprise/). That is, apps are distributed within the organization rather than publicly through the App Store, and all signing is managed in-house as well.

Additionally, it is worth noting that you would require a separate and distinct program, the Apple iOS **Developer Enterprise Program** (https://developer.apple.com/programs/enterprise/), in order to distribute your app in-house, such as to other staff members, bypassing the App Store.

Expiration of provisioning profiles

Development provisioning and ad hoc have a shelf life, or rather, have an expiration date dependent on the associative developer certificate, which expires after 12 months, preventing the app from running on the previously-provisioned devices. The developer would, therefore, need to request a new development certificate in order to create a new development provisioning profile, and, prior to using sigh, it would need to be done manually via the developer portal.

Introducing sigh

Armed with an understanding (or recap) of what provisioning profiles are and how they work, let's introduce the first lane, sigh (https://docs.fastlane.tools/actions/sigh). Sigh takes the process we mentioned in the previous section, that of creating a developer provisioning profile, and, simply put, makes the process more straightforward and automated. The following is the logo of sigh:

sigh (`https://docs.fastlane.tools/actions/sigh`) will help you create, download, and repair provisioning profiles through the command line, bypassing Xcode and/or the Apple developer portal, supporting development, ad hoc, Enterprise, and App Store provisioning profiles. As the official website outlines, sigh will, in fact, support the following tasks that would otherwise be mundane and in many cases laborious:

- Downloading the latest provisioning profile for your app
- Renewing a provisioning profile when it has expired
- Repairing a provisioning profile when it is broken
- Creating a new provisioning profile if it doesn't exist already
- Supporting App Store, ad hoc, and development profiles
- Supporting multiple Apple accounts, storing your credentials securely in the keychain
- Supporting multiple teams
- Supporting Enterprise profiles

With this book focusing on CD, sigh fits right into the developer's workflow, with the ability to integrate it easily into Jenkins or other popular CI tools, which we will cover in the later chapters of this book.

Usage

In its simplest usage form, you summon sigh by typing the following, including your app bundle identifier and username:

```
fastlane sigh -a com.acme.Firefox -u username
```

To specifically generate a development profile, we would enter:

```
fastlane sigh --development</strong>
```

For downloading and installing all of your provisioning profiles (development, ad hoc, App Store), you would type:

```
fastlane sigh download_all
```

There are additional advanced features you can do with sigh:

- `--skip_install`: Generates a profile but skips the installation of the profile
- `--skip-certificate_verification`: Skips verification of the code signing identity
- `--force`: Renews the provisioning profile, regardless of whether it's imminently expiring
- `--c CertificateName`: Allows you to forego the default approach of including all development profile certificates and instead set a specific certificate
- `repair`: As its namesake indicates, repairs all of your existing provisioning profiles which are either invalid or expired
- `resign`: Allows you to apply a different code signing identity to an existing `.ipa` file

List of sigh commands

Finally, you can get a list of all the available parameters and commands for a sigh by entering:

```
fastlane sigh --help
```

Our project problem

With what we've just learned, let's create a development provisioning profile for our Firefox for iOS project. At this stage, we are assuming there aren't any provisioning profiles created, so we will go ahead and create one. But first, we will need to register our own App ID to associate with our provisioning profiles. Our Firefox project already has an App ID, but for the purposes of this book, we will be creating our own so that we will have the access we need for our project, as shown in the following screenshots:

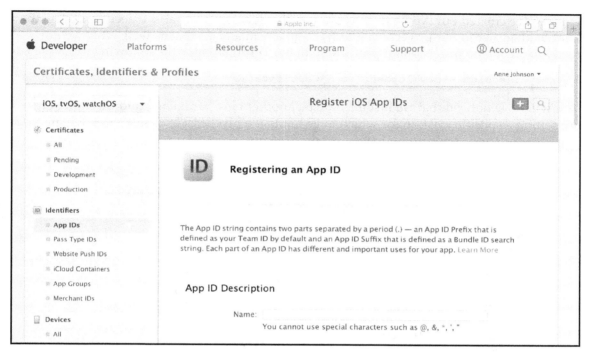

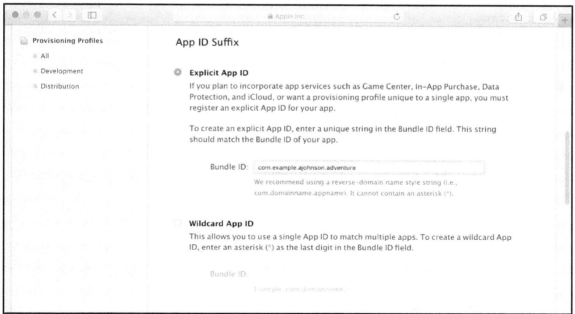

Once we've created our Apple ID in iTunes on the developer portal, we need to update the bundle identifier in our project via Xcode, so go ahead and do that as well. Now we are ready to create the provisioning profiles, so in the Terminal, type the following:

```
fastlane sigh --development -o ~*Certificates
```

You will have noticed that we just introduced another new parameter, and through -o, we are setting a specific location for which to generate the profiles. Go ahead and navigate to that directory and confirm you have your profiles and certificates set:

```
$ fastlane sigh --development -o ~*Certificates

+----------------------------------------+------------------------+
|                  Summary for sigh 2.41.0                        |
+----------------------------------------+------------------------+
| development                            | true                   |
| adhoc                                  | false                  |
| skip_install                           | false                  |
| force                                  | false                  |
| app_identifier                         | com.dktz.firefox |     |
| username                               | dktz@mac.com           | f
| team_id                                | UU98N6FWB5             |
| ignore_profiles_with_different_name    | false                  |
| skip_fetch_profiles                    | false                  |
| skip_certificate_verification          | false                  |
| platform                               | ios                    |
+----------------------------------------+------------------------+

[15:06:55]: Starting login with user 'dktz@mac.com'
[15:06:57]: Successfully logged in
[15:06:57]: Fetching profiles...
[15:06:58]: Verifying certificates...
[15:06:59]: Found 1 matching profile(s)
[15:06:59]: Downloading provisioning profile...
[15:07:01]: Successfully downloaded provisioning profile...
[15:07:01]: Installing provisioning profile...
*Users*doronkatz*Certificates*Development_com.doronkatz.firefox.mobileprovi
sion
```

Now, let's manage our list of provisioning profiles installed locally by typing the following:

```
$ fastlane sigh manage
[15:05:54]: Loading Provisioning profiles from
~*Library*MobileDevice*Provisioning Profiles*
[15:05:56]: Provisioning profiles installed
[15:05:56]: Valid:
[15:05:56]: com.doronkatz.firefox Development
```

```
[15:05:56]: iOS Team Provisioning Profile: com.doronkatz.packt
[15:05:56]:
[15:05:56]: Expired:
[15:05:56]: com.acme.AdHoc
[15:05:56]: com.acme.onroad AppStore
```

The output will produce a list of all the valid profiles, as well as those that are expired. Quite powerful, isn't it? We didn't have to jump into any website or on Xcode; we can manage what we need to via the Terminal, quickly and efficiently. The real power, however, comes through our continuous deployment workflow, where we can include this as part of our Fastfile workflow.

Updating our Fastfile

So, with an empty Fastfile, let's start by creating our first lane, which we will label beta. We will be adding more actions to it later on, but for now, we are simply going to call sigh every time we run a beta deployment, ensuring our provisioning profiles are always current through the use of force. Enter the following into a new lane, then hit save. Make sure to remove any other lines in the :beta lane. Ignore any other lanes for now; we will get to them at a later stage. Refer to the following code snippet:

```
lane :beta do
  sigh(force: true)
end
```

And that's it! We started creating a simple but functional lane. We can test our very first lane by typing the following in a Terminal:

```
fastlane beta
```

The output should produce something similar to the following:

```
14:50 $ fastlane beta
[14:52:08]: ---------------------------------------------------
[14:52:08]: --- Step: Verifying required fastlane version ---
[14:52:08]: ---------------------------------------------------
[14:52:08]: Your fastlane version 2.41.0 matches the minimum requirement of
2.41.0 ✅
[14:52:08]: -------------------------------
[14:52:08]: --- Step: default_platform ---
[14:52:08]: -------------------------------
[14:52:08]: Driving the lane 'ios beta' 🚀
[14:52:08]: ----------------------
[14:52:08]: --- Step: carthage ---
```

```
[14:52:08]: ----------------------
[14:52:08]: $ carthage bootstrap
[14:52:12]: > *** Checking out Alamofire at "4.3.0"
[14:52:13]: > *** Checking out GCDWebServer at "3.3.2"
[14:52:14]: > *** Checking out Fuzi at "1.0.1"
[14:52:14]: > *** Checking out Deferred at
"35b8927c1b94ce074e10793c57e1f80d0e2227fa"
[14:52:14]: > *** Checking out JSONSchema.swift at
"1c052b83baa8c497e12cde6a8afca0f54574612f"
[14:52:14]: > *** Downloading ios_sdk.framework binary at "CPU family and
min iOS version"
[14:52:15]: > *** Downloading EarlGrey.framework binary at "EarlGrey 1.9.0"
[14:52:15]: > *** Checking out EarlGrey at "1.9.0"
[14:52:15]: > *** Checking out KIF at "v3.5.1"
[14:52:16]: > *** Downloading Leanplum-iOS-SDK.framework binary at
"Leanplum iOS SDK 2.0.1"
[14:52:17]: > *** Checking out libPhoneNumber-iOS at "0.9.2"
[14:52:17]: > *** Checking out onepassword-extension at
"a614e290396346e3cb69e4951656eb8033390f8c"
[14:52:18]: > *** Checking out SDWebImage at "3.7.4"
[14:52:18]: > *** Checking out readability at
"ccc8e9bf4c5400814d9b7a3ea83c21540da4c76f"
[14:52:18]: > *** Downloading sentry-cocoa.framework binary at "3.0.3"
[14:52:18]: > *** Checking out SnapKit at "3.1.2"
[14:52:19]: > *** Checking out SwiftKeychainWrapper at "3.0.1"
[14:52:19]: > *** Checking out SwiftRouter at "2.0.0"
[14:52:21]: > *** Checking out XCGLogger at "Version_4.0.0"
[14:52:21]: > *** Checking out SwiftyJSON at "3.1.4"
[14:53:34]: > *** xcodebuild output can be found in
*var*folders*68*946ywfgx3jq3bwhy02std9tc0000gn*T*carthage-
xcodebuild.G6gpmd.log
[14:54:01]: > *** Building scheme "Alamofire iOS" in Alamofire.xcworkspace
[14:55:45]: > *** Building scheme "Alamofire tvOS" in Alamofire.xcworkspace
[14:57:00]: > *** Building scheme "Alamofire macOS" in
Alamofire.xcworkspace
```

The sequence above relates to Carthage rebuilding again, but we didn't request that in our lane. The reason being, there is another lane in the Fastfile, which will run regardless of which lane we call upon:

```
platform :ios do
  before_all do
    ...
    carthage
  end
```

This is quite useful if we have common actions we always want to run, regardless of what lane we are triggering. At this stage, we are only running Carthage, but in later chapters we will enable Slack, among other actions that we will want to run in each *fastlane* build. When we run our Fastfile, we encounter an error. Take a look at the following code snippet:

```
15:00:18]: Starting login with user 'dktz@mac.com'
[15:00:20]: Successfully logged in
[15:00:20]: Fetching profiles...
[15:00:21]: Verifying certificates...
[15:00:21]: No existing profiles found, that match the certificates you
have installed locally! Creating a new provisioning profile for you
+--------------------+----------+
|           Lane Context        |
+--------------------+----------+
| DEFAULT_PLATFORM | ios       |
| PLATFORM_NAME    | ios       |
| LANE_NAME        | ios beta |
+--------------------+----------+
[15:00:22]: Could not find a matching code signing identity for type
'AppStore'. It is recommended to use match to manage code signing for you,
more information on https:**codesigning.guide.If you don't want to do so,
you can also use cert to generate a new one: https:**fastlane.tools*cert


+-------+----------------------------------------------+-------------+
|                      fastlane summary                              |
+-------+----------------------------------------------+-------------+
| Step  | Action                                       | Time (in s) |
+-------+----------------------------------------------+-------------+
| 1     | Verifying required fastlane version          | 0           |
| 2     | default_platform                             | 0           |
| ☀     | sigh                                         | 3           |
+-------+----------------------------------------------+-------------+

[15:00:22]: fastlane finished with errors

[!] Could not find a matching code signing identity for type 'AppStore'. It
is recommended to use match to manage code signing for you, more
information on https:**codesigning.guide.If you don't want to do so, you
can also use cert to generate a new one: https:**fastlane.tools*cert
```

We essentially don't have a certificate to code sign our app. We will rectify this in the next chapter, on **cert** (https://github.com/fastlane/fastlane/tree/master/cert#readme), which is sigh's counterpart for certificates.

Summary

In this chapter, we started working with our first action, sigh (`https://docs.fastlane.tools/actions/sigh/`), to help manage our provisioning profiles. We delved into the process for creating and managing the different types of provisioning profiles the traditional way, before embarking on using sigh (`https://docs.fastlane.tools/actions/sigh/`) to generate and refresh our profiles seamlessly through the Command Prompt.

Working through the different parameters we could pass, we finally created our first Fastfile lane, a beta that will form part of the beta distribution deployment strategy of our Firefox for iOS application, in addition to downloading our provisioning profiles. In the next chapter, we will walk you through managing certificates using the cert.

4
Manage Code Signing Certificates with cert

We were not able to complete our first task in the previous chapter using sigh (`https://docs.fastlane.tools/actions/sigh`), as we lacked a certificate to codesign. In this chapter, we will complete the circle through the use of a related action, cert (`https://docs.fastlane.tools/actions/cert`), which will help us in managing our code-signing certificates, and will complete our exercise from the previous chapter and code sign our app.

While match (`https://docs.fastlane.tools/actions/match`) is normally the most appropriate tool for developers to automate and share code-signing credentials, and while it takes care of all the required certificate and profiles, working with cert (`https://docs.fastlane.tools/actions/cert`) allows you to exercise greater control over the certification process with your apps, and this chapter will serve as an insightful way to understand how certification works.

What you will learn

This chapter focuses on certificates, primarily managing development and production certificates. Certificates go hand-in-hand with provisioning, and we will first understand what certificates are, then demonstrate how we would normally manually create and manage certificates, and finally, show how cert can help automate the process. In a later chapter, we will cover match (`https://docs.fastlane.tools/actions/match`), which is fastlane's recommended way of managing certifications, distributively.

Skills learned

The following skills will be learned in this chapter. We will be working with cert through the command line to:

- Check and verify if you have an existing certificate.
- Create a new private key and signing request.
- Generate, download, and install/import the certificate into your keychain.
- Integrate the lane into our project Fastfile.

What are certificates?

If you are familiar with certificates you can go ahead and skip this section, but for those who want to know a bit more about the mechanics of how certificates work, before we get started with how to use cert (`https://docs.fastlane.tools/actions/cert`), we will give a basic overview of what certificates are, as well as how they work with the provisioning profiles, which we covered in the previous chapter.

As mentioned in the previous chapter, code signing provides assurances to both Apple and the end users that the app has been untampered with. Through the combination of certifying and provisioning for either the App Store or to distribute via TestFlight, the app comes from the original developer and has not been compromised by the addition of malicious software.

When you distribute your app to the App Store, Apple, in fact, re-signs it with their certificate before reaching the App Store, and your code-signing signature is used to ensure integrity is maintained so that Apple can, in turn, provide customers assurance of integrity through its own (re)certification of your app.

This certification process is a certification of trustworthiness, so the only way a developer can distribute the app internally or publish externally is by code signing a new build (`.ipa`) and reprovisioning, along with the appropriate certificate, for each new build. This is the developer's unique signature or a digital thumbprint of assurance.

In the code-signing workflow, certificates are created and stored in the developer portal together with your public key, associated with the app identifier (bundle). An intermediate certificate issued by Apple (certificate authority) is also stored in the developer's keychain, and it usually comes installed automatically, along with Xcode.

The public and private key used to create the certificate, cryptographically hashed, are stored in the developer's keychain. In order to authenticate your unique signature, the following needs to happen in sequence:

1. The public key, stored locally on the developer's keychain, and the public key will need to match. This ensures the identification matches, as shown in the following diagram:

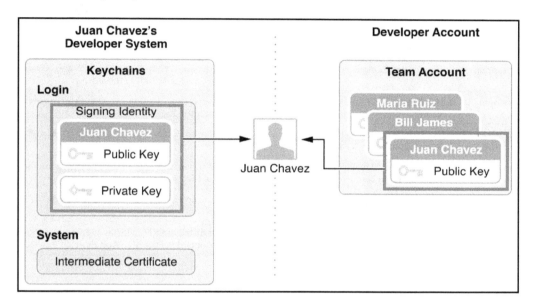

Developer and distribution certificates

There are two types of certificates that you will be working with the *development certificate* and the *distribution certificate*.

Development certificate

The *development certificate* associates an individual or team member to code sign an app with a development provisioning profile for beta-testing purposes. It identifies the person on your team and is used to run the app on your local physical device.

Distribution certificate

The *distribution certificate* identifies the team that will be in charge of distributing the app to the App Store, and the distribution certificate can be shared by team members that are provided with the appropriate permissions. There are a few types of *distribution certificates* that are used, as illustrated in the following table:

Certificate type	Certificate name	Description
iOS Development	iPhone Developer: Team Member Name	Used to run an iOS, tvOS, or watchOS app on devices and use certain app services during development.
iOS Distribution	iPhone Distribution: Team Name	Used to distribute your iOS, tvOS, or watchOS app on designated devices for testing or to submit it to the store.
Mac Development	Mac Developer: Team Member Name	Used to enable certain app services for a Mac app during development and testing.
Mac App Distribution	3rd Party Mac Developer Application: Team Name	Used to sign a Mac app before submitting it to the Mac App Store.
Mac Installer Distribution	3rd Party Mac Developer Installer: Team Name	Used to sign and submit a Mac Installer Package, containing your signed app, to the Mac App Store.
Developer ID Application	Developer ID Application: Team Name	Used to sign a Mac app before distributing it outside the Mac App Store.
Developer ID Installer	Developer ID Installer: Team Name	Used to sign and distribute a Mac Installer Package, containing your signed app, outside of the Mac App Store.

Source: Apple

Managing certificates manually

As a developer, you have two options when managing your certificates: from Xcode or via the developer portal.

Creating a certificate through Xcode

In Xcode, you are able to verify your certificates and provisioning profiles by going to **Xcode** | **Preferences** | **Accounts** and then selecting the team that corresponds to your account:

If you don't see your account, you may need to log in. Only users with the privileges of Agent or Admin are able to add signing identities.

You will then see a list of your provisioning profiles and certificates (sign-in identities), along with when they are set to expire. You are also able to create new signing identities from this dialog screen by selecting the **Create** button.

You can verify your signing certificates and provisioning profiles on the developer portal, which should match what you have on Xcode. Furthermore, if you choose to, you are also able to create your certificates through the developer portal, although it is a bit more cumbersome.

Creating a certificate through the developer portal

Through `https://developer.apple.com`, you will first need to upload a **Certificate Signing Request** (**CSR**). You will first choose the type of certificate (development or production) that you want to generate, as shown in the following screenshot:

For the trickiest part of the process, actually creating the CSR, you will need to open up keychain (located in /Utilities) and do the following:

1. Select **Keychain Access** | **Certificate Assistant** | **Request a Certificate** from a **Certificate Authority** from the drop-down menu.
2. Follow the rest of the steps, as shown in the following dialog box:

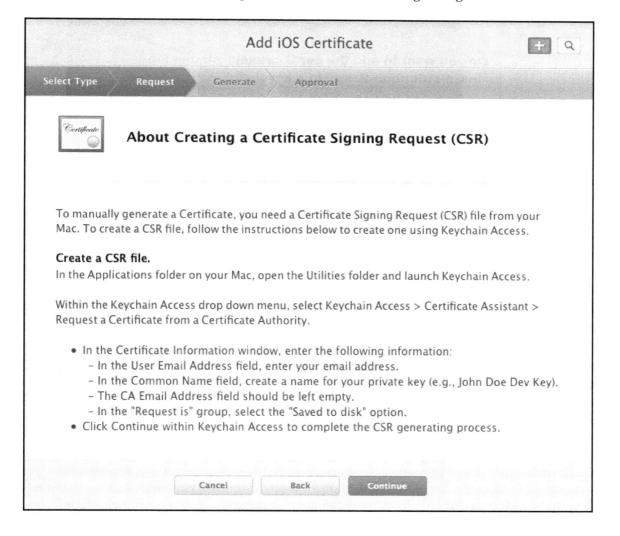

3. You will then be presented with a screen to download your certificate as a `.cer` file. You will need to ensure you back up this file somewhere, as it's critical you don't accidentally lose it.
4. You then double-click the `.cer` file to add the certificate to your **keychain**, as shown in the following screenshot:

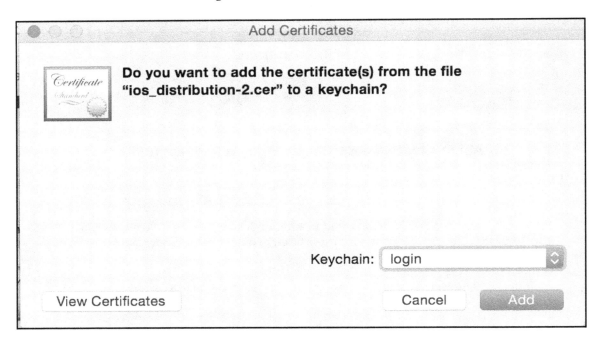

Verifying the private/public keys in keychain throughout this workflow, when using your certificate and provisioning profile, you need

The final piece is ensuring the developer's keychain has the appropriate private and public keys associated with the signing identities. When you either use Xcode or follow the steps on the developer portal to create a development or distribution certificate, you should automatically have the key pair installed on your keychain. You can verify that by going to **Keychain | login** and then selecting the category **Certificates**. Your certificates will be prefixed with the name `iPhone Developer...` or `iPhone Distribution...`, followed by your name, as illustrated in the following screenshot:

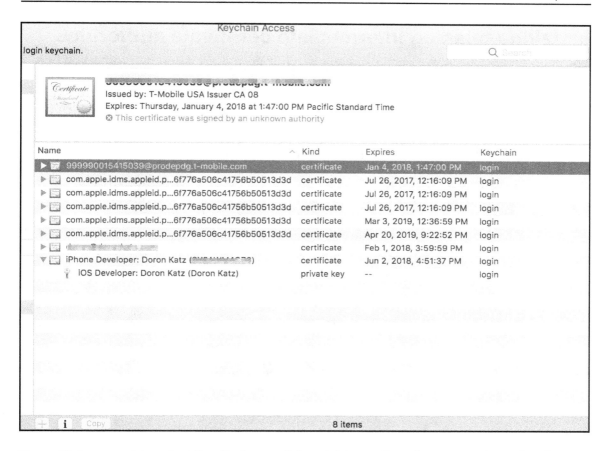

You will then need to select the disclosure (triangle) to confirm that your private key is listed below it; otherwise, you are missing your private key. When you have your certificates successfully installed, you are then able to associate them with a provisioning profile, as you had done in the previous chapter, and distribute your apps internally or publish them to the App Store. Next, we are going to introduce you to cert (`https://docs.fastlane.tools/actions/cert`) and how this action can work in concert with a sigh to automate your code-signing process.

Installing missing intermediate certificate authorities

Throughout this workflow, when using your certificate and provisioning profile, you need to have an active *intermediate certificate*, the *Apple Worldwide Developer Relations Certificate Authority*, in your keychain, which assures that the certificate was issued by a *trusted source*. This is usually installed when you install Xcode, but there may be a situation in which the intermediate certificate has accidentally been removed.

However, you are able to reinstall it again by doing the following:

1. Go to `http://www.apple.com/certificateauthority`, and under **Apple Intermediate Certificates**, click the link for the intermediate certificate you are missing.
2. You should have a `.cer` file downloaded in your `Downloads` folder. Double-click it to add it to your keychain, as shown in the following screenshot:

Recreating certificates

If your certificate happens to be invalidated, be it due to accidentally removing a private key in your keychain or a certificate being revoked or expired, the difficulty lies in that the collection of assets that encompass your *developer profile* resides both locally (on your Mac) as well as on the developer portal.

> Recreating your certificate (developer or distribution) doesn't affect the apps already submitted to the store, as far as your ability to update them is concerned. Nor does it affect your distribution or development provisioning profiles.

To recreate your certificate, first revoke your existing invalidated certificate, located in your developer portal, by going to the *Certificates, Identifiers, and Profiles* screen. Note that this will invalidate the associated provisioning profile/profiles.

If you have the code-signing identities in your keychain, you will need to remove those, too, by selecting the entry in your keychain and right-clicking and removing it. Then, create the certificate/certificates, as described in the previous section of this chapter.

Finally, you will need to regenerate and reassociate the provisioning profiles that belonged to the removed certificate with the new certificate, once again in the developer portal, and then finally, download the provisioning profile again, along with the certificate, and double-click to add them to your keychain. Next, we will show you how to back up your certificates and provisioning profiles.

Backing up certificates and provisioning profiles

A critical part of working with certificates and provisioning profiles is to ensure you always back up your *developer profile*, consisting of those important assets. If you happen to lose your certificate, you will need to create a new certificate and remove any broken/invalid certificates, a task which is certainly frustrating, as we just explained. To export your developer profile, do the following:

1. In **Xcode**, go to **Preferences**.
2. Select **Accounts**.

3. Click the gear icon on the lower-left and select **Export Developer Accounts...**, from the modal/pop-up menu, as shown in the following screenshot:

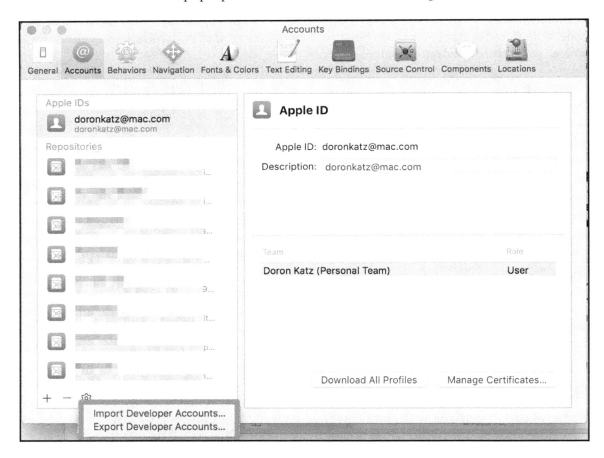

4. To reimport your developer account, you simply go to the same screen and select **Import Developer Accounts...**. As you can see, it's quite involved to maintain your certificates manually, but thankfully, we will introduce you to our next action, *cert*, which will automate the tasks we just mentioned. In the next chapter, we will discuss the match, another related action that will resolve the issue of backing up and restoring developer profiles as well as making the distribution of the profiles a lot easier.

Introducing cert

The **cert** is one-half of the code-signing process, working in tandem with the sigh (`https://docs.fastlane.tools/actions/sigh`), managing your development and distribution certificates, whereas sigh (`https://docs.fastlane.tools/actions/sigh`) takes care of managing the provisioning profiles. The first part of this chapter explained the process of managing certificates manually, and while it may not seem extremely cumbersome, the burden of effort does indeed add up.

Furthermore, certificates expire as profiles do, so providing other members of your development team with a way to automate the provisioning of certificates, as you do with provisioning profiles, ensures consistency and predictability universally, across the team and over time. The following is the logo of cert:

Usage

Like a sigh, cert also has a simple set of commands to work with. The most basic of those commands is to type `fastlane cert`. This will list and verify all the signing certificates on the machine, and output something like:

```
21:17 $ fastlane cert

+----------------+-----------------------------------------------------+
|                          Summary for cert 2.41.0                      |
+----------------+-----------------------------------------------------+
| development    | false                                               |
| force          | false                                               |
| username       | dktz@mac.com                                        |
| team_id        | UU98N6FWB5                                          |
| keychain_path  | /Users/doronkatz/Library/Keychains/login.keychain-db |
| platform       | ios                                                 |
+----------------+-----------------------------------------------------+

[21:17:32]: Starting login with user 'dktz@mac.com'
[21:17:33]: Successfully logged in
[21:17:33]: Couldn't find an existing certificate... creating a new one
[21:17:36]: Successfully generated Q97R4F6PJT which was imported to the
local machine.
```

```
[21:17:36]: Verifying the certificate is properly installed locally...
[21:17:36]: Successfully installed certificate Q97R4F6PJT
...
```

Cert will also automatically create a new private key, or signing request (CSR), as needed, and generate, download, and install the certificate, as well as finally import it into your keychain. In the preceding transcript, you can see that it did, in fact, generate a new certificate, as it didn't find a previous one.

This one command essentially takes care of all of the steps we mentioned in the previous section, which is quite an impressive feat. We can verify in the keychain that the distribution certificate was indeed installed:

	certificate	Jan 4, 2018, 1:47:00 PM
▶	certificate	Feb 1, 2018, 3:59:59 PM
	certificate	Apr 30, 2018, 9:41:04 PM
▶ iPhone Developer: Doron Katz (9X6AWM4CZ6)	certificate	Jun 2, 2018, 4:51:37 PM
▼ iPhone Distribution: Doron Katz (UU98N6FWB5)	certificate	Jul 1, 2018, 9:07:37 PM
Imported Private Key	private key	--
	ıte	Oct 11, 2018, 4:59:59 PM
	ıte	Mar 3, 2019, 12:36:59 PM

You can also be more specific in your commands, and rather than letting cert automatically figure out which certificate to install, you can opt to create a development certificate, as follows:

```
fastlane cert create --development "CERT_DEV_NAME"
```

For distribution, you can substitute development for distribution. You can also manually invoke the command revoke_expired, to remove expired certificates, like this:

```
fastlane cert —revoke-_expired
```

You can specify, like with sigh, an output path (directory) where all the certificates and private keys should be stored, say if you want to have it backed up and saved to a specific location:

```
fastlane cert -o "~/Certificates"
```

List of cert commands

Finally, you can get a list of all the available parameters and commands for sigh by entering:

```
fastlane cert --help
```

Our project problem

We already created an App ID for our Firefox project in the last chapter; in this chapter, we are going to combine sigh and cert into our beta lane, and together, code sign our app for development. If our certificates don't exist, it will create them, and the same for the provisioning profiles. Before we update our lane, let's create our certificates and have them located in the same folder that we did in the previous chapter for provisioning profiles:

```
fastlane cert --development -o ~/Certificates
```

The output is as follows:

```
+---------------+------------------------------------------------------+
|                        Summary for cert 2.41.0                        |
+---------------+------------------------------------------------------+
| development   | true                                                 |
| force         | false                                                |
| username      | dktz@mac.com                                         |
| team_id       | UU98N6FWB5                                           |
| keychain_path | /Users/doronkatz/Library/Keychains/login.keychain-db |
| platform      | ios                                                  |
+---------------+------------------------------------------------------+

[21:31:13]: Starting login with user 'dktz@mac.com'
[21:31:15]: Successfully logged in
[21:31:15]: Found the certificate 79R9953EUR (iOS Development) which is
installed on the local machine. Using this one.
[21:31:15]: Verifying the certificate is properly installed locally...
[21:31:15]: Successfully installed certificate 79R9953EUR
```

Looking at our `~/Certificates` directory, we can see our certificate has been created:

```
21:35 $ ls ~/Certificates
79R9953EUR.cer
```

We can also verify on the Apple developer portal that our certificate has been created:

Now let's update our Fastfile, incorporating cert into our workflow.

Updating our fastfile

Open up the fastfile we worked on from the previous chapter and go to the beta lane. We are simply going to add one line above the sigh command, so your lane should now look something like this:

```
lane :beta do
        cert
    sigh(force: true)
end
```

And that's it! We started creating a simple but functional lane. We can test our very first lane by typing the following in a Terminal:

```
fastlane beta
```

The output should produce something similar to the following:

```
21:45 $ fastlane beta
[21:45:33]: ------------------------------------------------
[21:45:33]: --- Step: Verifying required fastlane version ---
[21:45:33]: ------------------------------------------------
```

```
[21:45:33]: Your fastlane version 2.44.1 matches the minimum requirement of
2.41.0
[21:45:33]: ---------------------------------
[21:45:33]: --- Step: default_platform ---
[21:45:33]: ---------------------------------
[21:45:33]: Driving the lane 'ios beta'
[21:45:33]: ------------------
[21:45:33]: --- Step: cert ---
[21:45:33]: ------------------


+---------------+--------------------------------------------------------------+
|                            Summary for cert 2.44.1                           |
+---------------+--------------------------------------------------------------+
| development   | false                                                        |
| force         | false                                                        |
| username      | dktz@mac.com                                                 |
| team_id       | UU98N6FWB5                                                   |
| keychain_path | /Users/doronkatz/Library/Keychains/login.keychain-db         |
| platform      | ios                                                          |
+---------------+--------------------------------------------------------------+


[21:45:33]: Starting login with user 'dktz@mac.com'
[21:45:35]: Successfully logged in
[21:45:35]: Found the certificate Q97R4F6PJT (iOS Distribution) which is
installed on the local machine. Using this one.
[21:45:35]: Verifying the certificate is properly installed locally...
[21:45:35]: Successfully installed certificate Q97R4F6PJT
[21:45:35]: Use signing certificate 'Q97R4F6PJT' from now on!
[21:45:35]: ------------------
[21:45:35]: --- Step: sigh ---
[21:45:35]: ------------------


+----------------------------------------+----------------------+
|                     Summary for sigh 2.44.1                   |
+----------------------------------------+----------------------+
| force                                  | true                 |
| adhoc                                  | false                |
| development                            | false                |
| skip_install                           | false                |
| app_identifier                         | com.doronkatz.firefox|
| username                               | dktz@mac.com         |
| team_id                                | UU98N6FWB5           |
| ignore_profiles_with_different_name    | false                |
| cert_id                                | Q97R4F6PJT           |
| skip_fetch_profiles                    | false                |
| skip_certificate_verification          | false                |
| platform                               | ios                  |
+----------------------------------------+----------------------+
```

```
[21:45:35]: Starting login with user 'dktz@mac.com'
[21:45:36]: Successfully logged in
[21:45:36]: Fetching profiles...
[21:45:37]: Verifying certificates...
[21:45:37]: No existing profiles found, that match the certificates you
have installed locally! Creating a new provisioning profile for you
[21:45:37]: Creating new provisioning profile for 'com.doronkatz.firefox'
with name 'com.doronkatz.firefox AppStore' for 'ios' platform
[21:45:38]: Downloading provisioning profile...
[21:45:38]: Successfully downloaded provisioning profile...
[21:45:39]: Installing provisioning profile...
/Users/doronkatz/Development/Projects/firefox-
ios/AppStore_com.doronkatz.firefox.mobileprovision
[21:45:39]: Setting Provisioning Profile type to 'app-store'
```

```
+-------+----------------------------------+-------------+
|                 fastlane summary                       |
+-------+----------------------------------+-------------+
| Step  | Action                           | Time (in s) |
+-------+----------------------------------+-------------+
| 1     | Verifying required fastlane      | 0           |
|       | version                          |             |
| 2     | default_platform                 | 0           |
| 3     | cert                             | 1           |
| 4     | sigh                             | 3           |
+-------+----------------------------------+-------------+
```

```
[21:45:39]: fastlane.tools finished successfully
```

You should be able to see that *fastlane* has, in fact, created a provisioning profile for development, as well as in the App Store, successfully, whereas in the previous chapter, we failed because we didn't have a certificate setup. By adding cert before sigh, we ensure that we have a certificate prior to creating the provisioning profile and leveraging the existing or newly created certificate.

You can appreciate what we have just achieved with two lines of code to create a provisioning profile as well as an associated certificate, without having to deal with the intricacies of setting that up through Xcode as well as the developer portal.

Summary

In the last two chapters, we completed our first milestone of code signing our app in one lane, beta, through the use of cert and sigh, to manage our certificates and provisioning profiles. This chapter has really honed how easy it is through *fastlane*, as compared to the traditional approaches of managing certificates. It not only reduces the effort and burden, but makes onboarding new developers extremely easy while maintaining consistency across the development team when it comes to code signing.

In the next chapter, we are going to work through our final code-signing lane, match (`https://docs.fastlane.tools/actions/match/`), which takes managing certificates and provisioning profiles to even more collaborative convenience through the ability to sync those vital assets across teams easily, the way developers share code through Git.

5
Sync Profiles and Certificates with match

Following sigh (`https://docs.fastlane.tools/actions/sigh`) and cert (`https://docs.fastlane.tools/actions/cert/`), which automate the process of managing provisioning profiles and certificates, respectively, we are now going to show you a new approach to iOS code signing that goes beyond the two we just mentioned. That is, *sharing one code signing identity across your entire team, simplifying code signing set up and minimizing code signing issues.*

This is a radical change from the way code signing has traditionally been done (whereby each developer has her or his own code signing identity), in which developers share a common set of code signing identities that are accessed via a shared `Git` repository. This modern code signing management approach promises to make credential sharing more streamlined, easier to manage, and with fewer issues going forward.

This chapter provides a new and even easier solution for managing your provisioning profiles and certificates, beyond what we showed in the last two chapters with sigh and cert, respectively. We will explore match (`https://docs.fastlane.tools/actions/match`) in this chapter and will demonstrate how you can leverage this action to automate the process of managing all your app signing needs, as well as easily sharing your app signing credentials with other team members.

We will be working with cert through the command line to:

- Understand the collective code sharing approach
- Create a private `Git` repository to store certificates and provisioning profiles
- Secure the private `Git` repository
- Integrate the lane into our project Fastfile

Before we dive into match (`https://docs.fastlane.tools/actions/match`), let's first discuss the new best practices approach that the team at *fastlane* is advocating (`https://codesigning.guide`).

Collective code signing

Previously this book has discussed how we would automate and manage the process of creating certificates and provisioning profiles, and subsequently, code signing through public/private keys (separately, for both development and distribution). We discussed the theory and processes for working with profiles and certificates in great detail, and while *fastlane* has done a great job in allowing developers to not only manage but also repair their code signing assets with sigh and cert, there is one glaring problem—each developer still has an individual profile, and that leads to numerous profiles.

The number of profiles will grow as the teams grow, and, even with personnel leaving, they have to be pruned over time; needless to say, it's a model that isn't exactly scalable. Each new machine will require quite a bit of setting up using individual code signing credentials, with new provisioning profiles having to be set up each time a new device is added or removed, or in response to an expired certificate. Take a look at the following screenshot:

Source: fastlane (https://codesigning.guide/)

Scalability, when onboarding new developers with the right permissions to code sign your app, is a common concern, requiring a lot of manual intervention in order to get the right certificates and provisioning profiles generated for each user. *fastlane* thus advocates for a centralized provisioning and certification management approach, a *collective code signing* through a private `Git` repository. Developers who have access to the `Git` repository are able to access the code signing identity and profiles, setting them up once and working for teams of any size.

Whenever a certificate expires or a new provisioning profile needs to be generated, be it development or App Store, it will be done once and then synced across all of the development team. Through either a federated access to the `Git` repository or having numerous `Git` repository administrators, new developers will be onboarded effortlessly, and via a match, they will receive the latest credentials automatically. There are no lingering or orphaned profiles in the developer portal. Refer to the following diagram:

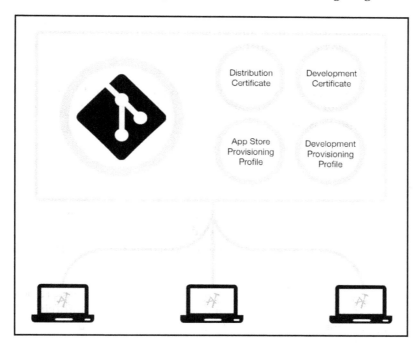

Source: *fastlane* (https://codesigning.guide/)

Security

Of course, when pushing critical assets to a shared, cloud-stored repository, security plays a critical factor, and through leveraging match, as well as best practices across your team, you can enjoy the convenience and robustness of this workflow along with the security coverage. In this section, we are going to discuss *access management*.

Portal access management

Alongside all the automation benefits match provides to its developers, it is a way of providing team access to the code signing assets without having to open up access to the developer portal, with developers only needing to have access to the private Git repository. match handles updates with new profiles so that developers automatically get the latest profiles each time match is run.

match also handles storing certificates and profiles of more than one team in a single repository through the use of Git branches, by denoting the branches in the match parameter.

 We will provide an example of how to work with multiple branches and projects using one Git repository, as well as onboarding new developers, later in the chapter.

Git access management

As mentioned, a private Git repository will be used and shared among developers. Whether you use an existing Git repository vendor like **GitHub** (https://github.com/) or **Bitbucket** (https://bitbucket.org/), you will need to ensure that correct access to the repository is maintained at all times.

Rather than merely using usernames and passwords, employ more secure best practices, from using **2-Factor Authentication** (**2FA**) for developer access to enforcing the use of ssh keys (https://help.github.com/articles/connecting-to-github-with-ssh/) to forego having to explicitly enter passwords altogether.

Encryption

Before committing and pushing the code signing assets, it is important to encrypt the files to ensure that if the Git repository access is compromised, the ever-important code signing assets aren't. You have various options for encrypting your files, but *fastlane* suggests OpenSSL as one solution, and in fact, match does it out of the box. match automatically encrypts both the keys and provisioning profiles using OpenSSL, using a passphrase which will be prompted the first time a new developer is on board with a new machine setup.

OpenSSL (https://openssl.org/) is freely available and built into macOS, and is most commonly used in encrypting communications to secure websites, denoted by a padlock icon in the address bar.

While you may not need to know how to encrypt and decrypt manually when you are using a match, it is good to be mindful of how you would go about manually encrypting and decrypting a file. To decrypt a file on macOS, enter the following in the Terminal:

```
openssl aes-256-cbc -k "<password>" -in "certs/certificate.cer" -out
"certs/certificate.cer.aes" -a
```

This simply creates an AES encryption and outputs a `.des` encrypted file. You will then be prompted for a password that you will need to confirm twice, and which will be used to encrypt your file. You should provide a separate and agreed upon password that your entire team knows and should also use for their encryption. You should encrypt all your code signing assets the same way.

If unencrypted files on the `Git` repository are compromised by external users, as long as the Apple developer portal credentials are still secured (for which 2FA is also highly recommended), there is a limit to the damage that can be done, according to *fastlane*. For one, Apple is required to resign for the App Store if the App Store profile is compromised, and without access to iTunes Connect credentials, which are stored in a Keychain and not in the repository, they cannot submit the app to the App Store.

Potential harm to development and ad hoc profiles is also limited in the absence of the intruder having access to the developer portal credentials; however, there is a vulnerability with Enterprise profiles whereby attackers could potentially distribute a signed version of your app to a high number of devices and end up being a breach of Apple's Enterprise provisioning policies, leading to a termination of the Enterprise agreements.

However, as mentioned, through employing best practices, the risk of a security breach would be minimal at best.

Introducing match

When implementing match (https://docs.fastlane.tools/actions/match/) into your team's workflow, you will see how the new collective code signing process works effortlessly, in a scalable way, to deprecate the use of cert and sigh (in most cases).

The easiest way to see how these workflows work is by example. Let's get started. The following is the logo of match:

Create a private Git repository

Assuming you already have a team Apple ID, the next step is to create a private `Git` repository that will serve to host the profiles and certificates. For the purpose of this example, we are going to create a new, private repository in Bitbucket, which is free. If you don't already have an account, please create a Bitbucket account and create a repository, as follows:

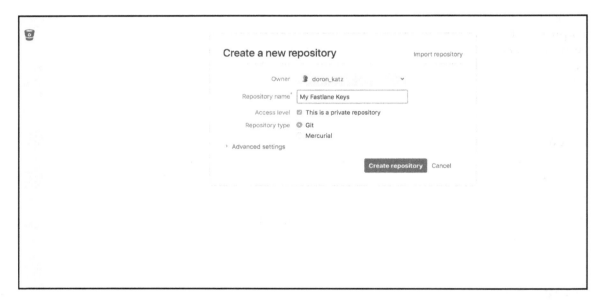

You will then clone this project into a local project folder by entering the following (substitute YOURTEAM, YOURPROJECTNAME, and FOLDERNAME with your Bitbucket team name, project name, and project folder location, as appropriate):

```
git clone git@bitbucket.org:YOUR_TEAM/YOUR_PROJECT_NAME.git
cd FOLDER_NAME
```

```
echo "# My project's README" >> README.md
git add README.md
git commit -m "Initial commit"
git push -u origin master
```

In the preceding set of commands, we created a README file which will serve as the onboarding instructions for any new member and is a great place for you to add project-specific information you would like to relay.

 It is important to ensure that access is restricted to only the appropriate team members.

Initialize match

In the project folder, initialize match by entering the following in a Terminal:

```
fastlane match init
```

You will then be prompted to enter the URL of the Git repository you just created, which can either be the HTTP URL or a Git URL:

```
[12:32:34]: Please create a new, private git repository
[12:32:34]: to store the certificates and profiles there
[12:32:34]: URL of the Git Repo:
https://bitbucket.org/YOUR_TEAM/YOUR_PROJECT
[12:33:13]: Successfully created './Matchfile'. You can open the file using
a code editor.
[12:33:13]: You can now run `fastlane match development`, `fastlane match
adhoc`, `fastlane match enterprise` and `fastlane match appstore`
[12:33:13]: On the first run for each environment it will create the
provisioning profiles and
[12:33:13]: certificates for you. From then on, it will automatically
import the existing profiles.
[12:33:13]: For more information visit
https://docs.fastlane.tools/actions/match
```

If you look at your project folder, match init created a Matchfile which is the configuration of match file, similar to a Fastfile, and may look similar to:

```
git_url "git@bitbucket.org:YOUR_TEAM/YOUR_PROJECT.git"
type "development" # The default type, can be: appstore, adhoc, enterprise
or development
#/ app_identifier ["tools.fastlane.app", "tools.fastlane.app2"]
```

```
#/ username "user@fastlane.tools" # Your Apple Developer Portal username
#/ For all available options run `fastlane match --help`
#/ Remove the # in the beginning of the line to enable the other options
```

Running match for the first time

It is recommended that you run a match for the first time by starting with a new set of certificates and profiles, so we will start off by using match's nuke command to revoke all certificates and profiles, by entering the following:

```
fastlane match nuke development
fastlane match nuke distribution
```

You should get a response similar to the following:

```
INFO [2017-07-12 15:51:44.68]: Successfully loaded
'/Users/YOU/Development/Projects/YOUR_FOLDER/Matchfile'

+---------+------------------------------------------+
|         Detected Values from './Matchfile'         |
+---------+------------------------------------------+
| git_url | git@bitbucket.org:YOUR_TEAM /YOUR_PRO|
|         | JECT.git                             |  |
| type    | development                          |  |
+---------+------------------------------------------+

INFO [2017-07-12 15:51:44.69]: Cloning remote git repo...
INFO [2017-07-12 15:51:44.69]: If cloning the repo takes too long, you can
use the `clone_branch_directly` option in match.
INFO [2017-07-12 15:51:44.69]: $ GIT_TERMINAL_PROMPT=0 git clone
'git@bitbucket.org:YOUR_TEAM/YOUR_PROJECT'
'/var/folders/68/946ywfgx3jq3bwhy02std9tc0000gn/T/d20170712-58445-146a4pd'
INFO [2017-07-12 15:51:44.70]: > Cloning into
'/var/folders/68/946ywfgx3jq3bwhy02std9tc0000gn/T/d20170712-58445-146a4pd'.
..
INFO [2017-07-12 15:51:53.29]: > warning: You appear to have cloned an
empty repository.
INFO [2017-07-12 15:51:53.39]:      Successfully decrypted certificates repo

+--------------------+------------------------------------+
|              Summary for match nuke 2.46.1              |
+--------------------+------------------------------------+
| verbose            | true                             |  |
| git_url            | git@bitbucket.org:YOUR_TEAM/YOUR_PROJ|
| type               | development                      |  |
```

```
| git_branch            | master          |                                          |
| keychain_name         | login.keychain  |                                          |
| readonly              | false           |                                          |
| force                 | false           |                                          |
| skip_confirmation     | false           |                                          |
| shallow_clone         | false           |                                          |
| clone_branch_directly | false           |                                          |
| force_for_new_devices | false           |                                          |
| skip_docs             | false           |                                          |
| platform              | ios             |                                          |
+-----------------------+-----------------+------------------------------------------+
```

```
INFO [2017-07-12 15:51:53.40]: Fetching certificates and profiles...
WARN [2017-07-12 15:51:53.41]: To not be asked about this value, you can
specify it using 'username'
 [2017-07-12 15:51:53.41]: Your Apple ID Username: dktz@mac.com
Loading session from '/Users/YOU/.fastlane/spaceship/YOU@mac.com/cookie'
```

```
+-----------------+------------+--------------+------------+
|             Certificates that are going to be revoked    |
+-----------------+------------+--------------+------------+
| Name            | ID         | Type         | Expires    |
+-----------------+------------+--------------+------------+
| iOS Development | XXX        | Development  | 2018-06-02 |
+-----------------+------------+--------------+------------+
```

```
+--------------+------------+---------+--------------+------------+
|          Provisioning Profiles that are going to be revoked     |
+--------------+------------+---------+--------------+------------+
| Name         | ID         | Status  | Type         | Expires    |
+--------------+------------+---------+--------------+------------+
| com.xxx      | LZNXS89HZJ | Active  | iOS          | 2018-06-25 |
| .xxxx        |            |         | Development  |            |
|              |            |         |              |            |
| Development  |            |         |              |            |
| XXXXXXX      | VMAN5UUJZ2 | Expired | iOS          | 2014-12-20 |
|              |            |         | Development  |            |
+--------------+------------+---------+--------------+------------+
```

```
ERROR [2017-07-12 15:52:12.98]: ---
ERROR [2017-07-12 15:52:12.98]: Are you sure you want to completely delete
and revoke all the
ERROR [2017-07-12 15:52:12.98]: certificates and provisioning profiles
listed above? (y/n)
ERROR [2017-07-12 15:52:12.98]: ---
 [2017-07-12 15:52:12.98]: Do you really want to nuke everything listed
above? (y/n)
y
```

```
INFO [2017-07-12 15:52:18.19]: ------------------------------------------------
INFO [2017-07-12 15:52:18.19]: --- Deleting 2 provisioning profiles... ---
INFO [2017-07-12 15:52:18.19]: ------------------------------------------------
INFO [2017-07-12 15:52:18.19]: Deleting profile 'xxx Development'
(LZNXS89HZJ)...
INFO [2017-07-12 15:52:18.89]: Successfully deleted profile
INFO [2017-07-12 15:52:18.89]: Deleting profile 'SomeProfile'
(VMAN23XUJZ2)...
INFO [2017-07-12 15:52:19.48]: Successfully deleted profile
INFO [2017-07-12 15:52:19.48]: ------------------------------------
INFO [2017-07-12 15:52:19.48]: --- Revoking 1 certificates... ---
INFO [2017-07-12 15:52:19.48]: ------------------------------------
INFO [2017-07-12 15:52:19.48]: Revoking certificate 'iOS Development'
(7JR9I53EUR)...
INFO [2017-07-12 15:52:19.90]: Successfully deleted certificate
INFO [2017-07-12 15:52:19.91]:    Successfully encrypted certificates repo
...
INFO [2017-07-12 15:52:23.28]: > To bitbucket.org:YOUR_TEAM/YOU_PROJECT.git
INFO [2017-07-12 15:52:23.28]: > * [new branch]      master -> master
INFO [2017-07-12 15:52:23.29]: Successfully cleaned your account
```

From the output, we can see that it has successfully pulled the latest from our Git repository and cleaned/revoked all of your certificates and provisioning profiles. We now have a clean code signing environment to begin recreating our development certificates and provisioning profiles, which we will do next. But before we do that, the final three lines show that match has pushed something back to our Git repo.

If we go to our Git repo via our browser, we can see that it has created a new README file, as well as uploaded match_version.txt, as shown in the following screenshot:

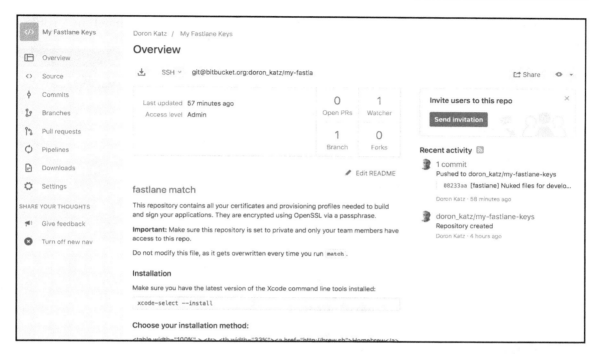

The README file now allows other developers to quickly be onboarded through a comprehensive list of instructions on installing *fastlane* and match, and to work with collective certificates and provisioning profiles.

Recreating development certificates and provisioning profiles

Next, let's start creating (or recreating) the development certificate and associated provisioning profiles, by simply entering:

```
fastlane match development
```

The match will ask you for a few more bits of information, the first of which is the bundle identifier for your app, which should already exist in your developer portal; otherwise, you can go ahead and create it. It then asks you for a passphrase to use for encryption purposes, so make sure you note it down and share it with the other developers in your team.

It will then push the newly generated encrypted developer certificate and matching profile straight to your `Git` repository. The resulting output should be:

```
[16:54:58]: Successfully loaded
'/Users/doronkatz/Development/Projects/Packt/my-fastlane-keys/Matchfile'
```

```
+---------+----------------------------------------+
|        Detected Values from './Matchfile'       |
+---------+----------------------------------------+
| git_url | git@bitbucket.org:YOUR_TEAM /YOUR_PRO|
|         | JECT.git                               |
| type    | development                            |
+---------+----------------------------------------+
```

```
+-----------------------+----------------------------------------+
|                     Summary for match 2.46.1                    |
+-----------------------+----------------------------------------+
| git_url               | git@bitbucket.org:YOUR_TEAM /YOUR_PRO|
|                       | JECT.git                               |
| type                  | development                            |
| git_branch            | master                                 |
| keychain_name         | login.keychain                         |
| readonly              | false                                  |
| verbose               | false                                  |
| force                 | false                                  |
| skip_confirmation     | false                                  |
| shallow_clone         | false                                  |
| clone_branch_directly | false                                  |
| force_for_new_devices | false                                  |
| skip_docs             | false                                  |
| platform              | ios                                    |
+-----------------------+----------------------------------------+
```

```
[16:54:58]: Cloning remote git repo...
[16:54:58]: If cloning the repo takes too long, you can use the
`clone_branch_directly` option in match.
[16:54:59]:    Successfully decrypted certificates repo
[16:54:59]: To not be asked about this value, you can specify it using
'username'
[16:54:59]: Your Apple ID Username: YOUR_TEAM@mac.com
[16:55:02]: Verifying that the certificate and profile are still valid on
the Dev Portal...
[16:55:03]: To not be asked about this value, you can specify it using
'app_identifier'
[16:55:03]: The bundle identifier(s) of your app (comma-separated):
com.yourbundle.yourapp
```

```
[16:55:13]: Couldn't find a valid code signing identity in the git repo for
development... creating one for you now

+---------------+------------------------------------+
|                 Summary for cert 2.46.1            |
+---------------+------------------------------------+
| development   | true                               |
| force         | true                               |
| username      | dktz@mac.com             |
| keychain_path | ...                                |
|                                                    |
|               | login.keychain-db                  |
| platform      | ios                                |
+---------------+------------------------------------+

[16:55:13]: Starting login with user 'YOUR_TEAM@mac.com'
[16:55:14]: Successfully logged in
[16:55:17]: Successfully generated P6J27D2843 which was imported to the
local machine.
[16:55:17]: Verifying the certificate is properly installed locally...
[16:55:17]: Successfully installed certificate P6Jc72D843

+-----------------------------------------+-------------------------+
|                  Summary for sigh 2.46.1                          |
+-----------------------------------------+-------------------------+
| app_identifier                          | com.yourbundle.yourApp  |
| username                                | YOUR_TEAM@mac.com       |
| force                                   | true                    |
| cert_id                                 | P6Jc72D843              |
| provisioning_name                       | match Development       |
|                                         | com.yourbundle.yourApp  |
| ignore_profiles_with_different_name     | true                    |
| platform                                | ios                     |
| development                             | true                    |
| adhoc                                   | false                   |
| skip_install                            | false                   |
| skip_fetch_profiles                     | false                   |
| skip_certificate_verification           | false                   |
+-----------------------------------------+-------------------------+

...
[16:55:20]: Successfully downloaded provisioning profile...
[16:55:20]: Installing provisioning profile...
...
[16:55:20]: Installing provisioning profile...
[16:55:21]: Enter the passphrase that should be used to encrypt/decrypt
your certificates
[16:55:21]: This passphrase is specific per repository and will be stored
```

```
in your local keychain
[16:55:21]: Make sure to remember the password, as you'll need it when you
run match on a different machine
[16:55:21]: Passphrase for Git Repo: ******
[16:56:54]: Type passphrase again: ******
[16:56:56]:        Successfully encrypted certificates repo
[16:56:56]: Pushing changes to remote git repo...


+--------------------+------------------------+------------------------+
|                        Installed Provisioning Profile                |
+--------------------+------------------------+------------------------+
| Parameter          | Environment Variable   | Value                  |
+--------------------+------------------------+------------------------+
...
[16:56:58]: All required keys, certificates and provisioning profiles are

installed
  ~/Development/Projects/Packt/my-fastlane-keys [master L|...1]
```

Let's take another peek at our Git repo via the browser, and you will notice that match added three new files:

- The development certificate
- A private key
- The development provisioning profile

Take a look at the following screenshot:

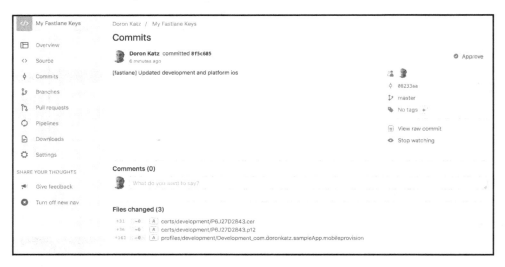

The directory structure is similar to the following:

```
├── Matchfile
├── README.md
├── certs
│   └── development
│       ├── J6Q27D2243.cer
│       └── P6J2QQ2243.p12
├── match_version.txt
└── profiles
    └── development
        └── Development_com.doronkatz.sampleApp.mobileprovision
```

As you can see, even though sigh and cert made the process of managing provisioning profiles and certificates significantly easier, the match takes this to a whole new level. With one command, you not only have a full development code signing identity, consisting of the certificate, private key, and provisioning profile, but you get encryption and Git synchronization thrown in for good measure. If you wanted to create a distribution code signing identity for the App Store, you would simply substitute development with appstore:

fastlane match appstore

Likewise, for Enterprise, you would do:

fastlane match enterprise

As it stands now, we have our development identities securely stored in our private Git repository. When a new team member gets introduced to the project, you will want to get her environment up and running right away. You will learn how to add a new team member next.

Adding new team members

We saw earlier that in the first push from `match` to our private repository, it created a great onboarding `README.md` file that thoroughly explains the process of setting up a new machine and obtaining the code signing credentials easily. Refer to the following screenshot:

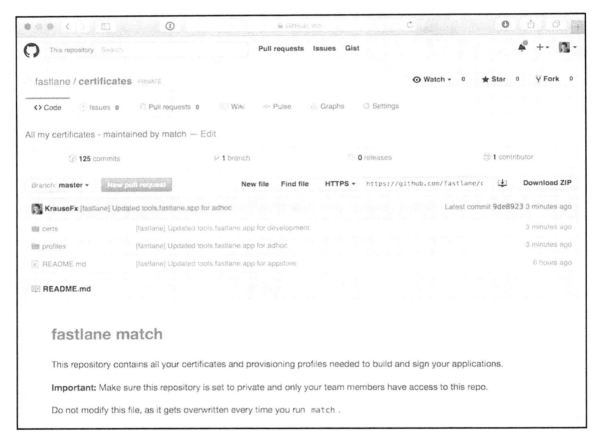

So, essentially, the new team member would install *fastlane* by again entering:

```
fastlane match development
```

The developer would be prompted for the passphrase only, which you would provide her with, and she would be ready to go. Xcode will configure automatically once the developer double-clicks the private key and the certificate to install it on the machine's keychain.

Handling multiple targets

If your app comprised more than one (iOS, Apple TV, watchOS) bundle, you would simply append the bundle identifiers, delimited by a comma:

```
fastlane match development -a com.packt.ios.sampleApp,
com.packt.watch.sampleApp
```

When using `Fastfile`, you would simply do as follows:

```
lane: codeSigning do
        match(app_identifier:["com.packt.ios.sampleApp",
"com.packt.watch.sampleApp"])
end
```

By running this lane, all the certificates, private keys, and profiles would be created for all the targets.

Adding new devices

Adding new devices to the development or ad hoc profile is another trivial process, thanks to `match`. The easiest way is to create a comma-delimited set of devices you want to maintain and store it in the private `Git` repo. You can create a `devices.txt` file, consisting of your device IDs and names, as shown here:

```
Device ID    Device Name
A12345678901234567890123456789012345678        DEVICE_NAME_1
B12345678901234567890123456789012345678        DEVICE_NAME_2
```

In future, all you need to do is maintain this text file and add/remove entries as necessary. You would then add the following, prior to calling the `match` in the Fastfile:

```
lane :development do
  register_devices(devices_file: "devices.txt")
  match(type: "development", force_for_new_devices: false)
end
```

`register_devices` will test if the device count has changed since the last match ran, and it will regenerate the appropriate profile as necessary.

Our project problem

This step will be an improvement on the previous chapters, whereby we replace the Fastfile's sigh and cert entries with the use of `match`.

 You can either use the keyword `match`, or the alias `sync_code_signing`, interchangeably. For instance: `sync_code_signing(type: "development", readonly: true)`

Edit the Fastfile, adding the following to automatically fetch the latest code signing certificates:

```
...
lane :beta do
    register_devices(devices_file: "devices.txt")
    match(git_url: "https://bitbucket.org/YOUR_TEAM/YOUR_PROJECT",
      type: "development",
      app_identifier: "com.yourname.firefox")
        # gym
    # sh "your_script.sh"
    # You can also use other beta testing services here (run `fastlane
actions`)
  end
...
```

We will be adding gym (`https://docs.fastlane.tools/actions/gym`) in a future chapter, to actually build our project, but for now, just create the `devices.txt` file in the root folder to match what we specified in `register_devices` in the preceding code snippet:

```
Device ID    Device Name
A12345678901234567890123456789    DEVICENAME1
B12345678901234567890123456789    DEVICENAME2
```

Finally, run the following to kick off lane beta:

```
fastlane beta
```

If everything ran successfully, we now have a new development code signing, set for Firefox for iOS:

```
21:23 $ fastlane beta
[21:23:52]: ---------------------------------------------------
[21:23:52]: --- Step: Verifying required fastlane version ---
[21:23:52]: ---------------------------------------------------
[21:23:52]: Your fastlane version 2.46.1 matches the minimum requirement of
```

```
2.41.0  ☑
[21:23:52]: ------------------------------
[21:23:52]: --- Step: default_platform ---
[21:23:52]: ------------------------------
[21:23:52]: Driving the lane 'ios beta'  🚀
[21:23:52]: ------------------------------
[21:23:52]: --- Step: register_devices ---
[21:23:52]: ------------------------------
[21:23:59]: Fetching list of currently registered devices...
[21:24:00]: Successfully registered new devices.
[21:24:00]: --------------------
[21:24:00]: --- Step: match ---
[21:24:00]: --------------------
```

```
+----------------------+-------------------------------------------+
|                      Summary for match 2.46.1                    |
+----------------------+-------------------------------------------+
| git_url              | xxx                                       |
|                      |                                           |
| type                 | development                               |
| app_identifier       | com.doronkatz.firefox                     |
| git_branch           | master                                    |
| username             | YOUR_TEAM@mac.com                         |
| keychain_name        | login.keychain                            |
| readonly             | false                                     |
| team_id              | UU98N6FWB5                                |
| verbose              | false                                     |
| force                | false                                     |
| skip_confirmation    | false                                     |
| shallow_clone        | false                                     |
| clone_branch_directly| false                                     |
| force_for_new_devices| false                                     |
| skip_docs            | false                                     |
| platform             | ios                                       |
+----------------------+-------------------------------------------+
```

```
[21:24:00]: Cloning remote git repo...
[21:24:00]: If cloning the repo takes too long, you can use the
`clone_branch_directly` option in match.
[21:24:03]: 🔓  Successfully decrypted certificates repo
[21:24:03]: Verifying that the certificate and profile are still valid on
the Dev Portal...
[21:24:05]: Installing certificate...
```

```
+--------------------+-------------------------------------------+
|                      Installed Certificate                     |
+--------------------+-------------------------------------------+
```

```
| User ID             | QW53HAMMWC                             |
...

+------------------------------------+----------------------+
|                   Summary for sigh 2.46.1                 |
+------------------------------------+----------------------+
| app_identifier                     | com.doronkatz.firefox |
...
```

[21:24:07]: Starting login with user 'dktz@mac.com'
[21:24:08]: Successfully logged in
[21:24:08]: Fetching profiles...
[21:24:08]: Verifying certificates...
[21:24:08]: No existing profiles found, that match the certificates you
have installed locally! Creating a new provisioning profile for you
[21:24:09]: Creating new provisioning profile for 'com.doronkatz.firefox'
with name 'match Development com.doronkatz.firefox' for 'ios' platform
[21:24:11]: Downloading provisioning profile...
[21:24:12]: Successfully downloaded provisioning profile...
[21:24:12]: Installing provisioning profile...
/var/folders/68/946ywfgx3jq3bwhy02std9tc0000gn/T/d20170712-62537-
uxf6dm/profiles/development/Development_com.doronkatz.firefox.mobileprovisi
on
[21:24:12]: Installing provisioning profile...
[21:24:13]: 🔒 Successfully encrypted certificates repo
[21:24:13]: Pushing changes to remote git repo...

```
+--------------------+----------------------+----------------------+
|                   Installed Provisioning Profile                 |
+--------------------+----------------------+----------------------+
| Parameter          | Environment Variable | Value                |
+--------------------+----------------------+----------------------+
| App Identifier     |                      | com.doronkatz.firefox |
| Type               |                      | development          |
| Platform           |                      | ios                  |
| Profile UUID       | sigh_com.doronkatz.fi | 9d52b5b7-4a7d-4260-bf |
|                    | refox_development    | 0f-6d900cc96e40      |
| Profile Name       | sigh_com.doronkatz.fi | match Development    |
|                    | refox_development_pro | com.doronkatz.firefox |
|                    | file-name            |                      |
| Profile Path       | sigh_com.doronkatz.fi | /Users/doronkatz/Libr |
|                    | refox_development_pro | ary/MobileDevice/Prov |
|                    | file-path            | isioning             |
|                    |                      | Profiles/9d52b5b7-4a7 |
|                    |                      | d-4260-bf0f-6d900cc96 |
|                    |                      | e40.mobileprovision  |
```

```
| Development Team ID | sigh_com.doronkatz.fi | UU98N6FWB5            |
|                     | refox_development_tea |                      |
|                     | m-id                  |                      |
+---------------------+-----------------------+----------------------+
```

[21:24:17]: All required keys, certificates and provisioning profiles are installed
[21:24:17]: Setting Provisioning Profile type to 'development'

```
+------+--------------------+-------------+
|              fastlane summary            |
+------+--------------------+-------------+
| Step | Action             | Time (in s) |
+------+--------------------+-------------+
| 1    | Verifying required | 0           |
|      | fastlane version   |             |
| 2    | default_platform   | 0           |
| 3    | register_devices   | 8           |
| 4    | match              | 17          |
+------+--------------------+-------------+
```

[21:24:17]: fastlane.tools finished successfully 🎉

And there you have it; it took care of sigh and cert, all through the one replacement command, match. Now, embedded within our Fastfile, we can automatically run this command each time we do a build for distribution internally, ensuring not only that the certificates and profiles are maintained, but that we can now bring in new team members and scale with extreme ease.

List of match commands

Finally, you can get a list of all the available parameters and commands for the match by entering:

```
fastlane match --help
```

Summary

In this chapter, we introduced a new concept and method of managing code signing, using a collective code sharing workflow that replaces the silos of development certificates and provisioning profiles that individual developers use (as we have relied on in the previous chapters) with a singular code signing certificate, private key, and profile that is stored in a private `Git` repository and shared among the development team.

match (`https://docs.fastlane.tools/actions/match#readme`) has allowed us to deprecate calling sigh and cert explicitly in our lane in lieu of this one command that not only manages the entire code signing set of assets but encrypts and synchronizes the assets into the `Git` repository automatically, meaning that onboarding new developers is extremely effortless.

In the next chapter, we are going to complete the first block of chapters that focus on the management of certificates and profiles by taking a look at pem (`https://docs.fastlane.tools/actions/pem#readme`), an action that allows us to automatically create and maintain push notification profiles the same way we do for our development provisioning profiles.

6
Manage Push Notification Profiles with pem

This chapter is all about understanding what push notifications are, how we enable our apps to receive push notifications the traditional way, and how pem will help us automatically manage creating, repairing, and refreshing our notification profiles the same way that match and sigh manages code signing provisioning profiles.

That is, we will be focusing on simplifying the creation and management of *push notification profiles*, similar to how we have been working with provisioning profiles, automatically generating a .pem file that you can upload to your push notification server.

The following skills will be learned in this chapter. We will be working with pem through the command line to:

- Create a new pem file, along with the required code signing identities needed for the server
- Integrate the lane into our project Fastfile

What push notifications are

Push notifications, or **Apple Notification Services** (**APNs**), are a mechanism for third-party developers to send notifications as packets of data to users who have their applications installed on their devices. Notifications display and notify the users, subtly, of important and time-sensitive news items. Displaying a transient bar in the top part of the screen, along with a nominated notification sound, notifications deliver a short message, as well as optional actions the users can take without being required to open the app.

Take a push notification from the Facebook Messenger (https://facebook.com). When a user sends a message to a friend, the friend receives a push notification with an excerpt of the message and a *bell sound* notifying the user. The following screenshot illustrates an icon when a new, unread notification is received, showing a badge-count on the top-right corner:

Along with the option to reply directly from within the notification widget, bypassing having to launch the app, the user is also presented with the option to send a quick emoticon reply back. This is what Apple calls *notification service app extensions*, and you can learn more about this framework by consulting Apple's User Notifications UI framework reference guide (https://developer.apple.com/documentation/usernotificationsui).

Push notifications also have the ability to send media files, such as an attached image, small sound files, or short videos, and have the user preview them without having to launch an app. Less common tasks that push notifications can do include performing background tasks without needing to wake up the device.

Push notifications are supported on iOS, watchOS, tvOS, and even macOS. Android devices have their own **Operating System Push Notification Service** (**OSPNS**), comparable to Apple's.

Push notifications, when executed correctly, provide developers with greater reach to their users, making their applications more engaging and ultimately increasing customer retention.

How push notifications work

The device and APNs establish a secure and encrypted connection when the application launches on the device, which persists for the duration of the life cycle of the app until it is relaunched. This opens up a channel for the APNs to send notifications to, and for the app to handle the notifications.

In order to send push notifications, you will need the following setup:

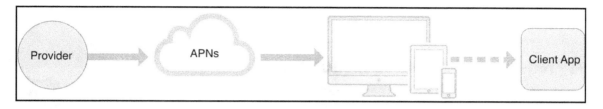

Source: Apple

Provider

The **provider** is a server that will be used to deploy and manage the APNs. The provider is tasked with accepting unique, app-specific device tokens that are sent from the app that is running on each device, allowing the provider to be aware of each instance of your app running.

The provider is also responsible for determining when and to whom notifications will be sent, through harvesting the list of devices that have an active device token stored and curated on the server.

Finally, the provider executes the process of sending the notification payload, consisting of a JSON dictionary (`https://developer.apple.com/library/content/documentation/NetworkingInternet/Conceptual/RemoteNotificationsPG/CreatingtheNotificationPayload.html#//apple_ref/doc/uid/TP40008194-CH10-SW1`), bundled with the aforementioned unique device token, as well as delivery information, that is then transported via an HTTP/2 request to the APNs gateway.

APNs

APNs are delivered through HTTP/2, and notifications essentially consist of payloads sent, with a maximum notification payload size of 4 kilobytes.

The APNs then attempt to deliver the payload to the designated devices, although delivery is not always guaranteed. Using a quality of service process of store and forward, the APNs will continue to attempt to redeliver the notification over a limited period of time, in case the device is offline or otherwise unable to receive notifications. If the APN is unable to send the notification successfully, the message will eventually be discarded.

The APNs also receive an encrypted certificate/token via the secure channel, to ensure that, like with provisioning profiles and certificates, the origin and target chain of communication is legitimate.

APNs-device trust connection

As mentioned previously, the APNs-to-device connection is encrypted using a private key that is securely stored on the device's operating system keychain. During activation, the APNs authenticate and validate the connection to the device. The device initiates the chain of trust through a TLS connection to the APNs, which is done because we registered the app for push notifications and set in the app's AppDelegate the intent to be able to handle push notification payloads. Refer to the following diagram:

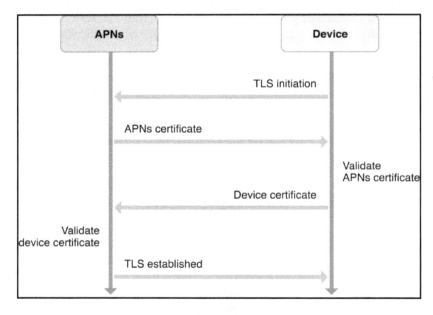

Source: Apple

The APNs then send a certificate back to the device, letting the device's operating system validate the certificate against its private key, and, when confirmed, establishing the persistent trust connection.

Local versus remote push notifications

The two types of notifications available on iOS are *local notifications* and *remote notifications*. The focus of this book will be on *remote push notifications*, but it is worth understanding what local notifications are so that you get a well-rounded knowledge of what Apple makes available to developers.

Local notifications set the configuration details locally on the device, having those details triggered and passed internally, without server intervention. They are the most straightforward to implement but lack the power of being remotely triggered. Initiated client/device-side, developers can schedule notifications to run and handle notifications appropriately, but notifications can only be logically triggered via code. For instance, you can schedule a local push notification to trigger every two weeks if a user hasn't logged in to the app in that period of time.

Remote notifications, on the other hand, allow marketing teams, for instance, to push new notification data to users independent of the client-side state, such as a sports ticketing app targeting a specific demographic of users near a location where new sporting event tickets are opening up.

Enabling push notifications

In order to set up push notifications on your app, there are a few things you will need. The provisioning aspect is the first criteria, whereby the app will need to be provisioned and registered with the APNs to receive push notifications. This is done via Xcode, which will be discussed shortly.

The second criteria is a server or provider (as we mentioned in the previous section) tasked with sending push notification payloads to the APNs conduit, which will then orchestrate the messages to the devices. This chapter will not focus much on the setup of a server, as it is beyond the scope of the book; however, there are some recommended free platforms that do provide push notification capabilities, including **Firebase** (https://firebase.google. com/) and **Urban Airship** (https://www.urbanairship.com/).

Another recommended tool to use for testing is the open source **NWPusher** (https:// github.com/noodlewerk/NWPusher), which will allow you to send JSON payload packets in a test environment in order to validate that your app is provisioned correctly. Take a look at the following screenshot:

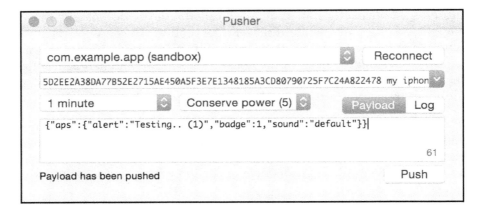

Enabling push notifications the traditional way via Xcode

The first thing we are going to do is enable push notifications in our Xcode project, which will add APNs entitlements to our project. This can be accomplished by simply going to the project's target, then selecting **Capabilities**:

Behind the scenes, what this does is associate push notifications entitlements in `https://developer.apple.com`. For the purpose of our project's example, as it was already associated with another project bundle previously, it wasn't able to add the entitlements successfully. First, let's remove the previous entitlements the project had associated with it:

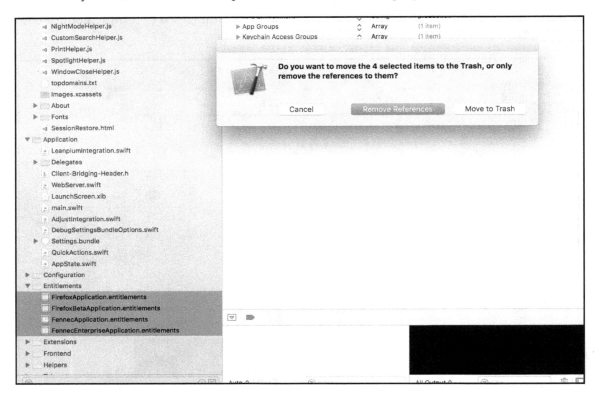

Also, ensure in the **Build Settings** that the **Provisioning Profile** matches the profiles we created in the previous chapters:

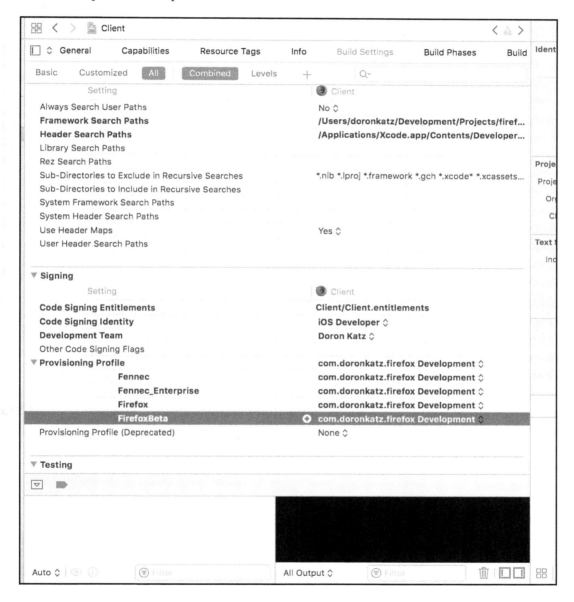

You will manually add the entitlements in the portal by selecting the **Edit** button and enabling **Push Notifications**. Ignore the section on adding certificates for now, as shown in the following screenshot:

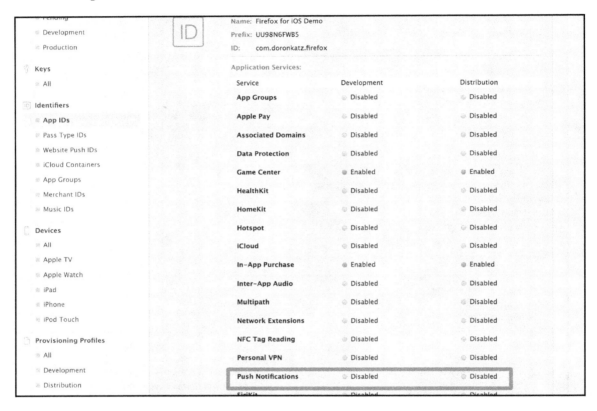

When everything is set up properly, we should get the following confirmation in our **Build Settings**:

As a final confirmation, you can also see that a `Client.entitlements` file has been generated in the `Client` folder. As you can see, while the task of creating the entitlements through Xcode isn't laborious in itself, repairing and renewing entitlements can become a bit of a hassle. This is where pem (`https://docs.fastlane.tools/actions/pem/`) comes in.

Introducing pem

The first half of this chapter explained what push notifications are, and the process by which a push notification is orchestrated from the provider/server, through the conduit that is APNs, and subsequently reaches the designated devices. The chapter has also illustrated how to enable push notifications manually via Xcode. This section will illustrate how pem can automate the process of push notifications and form part of the project workflow. You can either use the keyword pem, or the alias `get_push_certificate`. The following is the logo of pem:

pem (`https://docs.fastlane.tools/actions/pem/`) is one of the simplest of actions, yet it accomplishes a lot. Through a single command, pem is able to accomplish the following tasks:

- Creating a new push certification
- Creating a signing request
- Downloading the appropriate certificate
- Generating a new `.pem` file for uploading to the provider/server

Go ahead and enter the following in the project folder:

```
fastlane pem
```

Confirming a new push certificate has been created, you should see something similar to the following:

```
20:40 $ fastlane pem

+------------------+------------------------+
|         Summary for PEM 2.46.1           |
+------------------+------------------------+
| development      | false                  |
| generate_p12     | true                   |
| force            | false                  |
| save_private_key | true                   |
| app_identifier   | com.dktz.firefox       |
| username         | your_email@mac.com     |
| team_id          | 2U9RN6FWB5             |
| output_path      | .                      |
+------------------+------------------------+
```

```
[20:40:14]: Starting login with user 'dktz@mac.com'
[20:40:16]: Successfully logged in
[20:40:16]: Creating a new push certificate for app
'com.doronkatz.firefox'.
[20:40:18]: Private key: /Users/doronkatz/Development/Projects/firefox-
ios/production_com.doronkatz.firefox.pkey
[20:40:18]: p12 certificate: /Users/doronkatz/Development/Projects/firefox-
ios/production_com.doronkatz.firefox.p12
[20:40:18]: PEM: /Users/doronkatz/Development/Projects/firefox-
ios/production_com.doronkatz.firefox.pem
```

In the root folder, it will have created the following three files:

- `productioncom.yourname.firefox.p12`
- `productioncom.yournamefirefox.pkey`
- `productioncom.yourname.firefox.pem`

The basic command will only create a new certificate if you don't have an existing certificate, unless that certificate will expire within 30 days, in which case it will recreate it. You can override this behavior and force the creation of a new certificate by entering the following:

```
fastlane pem --force
```

To renew a certificate explicitly, enter the following command:

```
fastlane pem renew
```

So far, we have renewed production certificates. To renew a development certificate, enter the following:

```
fastlane pem --development
```

You should see a similar output for the initial command we entered:

```
20:49 $ fastlane pem --development

+------------------+-----------------------+
|          Summary for PEM 2.46.1          |
+------------------+-----------------------+
| development      | true                  |
| generate_p12     | true                  |
| force            | false                 |
| save_private_key | true                  |
| app_identifier   | com.doronktz.firefox  |
| username         | your_name@mac.com     |
```

```
| team_id           | UU98N6FWB5            |
| output_path       | .                    |
+-------------------+----------------------+

[20:50:07]: Starting login with user 'your_name@mac.com'
[20:50:08]: Successfully logged in
[20:50:09]: Creating a new push certificate for app
'com.doronkatz.firefox'.
[20:50:11]: Private key: /Users/doronkatz/Development/Projects/firefox-
ios/development_com.doronkatz.firefox.pkey
[20:50:11]: p12 certificate: /Users/doronkatz/Development/Projects/firefox-
ios/development_com.doronkatz.firefox.p12
[20:50:11]: PEM: /Users/doronkatz/Development/Projects/firefox-
ios/development_com.doronkatz.firefox.pem
```

The difference being, instead, development entitlements have been created:

- `developmentcom.yournamefirefox.p12`
- `developmentcom.dyourname.firefox.pem`
- `developmentcom.yourname.firefox.pkey`

To set a password for your `p12` file, you can enter:

```
fastlane pem -p "password"
```

Like the other *fastlane* actions, you can also choose the location to output the certificates:

```
fastlane pem -o ~/push/myCertificate.pem
```

List of pem commands

Finally, you can get a list of all the available parameters and commands for pem by entering:

```
fastlane pem --help
```

Updating our Fastfile

Open up the Fastfile we worked on in the previous chapter and go to the beta lane. We are simply going to add one line below the other commands, so your lane should now look something like this:

```
lane :beta do
  register_devices(devices_file: "devices.txt")
  match(git_url: "git@bitbucket.org:doron_katz/my-fastlane-keys.git",
    type: "development",
    app_identifier: "com.doronkatz.firefox")
    pem
end
```

Our lane is starting to look more comprehensive by the day. Let's run the entire lane again by typing the following in the Terminal:

```
fastlane beta
```

The output should produce something similar to the following:

```
[20:59:44]: ----------------------------------------------
[20:59:44]: --- Step: Verifying required fastlane version ---
[20:59:44]: ----------------------------------------------
[20:59:44]: Your fastlane version 2.46.1 matches the minimum requirement of
2.41.0 ✅
[20:59:44]: ------------------------------
[20:59:44]: --- Step: default_platform ---
[20:59:44]: ------------------------------
[20:59:44]: Driving the lane 'ios beta' 🚀
[20:59:44]: ------------------------------
[20:59:44]: --- Step: register_devices ---
[20:59:44]: ------------------------------
[21:00:00]: Fetching list of currently registered devices...
[21:00:02]: Successfully registered new devices.
[21:00:02]: --------------------
[21:00:02]: --- Step: match ---
[21:00:02]: --------------------

+------------------------+----------------------------------------+
|                       Summary for match 2.46.1                  |
+------------------------+----------------------------------------+
| git_url                | git@bitbucket.org:doron_katz/my-fas    |
|                        | tlane-keys.git                         |
| type                   | development                            |
| app_identifier         | com.doronkatz.firefox                  |
+------------------------+----------------------------------------+
```

```
| git_branch              | master                              |
| username                | dktz@mac.com                   |
| keychain_name           | login.keychain                      |
| readonly                | false                               |
| team_id                 | UU98N6FWB5                          |
| verbose                 | false                               |
| force                   | false                               |
| skip_confirmation       | false                               |
| shallow_clone           | false                               |
| clone_branch_directly   | false                               |
| force_for_new_devices   | false                               |
| skip_docs               | false                               |
| platform                | ios                                 |
+-------------------------+-------------------------------------+
```

[21:00:02]: Cloning remote git repo...
[21:00:02]: If cloning the repo takes too long, you can use the
`clone_branch_directly` option in match.

[21:00:27]:   Successfully decrypted certificates repo
[21:00:27]: Verifying that the certificate and profile are still valid on
the Dev Portal...
[21:00:31]: Installing certificate...

```
+--------------------+--------------------------------------------------+
|                         Installed Certificate                         |
+--------------------+--------------------------------------------------+
| User ID            | QW53HAMMWC                                       |
| Common Name        | iPhone Developer: Doron Katz (9X6AWM4CZ6)        |
| Organisation Unit  | UU98N6FWB5                                       |
| Organisation       | Doron Katz                                       |
| Country            | US                                               |
| Start Datetime     | Jul 12 23:45:16 2017 GMT                         |
| End Datetime       | Jul 12 23:45:16 2018 GMT                         |
+--------------------+--------------------------------------------------+
```

[21:00:37]: Installing provisioning profile...
[21:00:37]: 'match Development com.doronkatz.firefox' is available on the
Developer Portal, however it's 'Invalid', fixing this now for you

```
+----------------------------------+----------------------------+
|              Summary for sigh 2.46.1                         |
+----------------------------------+----------------------------+
| app_identifier                   | com.doronkatz.firefox |
| username                         | dktz@mac.com          |
| force                            | true                       |
| cert_id                          | P6J27D2843                 |
| provisioning_name                | match Development          |
```

```
|                                      | com.doronkatz.firefox |
| ignore_profiles_with_different_name  | true                  |
| team_id                              | UU98N6FWB5            |
| platform                             | ios                   |
| development                          | true                  |
| adhoc                                | false                 |
| skip_install                         | false                 |
| skip_fetch_profiles                  | false                 |
| skip_certificate_verification        | false                 |
+--------------------------------------+-----------------------+
```

```
[21:00:46]: Starting login with user 'dktz@mac.com'
[21:00:52]: Successfully logged in
[21:00:52]: Fetching profiles...
[21:00:53]: Verifying certificates...
[21:00:53]: No existing profiles found, that match the certificates you
have installed locally! Creating a new provisioning profile for you
[21:00:55]: Creating new provisioning profile for 'com.doronkatz.firefox'
with name 'match Development com.doronkatz.firefox' for 'ios' platform
[21:01:01]: Downloading provisioning profile...
[21:01:07]: Successfully downloaded provisioning profile...
[21:01:07]: Installing provisioning profile...
/var/folders/68/946ywfgx3jq3bwhy02std9tc0000gn/T/d20170715-92409-
ap5j7h/profiles/development/Development_com.doronkatz.firefox.mobileprovisi
on
[21:01:07]: Installing provisioning profile...
[21:01:09]: 🔒  Successfully encrypted certificates repo
[21:01:09]: Pushing changes to remote git repo...
```

```
+----------------------+-----------------------+------------------------+
|                     Installed Provisioning Profile                     |
+----------------------+-----------------------+------------------------+
| Parameter            | Environment Variable  | Value                  |
+----------------------+-----------------------+------------------------+
| App Identifier       |                       | com.doronkatz.firefox  |
| Type                 |                       | development            |
| Platform             |                       | ios                    |
| Profile UUID         | sigh_com.doronkatz.fi | aaed71eb-4d4b-4af5-87  |
|                      | refox_development     | 5e-14a9b811f2bc        |
| Profile Name         | sigh_com.doronkatz.fi | match Development       |
|                      | refox_development_pro | com.doronkatz.firefox  |
|                      | file-name             |                        |
| Profile Path         | sigh_com.doronkatz.fi | /Users/doronkatz/Libr  |
|                      | refox_development_pro | ary/MobileDevice/Prov  |
|                      | file-path             | isioning               |
|                      |                       | Profiles/aaed71eb-4d4  |
|                      |                       | b-4af5-875e-14a9b811f  |
```

```
|                     |                     | 2bc.mobileprovision  |
| Development Team ID  | sigh_com.doronkatz.fi | UU98N6FWB5          |
|                     | refox_development_tea |                     |
|                     | m-id                |                     |
+---------------------+---------------------+---------------------+
```

[21:01:14]: All required keys, certificates and provisioning profiles are installed
[21:01:14]: Setting Provisioning Profile type to 'development'

```
+------+---------------------+-------------+
|            fastlane summary              |
+------+---------------------+-------------+
| Step | Action              | Time (in s) |
+------+---------------------+-------------+
| 1    | Verifying required  | 0           |
|      | fastlane version    |             |
| 2    | default_platform    | 0           |
| 3    | register_devices    | 18          |
| 4    | match               | 72          |
+------+---------------------+-------------+
```

[21:01:14]: fastlane.tools finished successfully

Summary

Our lane is certainly doing a bit more now, but as you can see, it is starting to look more complete. So far, we have worked on our private `git` repository for our code-signing credentials and built the development and distribution certificates and the associated provisioning profiles, and we are now ensuring that our push notification provisioning is up to date. We are also maintaining our list of devices in a text file, which we started working on in the previous chapter.

In the next chapter, we are going to start working on something a bit different. We are going to create our apps on iTunes Connect, the developer portal, and the Google Play Store, using supply (https://github.com/fastlane/fastlane/tree/master/supply) and produce (https://github.com/fastlane/fastlane/tree/master/create_app_online).

7
Creating Our iOS and Android Apps with produce and supply

Now that we have our environment set up with the project, the first thing we are going to do is set up our project via **iTunes Connect** (https://itunesconnect.apple.com/login) and the **Apple Developer Portal** (https://developer.apple.com/). This chapter will set the framework for the rest of the book, especially the subsequent chapters where we start to work with certificates and provision our app. In this chapter, we are first going to demonstrate how a developer would go about registering a new device with Apple's Developer Program. To contrast it with this traditional workflow, we are then going to introduce you to the first *fastlane* action we will work with—**produce** (https://github.com/fastlane/fastlane/tree/master/create_app_online#readme). We will first show you how to make use of produce individually in the command line to not only register the app, but also work with metadata as you interface with the developer portal, all from Terminal. We will also introduce you to fastlane's Android cousin action, **supply** (https://github.com/fastlane/fastlane/tree/master/upload_to_play_store). Finally, we will conclude this chapter with the creation of our first lane, where we will add produce into our Fastfile workflow as part of our continuous delivery goals.

This chapter focuses on the creation of new iOS apps, bypassing iTunes Connect and the Developer Portal. Additionally, we will take a look at leveraging supply to create an Android app via *fastlane*, and publishing metadata on the Google Play Store.

In this chapter, we will be working with produce and supply through the command line to do the following:

- Register new apps on the developer portals
- Work with app groups
- Modify application services
- Integrate the lane into our project Fastfile
- Learn about supply, Android's metadata-updating counterpart utility

The process of creating an iOS

We will first go through the project development workflow, starting with this section, which will focus on the creation of your App ID using produce.

Registering your App ID with produce

Before we create our certificates and provisioning profiles, the first thing we are going to do is register an App ID in the **Developer Portal**, under **Certificates | Identifiers | Profiles**.

The first thing this screen will ask you for is your App ID name. Essentially, this is the name of your app, which in our case would be Firefox for iOS.

Along with the App ID name, we need to create a Bundle ID, a period-delimited identifier that is unique. The most common approach is to use a reverse-style domain name, say `com.packt.fastlane`, with the last part being the name of the app, and the second-to-last part being either a category, sub-company, or company name, depending on your organizational structure.

Finally, before completing this screen, you are asked to select the appropriate app services that your app will support, such as iCloud, App Groups, and HealthKit.

In this chapter, we are going to introduce you to the first *fastlane* action, produce, which will make this process more automated.

Provisioning your app

Next, you set your Developer, and either Ad-Hoc, App Store, or Enterprise profiles, depending on how you plan on distributing your app. Either way, you tie the provisioning profile to the App ID created in the previous step.

You will learn more about provisioning in `Chapter 3`, *Manage Provisioning Profiles with sigh*, and automate the process through sigh (`https://docs.fastlane.tools/actions/get_provisioning_profile/`).

Certificating your app

In order to complete the code signing of your app, you will need to create a developer or distribution certificate, which ties in with the associated provisioning profile.

You will learn more about certificates in `Chapter 4`, *Manage Code Signing Certificates with cert*, and automating the process through leveraging get_certificates (`https://docs.fastlane.tools/actions/get_certificates/`).

Distributing code-signing identities

Once you've set up the code-signing credentials, you will need to onboard new developers and make their environment setup easier. In `Chapter 5`, *Sync Profiles and Certificates with match*, we will take a look at how to distribute your code-signing certificates elegantly, using **match** (`https://github.com/fastlane/fastlane/tree/master/match`).

Managing push notifications

In addition to your certificates and provisioning profiles, you will most likely be supporting push notifications in your app.

In `Chapter 6`, *Manage Push Notification Profiles with pem*, you will learn how to make use of perm (`https://github.com/fastlane/fastlane/tree/master/pem`) to automate the process of handling the creation and maintenance of push notification profiles.

Building and packaging your app

Up until now, you will learn a few processes to automate the registration and provisioning of your app. This chapter focuses on the next logical step, which is to actually build your app. Through **gym** (https://github.com/fastlane/fastlane/tree/master/gym), you will learn how to automate building and packaging your app, getting it ready for distribution internally (beta distribution) or publishing externally to the App Store.

iTunes Connect versus Developer portal

To clear up any confusion, there are two closely connected portals in the Apple ecosystem—the all-encompassing **Apple Developer portal** (https://developer.apple.com/) and **iTunes Connect** (https://itunesconnect.apple.com/).

iTunes Connect is primarily used to actually publish and manage apps on the App Store, including setting metadata, screenshots, and so forth, whereas the Apple Developer portal is your first port of call in creating and managing certificates, identifiers, and profiles.

Adding capabilities

When you distribute your app on the App Store, if you require certain capabilities, they will need to be provisioned in order to be used, along with some additional configuration. Take a look at the following diagram:

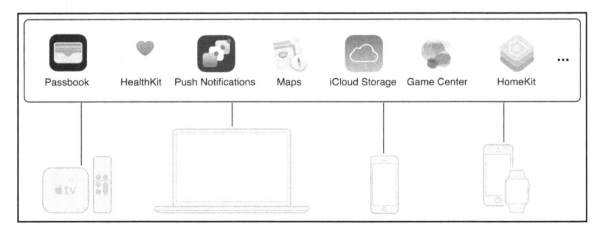

These include services such as CloudKit, Maps/Locations, Push Notifications, HealthKit, and so on. By letting Apple know the services you intend to support, the Developer portal provides Apple with the ability to implement an underlying security model to ensure that user-data privacy and security is protected even further.

Capabilities are usually signaled either at the time of registering/creating the app on iTunes Connect or via the Add Capabilities function within Xcode. Through the latter, Xcode automatically configures the project to use the capabilities and generates an entitlements list file, along with the code-signing and provisioning steps. Refer to the following screenshot:

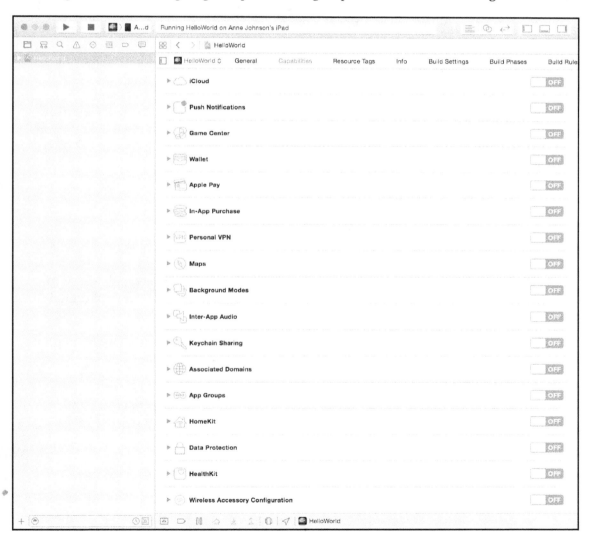

Refer to the `App Distribution Supported Capabilities` for the list of capabilities available on the various Apple platforms.

`Entitlements` is a provisioning configuration file that sets out a capability permission, granted to the app, that is included in the app's code-signature along with the certificate and provisioning profiles to request the operating system to grant access to said resources or system operations.

An entitlement extends the sandbox and capabilities of your app to allow a particular operation to occur. Let's take a look at how you would enable and configure the various capabilities, starting with iCloud support:

iCloud/CloudKit

Apple provides a robust cloud storage solution for storing your app's data and documents—**CloudKit** (`https://developer.apple.com/icloud/cloudkit/`). CloudKit works to ensure data is kept synced and up to date across all apps that are using the same CloudKit container, and Apple provides up to 1 PB of free data storage per app, which is quite generous.

To enable iCloud, in the Xcode project's **Capabilities** tab, toggle the iCloud property from off to on.

Passbook/Wallet

Apple Wallet (`https://developer.apple.com/wallet/`) provides users with access to manage their rewards cards, coupons, passes, and tickets as a dynamic form of digital payment for users to redeem using PassKit.

For information on how to work with Wallet, read Apple's documentation in the **Wallet Developer** (`https://developer.apple.com/library/content/documentation/UserExperience/Conceptual/PassKit_PG/index.html#//apple_ref/doc/uid/TP40012195`).

Enabling Wallet via Xcode involves the same process that we used to enable iCloud, toggling the Wallet property to on. Xcode will automatically add the relevant PassKit framework into your project.

Apple Pay

Similarly to Wallet, **Apple Pay** (https://www.apple.com/apple-pay/) allows users to make purchases with their bank cards and credit cards, safely and securely, through tapping their device at the card readers of supported merchants in their stores.

Rather than using the POS in the merchants' stores, developers have the ability to request payment from users for physical goods/services using Apple Pay. To enable Apple Pay, as we did with the other capabilities in Xcode, toggle the property option to on. A dialog box will appear requesting the Apple Pay identifiers.

For more information on how to work with Apple Pay, refer to the **Apple Pay Programming** (https://developer.apple.com/library/content/ApplePay_Guide/index.html#//apple_ref/doc/uid/TP40014764).

In-App Purchase

In-App Purchase—unlike Apple Pay, which is used for the purchasing of physical goods and services—is used for purchasing digital goods that provide greater access to content or functionality. Take a look at the following screenshot:

Toggling support for In-App Purchase in Xcode will automatically add the `StoreKit` framework to your project. For more information on how to work with In-App Purchase, refer to Apple's `In-App Purchase Programming`.

Map/Location

By enabling the Maps capability, you are able to create navigational-like routing apps and access greater and more persistent location information from the user.

Enable **Maps,** as well as the various modes of routing specific to your app, in the Xcode Capabilities tab, as shown in the following screenshot:

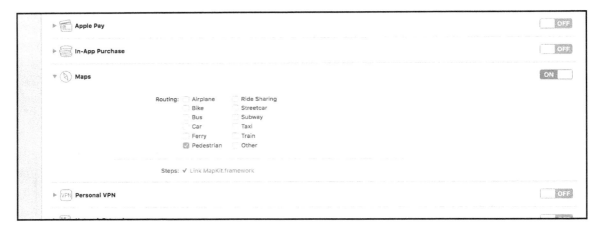

The modes of routing available to you include:

- **Airplane**
- **Bike**
- **Bus**
- **Car**
- **Ferry**
- **Pedestrian**

In order to support routing directions, you are required to perform additional configuration steps, which you can learn more about by consulting the `Location and Maps Programming`.

Background Modes

The **Background Modes** capability affords your app the ability to run in Background Mode for extended periods of time as a specific additional permission, as shown in the following screenshot:

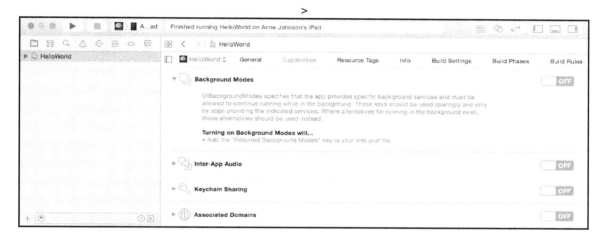

Enabling this capability in Xcode, you would then need to specify the reason for the use of extended background modes from a list, which includes the following:

- **Audio and AirPlay** and **Picture in Picture**
- **Location updates**
- **Voice over IP**
- **External accessory communications**
- **Uses Bluetooth LE accessories**
- **Background fetch**
- **Remote notifications**

App Groups

Finally, **App Groups** provides multiple apps with the ability to share data through a shared container sandbox, allowing for more intimate inter-app communications, as shown in the following screenshot:

Once you've enabled support for App Groups, a container ID would be downloaded from your developer account and be displayed in the Xcode capabilities subsection.

Inter-App Audio

Inter-App Audio provides apps with the ability to export audio data to other apps:

For more information on working with audio, refer to the Apple **Audio Toolbox** framework (`https://developer.apple.com/documentation/audiotoolbox`) guide.

HealthKit

HealthKit provides apps with the ability to access, store, and retrieve personal health information securely kept on the device.

For more information on working with HealthKit, refer to the **Apple Developer HealthKit** guide (`https://developer.apple.com/healthkit/`).

Data Protection

The Data Protection capability adds another layer of security to stored files within the app, using the device's hardware encryption capabilities for all the stored files within the container.

There are various modes of protection, from the default complete protection, where files are inaccessible when the device is locked. Please refer to the Apple Protecting Data Using On-Disk Encryption guide for other examples.

Adding HomeKit support

HomeKit is Apple's protocol for allowing apps to communicate with connected IoT home devices and accessories, for a connected-home experience. For more information on working with HomeKit, refer to the **Apple HomeKit Framework** guide(`https://developer.apple.com/documentation/homekit`).

Adding Associated Domains support

Associated Domains provides the app with domain-specific access to services, such as passwords saved in Safari .

Keychain sharing support

Keychain sharing allows apps to share secure credentials and passwords from one app to another app. Enabling this property setting will update the `entitlements` file by setting a `Keychain-access-groups` property to associate the app with that keychain group.

Push notifications

We will be covering push notification support in greater detail in Chapter 6, *Manage Push Notification Profiles with pem*.

Introducing produce

produce (`https://github.com/fastlane/fastlane/tree/master/create_app_online`) provides developers with the ability to directly orchestrate the process of creating new iOS applications on the Developer portal, and iTunes Connect, all from within the command line. The following is the logo of produce:

This utility provides the ability for developers to create and register new apps on iTunes Connect/Developer portal, and register and modify application services, such as providing access to CloudKit, App Groups, and associate App Groups with the Apple Developer portal.

produce (`https://github.com/fastlane/fastlane/tree/master/create_app_online`) also supports multiple Apple accounts, storing and containing each set of credentials securely in the keychain.

Usage

The first half of this chapter outlined the process and workflow by which a developer would register an app on iTunes Connect, as well as select the various capabilities that the app will support. In this section, we are going to demonstrate how *fastlane* and produce can be employed in lieu of the preceding manual steps, and automate the process of creating an app.

We will start off with entering the most basic of the action commands in the project folder in Terminal:

```
fastlane produce
```

This command creates the actual app for you in iTunes Connect by prompting you for your team ID (if you have multiple accounts), as well as the name of your app:

```
18:56 $ fastlane produce

+----------------+------------------------+
|         Summary for produce 2.46.1      |
+----------------+------------------------+
| username       | dktz@mac.com           |
| app_identifier | com.doronkatz.firefox  |
| sku            | 140086w4J9             |
| platform       | ios                    |
| language       | English                |
| skip_itc       | false                  |
| skip_devcenter | false                  |
| team_id        | PUX8N6FRBR             |
+----------------+------------------------+

[18:57:17]: To not be asked about this value, you can specify it using
'app_name'
[18:57:17]: App Name: firefox for iOS
[18:57:29]: Creating new app 'firefox for iOS' on iTunes Connect
[18:57:31]: Ensuring version number
[18:57:31]: Successfully created new app 'firefox for iOS' on iTunes
Connect with ID xxx
...
```

Let's jump to iTunes Connect to confirm that it has indeed created the new app:

And there you have it—it has created the app for us without the hassle of having to manually create it ourselves via the portal. You can also confirm on the Developer portal that the app ID is created for our Firefox app. Beyond the basic command, there are other options you have at your disposal through produce.

Enabling services

We talked about enabling services and capabilities in our app earlier, and demonstrated how to do it via Xcode. You can also use produce to enable or disable services just as easily. To enable iCloud and push notifications, you would enter the following:

```
fastlane produce enable_services —icloud cloudkit —-push-notification
```

It will confirm the services you have enabled, similar to the following:

```
. . .
[19:08:29]: Starting login with user 'XXXXXXX
[19:08:31]: Successfully logged in
[19:08:31]: [DevCenter] App found 'Firefox for iOS Demo'
[19:08:31]: Enabling services
[19:08:31]: Done! Enabled 2 services.
✔ ~/Development/Projects/firefox-ios
. . .
```

You can get a list of all the services that you can enable as a parameter by entering the following:

```
fastlane produce enable_services --help
```

Take a look at the following code snippet:

```
Examples:
   # Enable HealthKit, HomeKit and Passbook
   fastlane produce enable_services -a com.example.app --healthkit --
homekit --passbook
  Options:
     --app-group           Enable App Groups
     --apple-pay           Enable Apple Pay
     --associated-domains Enable Associated Domains
     --data-protection STRING Enable Data Protection,  suitable values are
"complete", "unlessopen" and
"untilfirstauth"
     --game-center         Enable Game Center
     --healthkit           Enable HealthKit
     --homekit             Enable HomeKit
```

```
   --wireless-conf       Enable Wireless Accessory Configuration
   --icloud STRING       Enable iCloud, suitable values are "legacy" and
"cloudkit"
```

Optional parameters

In addition to the basic commands for creating your app on iTunes Connect, *fastlane* provides additional parameters that we can pass in.

App and bundle ID

You can pass in the app ID parameter by entering `fastlane` and an `app_identifier` (that is, `com.doronkatz.firefox`) to explicitly set the app ID with which to associate the iTunes app registration. The same can be done when adding the bundle ID :

```
fastlane -e budle_identifier.*
```

Skipping iTunes Connect or Dev Center

You can also explicitly ask produce to skip the creation of the zoo on iTunes Connect or Developer portal by entering the parameter `fastlane -i etc [value]` or `fastlane -d dev_center_value` respectively.

Creating and associating a new app group

To create a new app group, enter the following syntax in Terminal:

```
fastlane produce group -g group.packt -n "FireFox Family Group"
```

Terminal will output the following confirmation:

```
[19:24:11]: Starting login with user 'XXXXX'
[19:24:13]: Successfully logged in
[19:24:13]: Creating new app group 'FireFox Family Group' with identifier
'group.packt' on the Apple Dev Center
[19:24:13]: Created group X2CQ4LRTAG
[19:24:14]: Finished creating new app group 'FireFox Family Group' on the
Dev Center
```

You can confirm that the group was created in the Developer portal using the identifier stated in the preceding code. To associate an app with the group, enter the following (substituting your settings):

```
fastlane produce associate_group -a com.doronkatz.firefox group.packt
```

The output would then be as follows:

```
[19:26:15]: Starting login with user 'XXXXXX'
[19:26:17]: Successfully logged in
[19:26:17]: Validating groups before association
[19:26:18]: Finalising association with 1 groups
[19:26:19]: Done!
```

Updating our Fastfile

So with an empty Fastfile, let's start by creating our first lane, which we will label `release`. In the next chapter, we will start working on a separate release for beta releases. Our first lane will only have one action for now, and that's `produce`. We will add more to it in future chapters.

Enter the following in your Fastfile:

```
lane :release do
    produce(
    username: 'your@email_address.com',
    app_identifier: 'com.doronkatz.firefox',
    app_name: 'Firefox for iOS',
    language: 'English',
    app_version: '1.0',
    team_name: 'Doron Katz' # only necessary when in multiple teams
    )
  end
```

Run the lane by entering the following:

```
fastlane release
```

And that's it! We started creating a simple but functional lane. We can test our very first lane. The results will confirm that we integrated our app creation into our Fastfile workflow by showing us something similar to the following:

```
[19:45:19]: ------------------------------------------------
[19:45:19]: --- Step: Verifying required fastlane version ---
[19:45:19]: ------------------------------------------------
```

```
[19:45:19]: Your fastlane version 2.47.0 matches the minimum requirement of
2.41.0  ✅
[19:45:19]: ------------------------------
[19:45:19]: --- Step: default_platform ---
[19:45:19]: ------------------------------
[19:45:19]: Driving the lane 'ios release'  🚀
[19:45:19]: --------------------
[19:45:19]: --- Step: produce ---
[19:45:19]: --------------------

+-----------------+-----------------------+
|       Summary for produce 2.47.0        |
+-----------------+-----------------------+
| username        | your_email_address    |
| app_identifier  | com.doronkatz.firefox |
| app_name        | Firefox for iOS       |
| language        | English               |
| app_version     | 1.0                   |
| team_name       | Doron Katz            |
| sku             | XXXXXXXXXX            |
| platform        | ios                   |
| skip_itc        | false                 |
| skip_devcenter  | false                 |
| team_id         | XXXXXXXXXX            |
+-----------------+-----------------------+


...


+------+---------------------+------------+
|              fastlane summary           |
+------+---------------------+------------+
| Step | Action              | Time (in s)|
+------+---------------------+------------+
| 1    | Verifying required  | 0          |
|      | fastlane version    |            |
| 2    | default_platform    | 0          |
| 3    | produce             | 52         |
+------+---------------------+------------+

[19:46:11]: fastlane.tools finished successfully  ▲
```

Introducing supply

While this chapter has focused heavily on iOS, *fastlane* does indeed also have an Android counterpart to produce called supply, which can be found at `https://docs.fastlane.tools/`. The following is the logo of supply:

Like the action produce, supply provides developers with the capability to update and retrieve Android apps (although it cannot create new apps) on the Google Play Store, as well as upload new APK builds to the store. In addition, supply is capable of uploading app icons, promotional graphics, and screenshots.

If you have not already done so, the first step in this process is to register as a Google developer, as explained next.

Setting up a Google Play developer account

To be able to publish Android apps on the Google Play Store, you must first register as a developer. There is a one-off registration fee of $25 in order to create your own account.

To register as a Google Play Store developer, you need to do the following:

1. Begin by signing in with your Google account at `play.google.com/`.
2. Read and agree to the Developer Distribution Agreement.
3. Pay the registration fee. This can be done with most credit and debit cards, but availability differs widely, depending on location.
4. Finally, complete your details. Your developer name can be anything you like up to 50 characters long, and will appear under your apps' titles in the Play Store. Refer to the following screenshot:

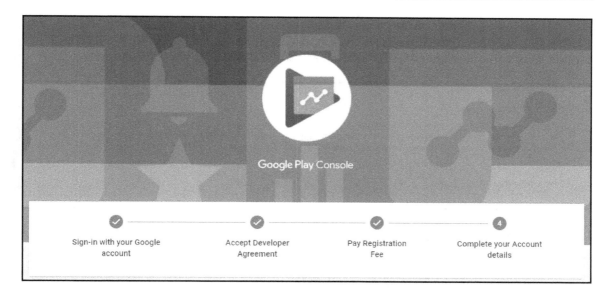

As a registered developer, you can now leverage fastlane's supply action with your Google Play Store and Developer Console. We will briefly go through setting up *fastlane* with Google Developer Console in the next section.

Setting up *fastlane* and supply

From the API access page of your console, you can configure and update Android applications using third-party software packages. We will configure the API access to allow us to use *fastlane*.

Before clicking on the **CREATE NEW PROJECT** button, it is worth taking note of the security disclaimer on the page before moving on. If you encounter any errors when setting up your new project, do the following:

1. In your project Terminal, run the following:

    ```
    fastlane init
    ```

2. When prompted, enter your package name.
3. Next, enter your JSON secret file.
4. Finally, enter N when asked if you intend to upload to the Play Store. This is something you will manually do later on.

fastlane will now generate the appropriate *fastlane* directory, containing both the Appfile and Fastfile files. Return to the developer console and click on the **CREATE NEW PROJECT** button. This will open a page with a dialog, as shown in the following screenshot:

Service Accounts

Service accounts allow access to the Google Play Developer Publishing API on behalf of an application rather than an end user. Service accounts are ideal for accessing the API from an unattended server, such as an automated build server (e.g. Jenkins). All actions will be shown as originating from the service account. You can configure fine grained permissions for the service account on the 'User Accounts & Rights' page.

There are no service accounts associated with your project.

CREATE SERVICE ACCOUNT

Follow these steps to complete the setup of this account:

1. Begin by entering a suitable name for the account.
2. Select **Project | Service Account Actor** as a role.
3. Check **Furnish** to furnish a new private key.
4. Select **JSON** as the **Key type** and click on **Create**. This will download a file onto your computer.
5. Make a note of this filename.
6. Click **Done** to close the console dialog.
7. Click on **Grant Access**, and select **Release Manager** from the **Role** dropdown.
8. Click **Add User** to close the dialog.
9. Finally, edit the `json_key_file` line to read as follows:
   `json_key_file "your_downloaded_key_path.json"`

You are now ready to use supply, and we will explore the features available to us next.

Using supply

First up, you will see how easy it is to update your app's metadata directly through supply. From the Terminal, within your project's folder, enter the following command:

```
fastlane supply init
```

This will allow you to download your app's metadata, including images, to a location of your choice. Make the metadata changes you require, such as adding new images or including an APK. Enter the following command to upload your changes to the Play Store:

```
fastlane supply run
```

You could also enter `fastlane supply` (omitting `run`) to upload data to the store. Useful information about available commands and environmental variables can be summoned with the following:

```
fastlane action supply
```

Uploading an APK to the store is even easier. Simply run the following command:

```
fastlane supply --apk your_path/to/your_app.apk
```

Finer-grained control over promotional images is also provided by making use of the `images` folder within our local directories. You are able to change the following forms of promotional graphics, within the folder, by adhering to the following file names:

- `featureGraphic`
- `icon`
- `promoGraphic`
- `tvBanner`

The files can have .png, .jpg, or .jpeg file extensions.

It is also possible to upload screenshots by creating directories with the following file names:

- `phoneScreenshots`
- `sevenInchScreenshots`
- `tenInchScreenshots`
- `tvScreenshots`
- `wearScreenshots`

The files can have .png, .jpg, or .jpeg file extensions.

 Be aware that these folders will replace all images previously uploaded to the store.

We have only touched the surface of what you can do with supply; there are more advanced options available, including integrating supply with the Espresso testing support library, which is beyond the scope of this book.

If you are interested in exploring more advanced development topics with supply, refer to `github.com/fastlane/fastlane/tree/master/upload_to_play_store`, as well as `https://docs.fastlane.tools/actions/upload_to_play_store/`

As we have seen in this section, supply is Android's counterpart to produce on the iOS side, enabling you to easily upload Android apps to the Google Play Store, along with updating your metadata and images in a convenient manner. The benefits of managing your app by publishing through *fastlane* lie in being able to version control your store content locally, as part of your automated workflow. Our automated workflow means that you don't have to do your own mabling, allowing you to easily upload your Android app with Espresso testing, which would otherwise be lengthy and prone to human error.

Summary

And we are done with our first Fastfile lane, as we worked our way through creating our app through produce (`https://docs.fastlane.tools/actions/create_app_online/`) and even learned a bit about its Android counterpart, supply (`https://docs.fastlane.tools/actions/upload_to_play_store/`). In this chapter, you learned how to work with the individual commands that produce uses to create an iTunes Connect app, as well as how to embed the action within our Fastfile workflow.

In the next chapter, we will work through the various actions in *fastlane* that will help us provision our app. We will also be working with certificates and code-signing our apps through automation without having to jump into iTunes Connect or the Developer portal.

8
Build and Package Apps for the App Store with gym

Up until now, we have been working with the various *fastlane* actions to create and distribute certificates and provisioning profiles and to communicate with iTunes Connect and the Developer portal through the command line. We will finally start to implement the real workhorse actions from this chapter, starting with gym (`https://docs.fastlane.tools/actions/gym/`), an action that will help us automate the process of building and packaging our app.

The actions so far have helped us set the stage by ensuring all our configurations are in place for this chapter and beyond, where we will work on the building and packaging aspects as well as the generation of snapshots in the subsequent chapters.

This chapter will focus on building and packaging our iOS app into a `.ipa` file and demonstrate how we would package it for local distribution (beta testing) versus deployment to the App Store and Enterprise customers.

We will be working with gym from the command line to:

- Build an app for developer distribution
- Build an app for ad hoc and Enterprise distribution
- Build an app for App Store distribution
- Create a Gymfile to store build configurations
- Create a manifest file for app thinning
- Integrate the lane into our project Fastfile

Traditional process of building an app

As your development progresses and it becomes time for you to test features in a truly agile way with others, you will want to distribute your app to beta testers internally, and eventually get your app to a state that is ready to be published to the App Store.

In the previous chapter, we had a text file that we included with a list of devices we wanted to register as part of our beta lane, but presuming we didn't have that, we would normally have to resort to registering the devices by supplying the device IDs through the Apple Developer portal (`https://developer.apple.com/library/content/documentation/IDEs/Conceptual/AppDistributionGuide/MaintainingProfiles/MaintainingProfiles.html#//apple_ref/doc/uid/TP40012582-CH30-SW10`).

Next, we will show you how you would traditionally go about building your app to test it with registered devices using the ad hoc provisioning profile and Xcode.

Using Xcode to build an app

You will need to archive your app, which you can accomplish by performing the following steps in Xcode:

1. Select the generic iOS device from the Scheme toolbar.
2. Select **Product** | **Archive** from the menu.

Xcode will then validate the app by running a few tests, including provisioning integrity, and will subsequently complete the process of archiving the app. If there are any issues, Xcode will output a warning or error.

We then reach the **Organizer** window, which displays our just-built archive. From this point, we have the option to distribute the app to our beta testers or distribute to the App Store. The choice you make will sign your app accordingly, but either way, it will produce a file with a `.ipa` extension.

For beta-testing purposes, from this screen, we select the **Export...** button and choose **Save for Ad Hoc Deployment**, and the app will be code-signed with the distribution certificate we created in the previous chapters. Refer to the following screenshot:

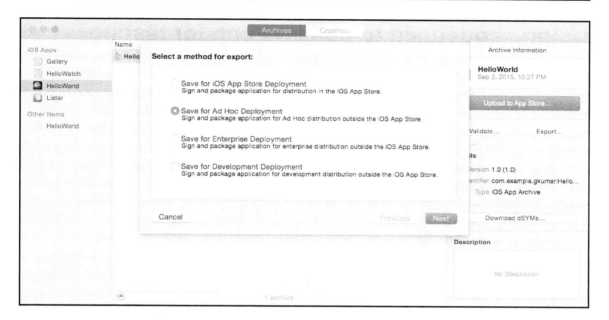

You will then be prompted to choose the development team, from which you would select the appropriate development user account. You will also have the option to select whether to export the app as a universal app or a specific device variant (that is iPhone only).

Finally, you will also be asked if you have any on-demand resources that you will need to upload, including a manifest file for over-the-air installations, for app-thinning purposes. We will talk about manifest files in detail later in this chapter.

Xcode will create the `.ipa` file in a folder you have nominated, from which you can distribute to your users.

Distributing your app for testing

We have a dedicated chapter on distributing your app for testing, but essentially, once you have the `.ipa` file, you can email it to users, put it up on a central location for download, or use a popular testing distribution platform, such as Apple's **TestFlight** (https:// developer.apple.com/testflight/) or **HockeyApp** (https://www.hockeyapp.net/).

Using xcodebuild to build an app for testing

Xcode is the most common avenue for developers; you are also able to make use of the command line tool that Xcode provides, called `xcodebuild`, which you can leverage to build your apps outside of Xcode. This is a more common approach for development environments where teams make use of automated scripts to build their projects.

With `xcodebuild`, you can choose to build a specific scheme that is part of a `.xcworkspace` or a `.xcodeproj`. To build for a workspace, enter the following in Terminal:

```
xcodebuild clean archive -archivePath build/FireFox -scheme Client -
workspace Firefox.xcworkspace
...
xcodebuild -exportArchive \
        -exportFormat ipa \
        -archivePath "build/Firefox.xcarchive" \
        -exportPath "build/Firefox.ipa" \
        -exportProvisioningProfile "ProvisioningDevProfile"
```

The two commands in sequence will build and archive the workspace project to a build folder and then create a `.ipa`, respectively. The provisioning profile selected will determine whether you are building to distribute to beta testers or for the App Store.

While it's not expected, developers will most commonly opt for the second option, using Xcode and the UI as a visual guide. While being an easier proposition for developers, it is still cumbersome and requires a bunch of pointing-and-clicking and manual intervention. It is worth noting that the use of `xcodebuild` is essentially how gym works under the hood, only it integrates with other utilities to accomplish more and make the process more automated.

The hope is that this chapter will demonstrate how through a single command-line, gym can package your app as part of the automating process we are building as part of our development workflow.

Next, we will introduce you to gym (`https://docs.fastlane.tools/actions/gym/`) and how you can substitute its simple command line syntax in lieu of the preceding steps to build and package your app.

Introducing gym

As the official project page states, gym automates the process of building and packaging iOS apps, taking care of the heavys workload, from manually archiving to code signing your app for testing or publishing purposes. You can either use the keyword `gym`, or the alias `build_ios_app`. The following is the logo of gym:

Usage

As with any of the other *fastlane* utilities, gym works even better in concert with other utilities as part of a lane, and we will show you how to integrate gym into our Fastfile later on. For now, let's start off with the simplest command:

```
fastlane gym
```

When prompted for the scheme, select `Client`.

You will get a whole bunch of Terminal text that resembles the following:

```
. . .
[17:45:02]: $ xcodebuild -list -project ./Client.xcodeproj
. . .
. . .
[17:45:13]: $ set -o pipefail && xcodebuild -scheme Fennec -project
./Client.xcodeproj -destination 'generic/platform=iOS' -archivePath
/Users/doronkatz/Library/Developer/Xcode/Archives/2017-07-29/Client\
2017-07-29\ 17.45.13.xcarchive archive | tee
/Users/doronkatz/Library/Logs/gym/Client-Fennec.log | xcpretty
[17:45:14]: > 2017-07-29 17:45:14.306 xcodebuild[75305:5197460] [MT]
PluginLoading: Required plug-in compatibility UUID DFFB3951-
EB0A-4C09-9DAC-5F2D28CC839C for plug-in at path '~/Library/Application
Support/Developer/Shared/Xcode/Plug-ins/XcodeColors.xcplugin' not present
in DVTPlugInCompatibilityUUIDs
[17:45:14]: > 2017-07-29 17:45:14.306 xcodebuild[75305:5197460] [MT]
PluginLoading: Required plug-in compatibility UUID DFFB3951-
EB0A-4C09-9DAC-5F2D28CC839C for plug-in at path '~/Library/Application
Support/Developer/Shared/Xcode/Plug-ins/RealmPlugin.xcplugin' not present
in DVTPlugInCompatibilityUUIDs
[17:45:14]: > 2017-07-29 17:45:14.307 xcodebuild[75305:5197460] [MT]
```

```
PluginLoading: Required plug-in compatibility UUID DFFB3951-
EB0A-4C09-9DAC-5F2D28CC839C for plug-in at path '~/Library/Application
Support/Developer/Shared/Xcode/Plug-ins/RealmBrowser.xcplugin' not present
in DVTPlugInCompatibilityUUIDs
[17:45:14]: > 2017-07-29 17:45:14.307 xcodebuild[75305:5197460] [MT]
PluginLoading: Required plug-in compatibility UUID DFFB3951-
EB0A-4C09-9DAC-5F2D28CC839C for plug-in at path '~/Library/Application
Support/Developer/Shared/Xcode/Plug-ins/OMQuickHelp.xcplugin' not present
in DVTPlugInCompatibilityUUIDs
[17:45:14]: > 2017-07-29 17:45:14.307 xcodebuild[75305:5197460] [MT]
PluginLoading: Required plug-in compatibility UUID DFFB3951-
EB0A-4C09-9DAC-5F2D28CC839C for plug-in at path '~/Library/Application
Support/Developer/Shared/Xcode/Plug-ins/OMQuickHelp 2.xcplugin' not present
in DVTPlugInCompatibilityUUIDs
[17:45:14]: > 2017-07-29 17:45:14.308 xcodebuild[75305:5197460] [MT]
PluginLoading: Required plug-in compatibility UUID DFFB3951-
EB0A-4C09-9DAC-5F2D28CC839C for plug-in at path '~/Library/Application
Support/Developer/Shared/Xcode/Plug-ins/NCSimulatorPlugin.xcplugin' not
present in DVTPlugInCompatibilityUUIDs
[17:45:14]: > 2017-07-29 17:45:14.308 xcodebuild[75305:5197460] [MT]
PluginLoading: Required plug-in compatibility UUID DFFB3951-
EB0A-4C09-9DAC-5F2D28CC839C for plug-in at path '~/Library/Application
Support/Developer/Shared/Xcode/Plug-ins/CocoaPods.xcplugin' not present in
DVTPlugInCompatibilityUUIDs
[17:45:14]: > 2017-07-29 17:45:14.309 xcodebuild[75305:5197460] [MT]
PluginLoading: Required plug-in compatibility UUID DFFB3951-
EB0A-4C09-9DAC-5F2D28CC839C for plug-in at path '~/Library/Application
Support/Developer/Shared/Xcode/Plug-ins/Alcatraz.xcplugin' not present in
DVTPlugInCompatibilityUUIDs
[17:45:14]: > 2017-07-29 17:45:14.309 xcodebuild[75305:5197460] [MT]
PluginLoading: Required plug-in compatibility UUID DFFB3951-
EB0A-4C09-9DAC-5F2D28CC839C for plug-in at path '~/Library/Application
Support/Developer/Shared/Xcode/Plug-ins/AdjustFontSize.xcplugin' not
present in DVTPlugInCompatibilityUUIDs
[17:45:16]: > Building Client/Shared [Fennec]
[17:45:16]: > Check Dependencies
[17:45:16]: > Processing Info.plist.
...
[17:45:49]: > Compiling NSCoderExtensions.swift
[17:45:49]: > Compiling AppConstants.swift
[17:45:50]: > Compiling NotificationConstants.swift
[17:45:50]: > Compiling StringExtensions.swift
[17:45:53]: > Compiling AssertionUtils.swift
[17:45:53]: > Compiling DictionaryExtensions.swift
[17:45:53]: > Compiling Error.swift
[17:45:53]: > Compiling NSURLExtensions.swift
[17:45:53]: > Compiling Reachability.swift
[17:45:53]: > Compiling KeyboardHelper.swift
```

```
[17:45:53]: > Compiling NSURLProtectionSpaceExtensions.swift
[17:45:53]: > Compiling SupportUtils.swift
[17:45:53]: > Compiling Loader.swift
[17:45:53]: > Compiling UserAgent.swift
[17:45:53]: > Compiling WeakList.swift
[17:45:53]: > Compiling UIImageExtensions.swift
[17:45:53]: > Compiling NSScannerExtensions.swift
[17:45:53]: > Compiling HexExtensions.swift
[17:45:53]: > Compiling Result.swift
[17:45:53]: > Compiling UIColorExtensions.swift
[17:45:53]: > Compiling DeferredUtils.swift
[17:45:53]: > Compiling AppInfo.swift
[17:45:53]: > Compiling MutableBox.swift
[17:45:53]: > Compiling NSCharacterSetExtensions.swift
[17:45:53]: > Compiling Logger.swift
[17:45:54]: > Compiling AsyncReducer.swift
[17:45:54]: > Compiling JSONExtensions.swift
[17:45:54]: > Compiling NSMutableAttributedStringExtensions.swift
[17:45:54]: > Compiling SystemUtils.swift
[17:45:55]: > Compiling SetExtensions.swift
[17:45:55]: > Compiling PhoneNumberFormatter.swift
[17:45:55]: > Compiling NSStringExtensions.swift
[17:45:58]: > Compiling AlamofireExtensions.swift
...
[17:48:46]: > ** ARCHIVE SUCCEEDED **
```

It will take a little while to complete, but essentially, what we've done with one command is compile and build our client scheme app using default properties, creating an archive. Let's take a look at some options we have with gym next.

Parameters and options

By passing in --scheme, we can pre-empt the prompt, so to speak, and select Fennec, as shown in the following command:

```
fastlane gym --workspace "Client.xcworkspace" --scheme "Fennec"
```

By adding the --clean parameter, we can ensure we do a clean-and-build, akin to *Command* + *K* in Xcode. If we had multiple Xcode applications installed, say Xcode 8 and 9, we could nominate which one we wanted gym to run against by adding the following parameters:

```
fastlane gym —-xcode-select "/Applications/Xcode6.2.app" gym
```

We can also explicitly set an `export` method, say to export as `ad-hoc`, by entering the following:

```
fastlane gym --export_method ad-hoc
```

To export to the App Store, use `app-store`. To add an `output` directory explicitly, add:

```
fastlane gym --output_directory "Export_Folder"
```

Manifest files/app thinning

App thinning (`https://developer.apple.com/library/content/documentation/IDEs/Conceptual/AppDistributionGuide/AppThinning/AppThinning.html`) is a feature that was added back in iOS 9 as a way of optimizing the installation of iOS apps on the user's device, *"by tailoring app delivery to the capabilities of the user's particular device, with minimal footprint"* (Source: Apple). That is, developers can distribute apps that will result in faster downloads and leave more space available on the end user's devices.

App thinning automatically detects the device type and downloads only the relevant content for that device, at the correct resolution, from the resource catalog.

Slicing is an aspect of app thinning which delivers a different version of the app bundle for different target devices, as opposed to encompassing all the types of target devices within the one ipa. By slicing the file via iTunes Connect, the user will get the image resources according to their device resolution capabilities. If you noticed during the exporting exercise in Xcode, you had the option to export variants from the archive. Take a look at the following diagram:

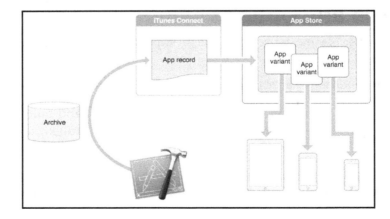

In fact, during normal development workflows, when running the app via Simulator, Xcode automatically slices the app and asset catalogs appropriately, with a variant to improve debug and build times.

Bitcode, on the other hand, is an *intermediate representation* of the app you have on iTunes Connect that contains bitcode that will subsequently be compiled and linked to the store. *"Including* bitcode *will allow Apple to re-optimize your app binary in the future without the need to submit a new version of your app to the store."* (Source: Apple)

Bitcode is on by default for iOS but can be removed. With the gym, you can opt to add or remove bitcode, and include the **dSYMs (Debug Symbols Files)** accordingly:

```
fastlane gym --include_bitcode true --include_symbols false
```

 dSYM or **Debug Symbols** files store debug symbols for your iOS or macOS apps, and various tools can be used to substitute the symbols for the actual methods in your crash logs, making it harder to reverse engineer your app. You pass the dSYM file to a third-party tool like Crashlytics to allow that service to translate the obfuscated log file into meaningful crash logs with actual method names.

Storing gym configurations externally with a Gymfile

As you may have noticed, the gym commands could end up having a lot of parameters and having to remember the attributes you need to specify the parameters can be cumbersome each time you want to do a build manually. We will see in the next section how, by adding gym to our Fastfile, we can ensure the parameters are always included; but there may be times when we want to run gym with the parameters but not within a Fastfile. This is where Gymfile comes in handy, a way in which you can persist with your default parameters so that every time you call gym, the default parameters will be included.

We are going to initialize and create a Gymfile now, so in your project folder in Terminal, enter the following:

```
fastlane gym init
```

The console should return the following:

```
[11:36:38]: Successfully created './fastlane/Gymfile'.
```

Open up the file in the location specified above using a simple code-editor, and you will observe that a default/generic Gymfile has been created, with some comments included:

```
# For more information about this configuration visit
# https://github.com/fastlane/fastlane/tree/master/gym#gymfile

# In general, you can use the options available
# fastlane gym --help

# Remove the # in front of the line to enable the option

# scheme "Example"

# sdk "iphoneos9.0"

output_directory "./"
```

Go ahead and remove the comments and change the file so that we can target our project. The file should now contain the following:

```
# For more information about this configuration visit
# https://github.com/fastlane/fastlane/tree/master/gym#gymfile

# In general, you can use the options available
# fastlane gym --help

# Remove the # in front of the line to enable the option

scheme "Fennec"

sdk "iphoneos10.3"

output_directory "./build"

output_name "Firefox"

clean true
```

We just specified the scheme we are using, the SDK version, where we want the output .ipa to be stored, as well as the name of the .ipa file. We also ensured with the last line that we always clean the project prior to compilation and archiving. Give it another try by typing in fastlane gym, and you should see that it will pick the preferences from the Gymfile we just created.

Exporting plist files

Additionally, gym provides you with the capabilities to export a plist file with optional parameters that you can modify for purposes like creating a manifest file for app thinning. You can easily provide the plist file by adding the `export_options` `"./propertyFile.plist"` parameter, pointing to your file, or by adding the key/values directly in the Gymfile:

```
export_options(
  method: "ad-hoc",
        provisioningProfiles: {
    "com.doronkatz.firefox": "Provisioning Profile Name"
  },
  manifest: {
    appURL: "https://yourapp.com/yourapp.ipa",
  },
  thinning: "<thin-for-all-variants>"
)
```

(Source: *fastlane)*

Updating our Fastfile

Let's make this even more efficient by adding a gym to our Fastfile workflow. Open up the Fastfile and go to the beta lane:

```
lane :beta do
    register_devices(devices_file: "devices.txt")
    match(git_url: "git@bitbucket.org:doron_katz/my-fastlane-keys.git",
      type: "development",
      app_identifier: "com.doronkatz.firefox")
    gym(scheme: "Fennec",
      output_name: "firefox.ipa",
                configuration: "development",
                export_method: 'ad-hoc',
      silent: false,
      output_directory: "./Export"
    )
    # sh "your_script.sh"
    # You can also use other beta testing services here (run `fastlane
actions`)
  end
```

Let's run *fastlane* beta and confirm our build action is working:

```
$ fastlane beta
[13:34:34]: -----------------------------------------------------
[13:34:34]: --- Step: Verifying required fastlane version ---
[13:34:34]: -----------------------------------------------------
[13:34:34]: Your fastlane version 2.49.0 matches the minimum requirement of
2.41.0 ✅
[13:34:34]: -----------------------------------
[13:34:34]: --- Step: default_platform ---
[13:34:34]: -----------------------------------
[13:34:34]: Driving the lane 'ios beta' 🚀
[13:34:34]: -----------------------------------
[13:34:34]: --- Step: register_devices ---
[13:34:34]: -----------------------------------
[13:34:52]: Fetching list of currently registered devices...
[13:35:36]: Successfully registered new devices.
[13:35:36]: -------------------
[13:35:36]: --- Step: match ---
[13:35:36]: -------------------


+----------------------+----------------------------------------------------
-+
|                                Summary for match 2.49.0
|
+----------------------+----------------------------------------------------
-+
| git_url              | git@bitbucket.org:doron_katz/my-fastlane-keys.git
|
| type                 | development
|
| app_identifier       | com.doronkatz.firefox
|
| git_branch           | master
|
| username             | dktz@mac.com                                      |
| keychain_name        | login.keychain
|
| readonly             | false
|
| team_id              | UU98N6FWB5
|
| verbose              | false
|
| force                | false
|
| skip_confirmation    | false
```

```
|
| shallow_clone        | false
|
| clone_branch_directly | false
|
| force_for_new_devices | false
|
| skip_docs            | false
|
| platform             | ios
|
+----------------------+-------------------------------------------------
--+
```

```
[13:35:36]: Cloning remote git repo...
[13:35:36]: If cloning the repo takes too long, you can use the
`clone_branch_directly` option in match.
[13:35:52]: 🔓  Successfully decrypted certificates repo
[13:35:52]: Verifying that the certificate and profile are still valid on
the Dev Portal...
[13:36:26]: Installing certificate...
```

```
+------------------+----------------------------------------------------+
|                            Installed Certificate                       |
+------------------+----------------------------------------------------+
| User ID          | QW53HAMMWC                                         |
| Common Name      | iPhone Developer: Doron Katz (9X6AWM4CZ6)          |
| Organisation Unit | UU98N6FWB5                                        |
| Organisation     | Doron Katz                                         |
| Country          | US                                                 |
| Start Datetime   | Jul 12 23:45:16 2017 GMT                           |
| End Datetime     | Jul 12 23:45:16 2018 GMT                           |
+------------------+----------------------------------------------------+
...
```

```
+--------------------------------------------------------+------------------
---------------------------------------------+
|                                                     Summary for gym 2.49.0
|
+--------------------------------------------------------+------------------
---------------------------------------------+
| scheme                                                 | Fennec
|
| export_method                                          | ad-hoc
|
| output_name                                            | firefox
|
```

```
| silent                                          | false
|
| output_directory                               | ./Export
|
| export_options.provisioningProfiles.com.doronkatz.fi | match Development
com.doronkatz.firefox                   |
| refox                                           |
|
| sdk                                             | iphoneos10.3
|
| clean                                           | true
|
| project                                         |
./Client.xcodeproj                  |
| destination                                     |
generic/platform=iOS                |
| build_path                                      |
/Users/doronkatz/Library/Developer/Xcode/Archives/20 |
|                                                 | 17-07-30
|
| skip_package_ipa                                | false
|
| buildlog_path                                   |
~/Library/Logs/gym                 |
| xcode_path                                      |
/Applications/Xcode.app            |
+----------------------------------------------------------+------------------
-------------------------------------+
...
[13:37:01]: > Check Dependencies
[13:37:01]: > Check Dependencies
[13:37:01]: > Check Dependencies
[13:37:01]: > Cleaning Client/Shared [Fennec]
[13:37:01]: > Check Dependencies
[13:37:01]: > Cleaning Client/Telemetry [Fennec]
[13:37:01]: > Check Dependencies
[13:37:01]: > Cleaning Client/Account [Fennec]
[13:37:01]: > Check Dependencies
[13:37:01]: > Cleaning Client/Storage [Fennec]
[13:37:01]: > Check Dependencies
[13:37:01]: > Cleaning Client/Sync [Fennec]
[13:37:01]: > Check Dependencies
[13:37:01]: > Cleaning Client/ReadingList [Fennec]
[13:37:01]: > Check Dependencies
[13:37:01]: > Cleaning Client/Client [Fennec]
[13:37:01]: > Check Dependencies
[13:37:01]: > Clean Succeeded
[13:37:07]: > Building Client/Shared [Fennec]
```

```
[13:37:07]: > Check Dependencies
[13:37:09]: > Processing Info.plist
...
[13:42:32]: > Touching Client.app
[13:42:40]: > Signing
/Users/doronkatz/Library/Developer/Xcode/DerivedData/Client-
fbzuyxhiifcmtcdzbwjjmexdybae/Build/Intermediates/ArchiveIntermediates/Fenne
c/InstallationBuildProductsLocation/Applications/Client.app
[13:42:43]: > Touching Client.app.dSYM
[13:42:46]: > Archive Succeeded
[13:42:46]: Generated plist file with the following values:
[13:42:46]: > -----------------------------------------
[13:42:46]: > {
[13:42:46]: >    "provisioningProfiles": {
[13:42:46]: >       "com.doronkatz.firefox": "match Development
com.doronkatz.firefox"
[13:42:46]: >    },
[13:42:46]: >    "method": "development"
[13:42:46]: > }
[13:42:46]: > -----------------------------------------
[13:42:46]: $ /usr/bin/xcrun
/Users/doronkatz/.rvm/gems/ruby-2.4.0/gems/fastlane-2.49.0/gym/lib/assets/w
rap_xcodebuild/xcbuild-safe.sh -exportArchive -exportOptionsPlist
'/var/folders/68/946ywfgx3jq3bwhy02std9tc0000gn/T/gym_config20170730-28186-
12rqpvb.plist' -archivePath
/Users/doronkatz/Library/Developer/Xcode/Archives/2017-07-30/firefox\
2017-07-30\ 14.31.08.xcarchive -exportPath
'/var/folders/68/946ywfgx3jq3bwhy02std9tc0000gn/T/gym_output20170730-28186-
1q5x3wt'
...
[13:43:56]: Successfully exported and compressed dSYM file
[13:43:56]: Successfully exported and signed the ipa file:
[13:43:56]: /Users/doronkatz/Development/Projects/firefox-
ios/Export/firefox.ipa
```

```
+------+----------------------------+-------------+
|                fastlane summary                 |
+------+----------------------------+-------------+
| Step | Action                     | Time (in s) |
+------+----------------------------+-------------+
| 1    | Verifying required fastlane | 0          |
|      | version                    |             |
| 2    | default_platform           | 0           |
| 3    | register_devices           | 64          |
| 4    | match                      | 64          |
| 5    | gym                        | 772         |
+------+----------------------------+-------------+
```

```
[13:43:56]: fastlane.tools just saved you 15 minutes!
```

Provided there were no errors, we can verify in the Export folder that our .ipa has indeed been created:

```
14:44 $ tree Export
Export
├── firefox.app.dSYM.zip
└── firefox.ipa
```

 To get a list of all available commands for gym, enter: fastlane gym --help

Summary

Our workflow is starting to take shape now, as we've accomplished the feat of building and packaging our app into an ipa. You've learned about the gym and its capabilities, and how to use the gym to build and package your app through the Terminal, as well as how to integrate the action in the beta lane of our Fastfile.

We compared gym to the traditional way of building and archiving apps using Xcode, and manually through xcodebuild, and how the packaging automation gym saves you time and labor. The next step in this beta lane is to distribute our app via two popular testing platforms: TestFlight and HockeyApp.

9
Distribute to Testers with TestFlight and Crashlytics

This chapter is all about distributing your app to testers and integrating beta-testing distribution into your *fastlane* workflow. Beta testing is the process of getting your app to testers before releasing your app publicly. Whether they are testers within the walls of your company or nominated external testers, testing plays a crucial role in the development cycle of products, from quality control to discovering bugs, a final check prior to your app being in the public's eyes and hands.

The objectives of this chapter are to learn how to manage and distribute to beta testers in iOS and to illustrate which tools are the most prominent. This chapter will also discuss how to manage and onboard your test users.

Finally, you will learn how developers like you can automate the processes by integrating the lane into your Fastfile as part of your workflow working.

The following skills will be learned in this chapter. We will be working with TestFlight and Crashlytics through the command line to:

- Onboard new users
- Manage users
- Integrate the lane into our project Fastfile

An overview of testing

In a crowded and competitive app market, delivering applications that are not only high in quality but which address users' needs with minimal bugs, is imperative. This is where testing plays a pivotal role in determining whether your app gets a one-star or five-star rating when you eventually launch it on the App Store.

Beta distribution provides development and business teams with critical insights into:

- **Release Quality**: As much as you test the code and app yourself, it can't ever be a substitute for putting the app in the hands of testers. Product owners, who are responsible for the vision of the product and who can get their hands on iterative beta releases, can discover quality issues, glitches, and quirks which can be ironed out with rapid feedback.

- **Idea Validation**: Another aspect that the product owner can get greater insight on is the validation of hypotheses. While your app may be functioning the way you intended, has the overall idea been validated? What about at a more micro level, going down to individual features, screens, and components; do the ideas resonate with users? You can use beta testing to validate different hypotheses and to A/B test certain features by providing certain users with one feature implementation and other users with another feature implementation, prior to deciding which approach to go with during your next release.

- **Discovering Crashes**: Unit testing and integration testing, which will form part of our continuous delivery mantra, are fantastic automation implementations, but even with as many use cases as you can write, you won't be able to catch all the crashes.

By putting your app in the hands of many testers, you can simulate different use cases (as opposed to simulating theoretical uses cases) and catch the edge cases. This will allow users to create real profiles and real interactions in different environments (low-signal situations), allowing you to catch crashes through as many unanticipated flows as possible, prior to releasing your next version to the App Store.

Continuous delivery and testing

The emphasis of this book is on continuous delivery, so it's not only important to include testing in your workflow but also to be able to distribute to testers continuously and effortlessly. Most projects these days at least practice a form of agile development, which means working in sprints.

A sprint is an agile concept which time-boxes durations of around three to four weeks, in which a development feature is completed. The completion of features in a sprint is based not only on development completion but more importantly, test completion.

During this rapid development mini-iteration series, it is imperative that developers release a feature for testing, testers discover bugs, developers resolve, and testers verify once more until the project passes test completion. This is essentially what constitutes an agile sprint that progresses towards feature completion.

Before a feature can satisfy the **Definition of Done** (**DoD**) (`https://www.scruminc.com/definition-of-done/`), which is the team's acceptance criteria, it needs to pass the product owner's acceptance criteria, which is why testing should not only be in the hands of end users but also available for your company's product owners and stakeholders to interact with.

Next, we are going to introduce you to the prominent tools that are heavily advocated in the iOS community for beta testing. We are then going to cover how to upload a build to TestFlight and Crashlytics in the absence of *fastlane*, and then how *fastlane* will help make the process of continuous testing achievable through automation.

Beta testing tools

The two prominent tools for beta testing on iOS are TestFlight (`https://developer.apple.com/testflight/`) and Crashlytics (`https://try.crashlytics.com/`). There are other testing distribution tools, such as HockeyApp (`https://www.hockeyapp.net/`), worth mentioning (and, in fact, also compatible with *fastlane*), but for the purposes of this chapter, we are going to concentrate on the first two, starting with TestFlight.

Overview of TestFlight

TestFlight was one of the first over-the-air distribution services for testing mobile applications, starting out cross-platform back in 2010, supporting both Android and iOS. TestFlight was purchased by Apple back in 2014 and integrated as part of its development platform a few months later, with Apple removing support for Android.

TestFlight has always been a favorite amongst mobile developers. TestFlight is triggered by uploading a beta of your app to iTunes Connect and using the same portal for managing the testers of your app. Take a look at the following screenshot:

On the other hand, the end users testing your app would download TestFlight on the App Store (`https://itunes.apple.com/us/app/testflight/id899247664?mt=8`), await an invitation from the developer for the current beta release, download the app using TestFlight, and provide rapid feedback.

TestFlight categorizes testers into either internal or external testers. Internal testers are actually part of your iTunes Connect developer team, whereas external testers are external users that have been invited through an email address.

As of recently, Apple has enabled up to 100,000 external testers and up to 100 apps at one time through a single iTunes Connect account. TestFlight now also lets developers distribute different builds at the same time so that testers can work with different versions of your app.

Next, we are going to show you how to set up TestFlight in order to distribute your app to your testers.

Setting up TestFlight

To navigate to TestFlight, log in to iTunes Connect and then navigate to the **My Apps** section, and then the **TestFlight** tab:

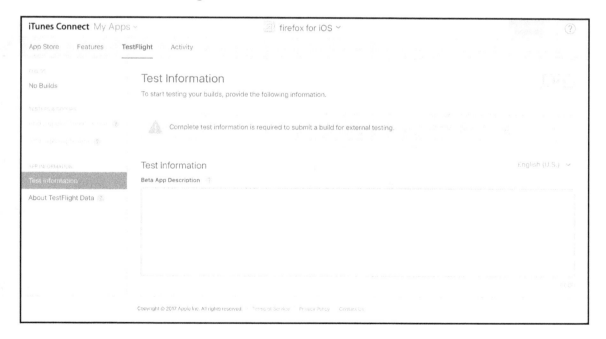

App information

The first thing we will need to do is add the information on your app that will be used by Apple for the Beta App Review process. Go ahead and enter the required information. Refer to the following screenshot:

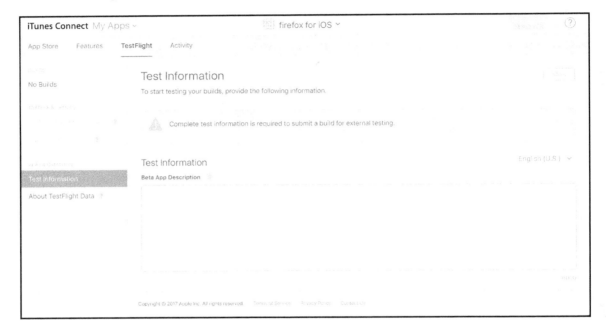

Things that you will need to add beyond a brief description include:

- A feedback URL for your testers
- A marketing URL for the testers' benefit
- A privacy policy
- The Beta App Review information, which includes a few fields from the contact information for Apple to contact in case of questions, review notes, and a username/password, if needed for a demo account

Upload your test build

Before you can add testers, you will need to upload at least one build, which will need to be reviewed prior to it being available for your testers. Go ahead and submit your first build with the information entered in the previous step. Refer to Apple's documentation on submitting your app for **TestFlight Build Review** (`https://developer.apple.com/ library/content/documentation/LanguagesUtilities/Conceptual/iTunesConnect_ Guide/Chapters/UploadingBinariesforanApp.html#//apple_ref/doc/uid/TP40011225- CH38-SW1`).

Managing and adding internal and external testers

Next up, you will be adding internal testers first, which you can do once you've submitted your first test build and had it approved.

As mentioned before, you are able to add up to 25 internal testers for TestFlight. To get started, from iTunes Connect, within the **TestFlight** tab, on the left-hand side under **Testers & Groups**, select **iTunes Connect Users**:

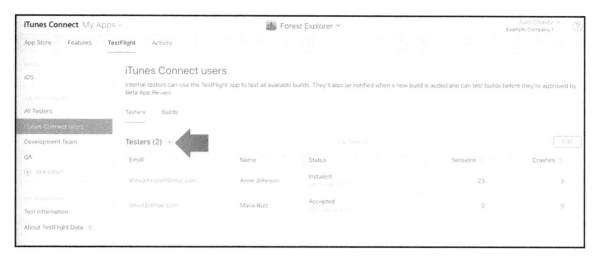

Select the (+) button to add an available internal tester/testers. When a build is available, your internal testers will receive an invitation email. Internal testers have up to 90 days to test each build before the invitation expires.

External testers are users that are outside your iTunes Connect organization and are invited via their email addresses. When working with external users, you first create a group, then add your external testers to that group, which you then associate with a release build.

To create a group, from the **TestFlight** tab once again, under **Testers & Groups,** select **Add External Group**, and come to the group when the dialog appears:

Within the same link, **Testers & Groups**, and within the newly created group, select the (+) button to add a new tester. You are also able to import testers in bulk via CSV. You would then associate a build with that group, which allows you to create different builds for different groups for testing purposes, akin to A/B testing different versions. To add the build, select **Builds** and then select the (+) add button. Take a look at the following screenshot:

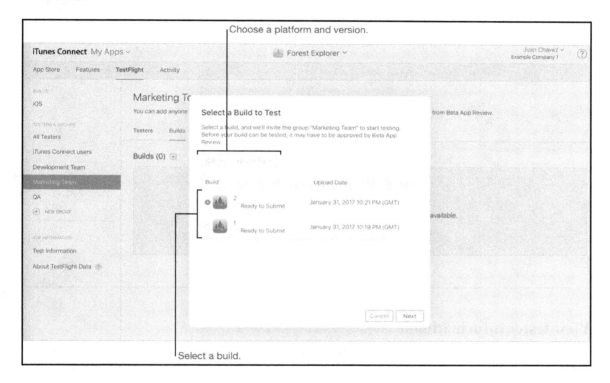

You will then be given the chance to select the build revision as well as testing information, such as what the testers should be focusing their testing on. You can optionally choose whether to release the build to the testers automatically, or delay. If you opt for the latter (when the build has been approved by Apple), you go back to this section, go to the build version, and then select **Automatically notify testers**:

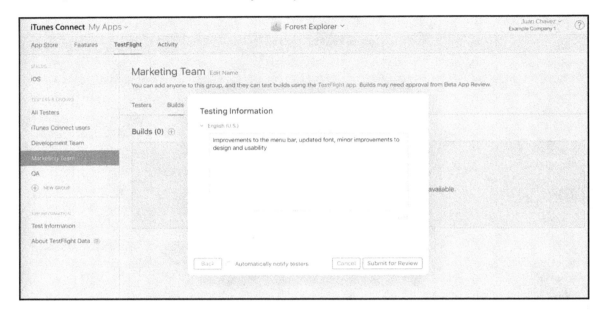

View tester information

Finally, you can view information on your testers at any time by going to **All Testers**. You will be able to see analytical information, such as their status (whether they have accepted and installed the build) as well as the number of sessions and crashes:

Next, we explore Crashlytics, one of the prominent alternatives to TestFlight.

Crashlytics

Crashlytics (http://try.crashlytics.com/) has also had a rich and interesting history, having been founded in 2011 before being integrated as part of a larger collection of mobile tools, Fabric. In 2013, it was acquired by Twitter, before being acquired once again by Google in 2017, to form part of the Firebase (https://firebase.google.com/) mobile solution that the internet giant is promoting.

Setting up Crashlytics

To get started with Crashlytics, the easiest way is to use CocoaPods, the very same toolchain we use for *fastlane*. Within your Podfile, add the following:

```
use_frameworks!
pod 'Fabric'
pod 'Crashlytics'
```

Next, you will need to create an account on Fabric, so go ahead and sign up at the **Fabric** home page (`https://fabric.io/kits?show_signup=trueutm_campaign=fabric-marketingutm_medium=natural`). Once you've completed your signup process, you will need to generate a build secret, which you will then use in Xcode, by going to Build Phases in your project target. You generate a build secret from Crashlytics by going to the organization name and selecting the respective credential link, where you will see your unique build secret.

Next, add the following new run script phase:

```
"${PODSROOT}/Fabric/run" <FABRICAPIKEY> <BUILDSECRET>
```

Finally, edit your `info.plist` file and add the following (replacing `FABRICAPIKEY` with your own account key):

```xml
<?xml version="1.0" encoding="UTF-8"?>
<!DOCTYPE plist PUBLIC "-//Apple//DTD PLIST 1.0//EN"
"http://www.apple.com/DTDs/PropertyList-1.0.dtd">
<plist version="1.0">
<dict>
  <key>Fabric</key>
  <dict>
    <key>APIKey</key>
    <string><FABRIC_API_KEY></string>
    <key>Kits</key>
    <array>
      <dict>
        <key>KitInfo</key>
        <dict/>
        <key>KitName</key>
        <string>Crashlytics</string>
      </dict>
    </array>
  </dict>
</dict>
</plist>
```

You will need to initialize Crashlytics in your code, and in particular, in your `AppDelegate.swift` file, and then build and run your app for the first time, to register the app with your account:

```swift
import UIKit
import Fabric
import Crashlytics
```

```
@UIApplicationMain
class AppDelegate: UIResponder, UIApplicationDelegate {
    func application(_ application: UIApplication,
didFinishLaunchingWithOptions launchOptions:
[UIApplicationLaunchOptionsKey: Any]?) -> Bool {
        Fabric.with([Crashlytics.self])
        return true
    }
}
```

And that's it; you are all set as far as setting up Crashlytics goes. Next, we will look at how to distribute your beta application to your testers in Crashlytics.

Distributing to Crashlytics manually

To distribute your app on Crashlytics, the first thing you will do is create an archive of your project through Xcode (**Product | Archive**), at which point you will notice a notification appear prompting you on whether you want to distribute your app. Fabric detects each archive build and prompts you each time. Take a look at the following screenshot:

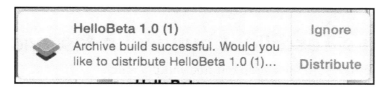

It will then bring up a window with testers/users you wish to invite, followed by a section for entering your release notes. The tester will then attempt to install the app after receiving an email notification, but will instead (the first time) be redirected to downloading a profile certificate that will provide Fabric and the developer with your device'sq UDID. In the next beta release, the tester's device will be provisioned to be able to install the beta.

On the developer's side, once the tester has accepted his or her invitation, the developer will receive a text file containing the device UDIDs, from which the developer would then add the tester in the developer portal, thus provisioning the device with the provisioning profile for testing.

As you can see, Crashlytics is quite involved, but hopefully, with *fastlane*, we will be able to improve our workflow regardless of which testing tool we use and make it a lot easier and more automated, starting with **Pilot** (https://github.com/fastlane/fastlane/tree/master/pilot#readme).

Introducing Pilot

Pilot is a very versatile *fastlane* tool, and as its namesake suggests, it allows you to pilot your test initiatives quite easily. Whereas in the previous section we saw all the steps needed to add and manage internal and external testers, Pilot (or autopilot, as it should be called) will help automate these tedious and laborious tasks. The following is the logo of Pilot:

Pilot provides developers with the ability not only to manage their testers, including adding/removing and viewing tester device information, but also to upload and distribute their builds, all directly from the command line (or Fastfile). Later on, we are going to demonstrate how we will automate building and distribution with Crashlytics.

So, let's start off by uploading a new build, followed by managing your TestFlight users.

Uploading a TestFlight build with *fastlane*

To upload a new build from the command line, simply enter:

```
fastlane pilot upload
```

To add a change log, simply append the following:

```
fastlane pilot upload --changelog "some changes to test"
```

It will look for a `.ipa` file in the current directory and use your current credentials from your existing *fastlane* session.

Listing all the builds

You can get a list of all the TestFlight builds by entering:

```
fastlane pilot builds
```

This will produce a list in the console of all the builds:

```
+-----------+---------+-------------+-----------+----------+
|                  Firefox for iOS  App Builds            |            |
+-----------+---------+-------------+-----------+----------+
| Version # | Build # | Testing     | Installs  | Sessions |
+-----------+---------+-------------+-----------+----------+
| 0.6.12    | 1       | Expired     | 1         | 2        |
| 0.6.11    | 1       | Expired     | 0         | 0        |
| 0.6.10    | 1       | Activr      | 0         | 0        |
| 0.6.9     | 2       | Internal    | 5         | 12       |
+-----------+---------+-------------+-----------+----------+
```

Managing TestFlight users with *fastlane*

Bypassing having to deal with the developer portal, you can also interact with your list of testers straight from within *fastlane* and Pilot. To get a list of all your registered testers on TestFlight, you simply enter:

```
fastlane pilot list
```

You will get a response back from *fastlane* similar to:

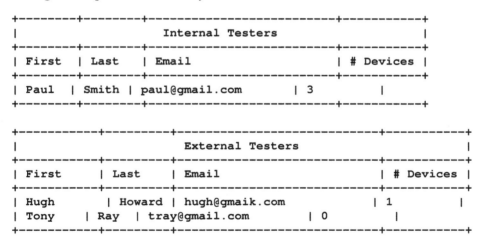

```
+--------+--------+----------------------------+-----------+
|                    Internal Testers                      |
+--------+--------+----------------------------+-----------+
| First  | Last   | Email                      | # Devices |
+--------+--------+----------------------------+-----------+
| Paul   | Smith  | paul@gmail.com        | 3         |
+--------+--------+----------------------------+-----------+


+-----------+---------+----------------------------+-----------+
|                      External Testers                       |
+-----------+---------+----------------------------+-----------+
| First     | Last    | Email                      | # Devices |
+-----------+---------+----------------------------+-----------+
| Hugh      | Howard  | hugh@gmaik.com        | 1         |
| Tony      | Ray     | tray@gmail.com        | 0         |
+-----------+---------+----------------------------+-----------+
```

To add a new tester, as well as associate the tester with the app (or just the latter, if the user happens to already exist as a tester), enter the following:

```
fastlane pilot add john@gmail.com
```

You can find out information about a specific user by searching for the user via email:

```
fastlane pilot find john@gmail.com
```

fastlane will search for the user and produce their information, including their registered devices. Finally, you can bulk import users using a CSV file, similar to how you would do it through the developer portal, by entering:

```
fastlane pilot import -c ~/Desktop/testers.csv
```

Onboard new testers on TestFlight with onboard

There is one more *fastlane* utility we wanted to squeeze into this chapter, and it's called **boarding** (https://github.com/fastlane/boarding). The following is the logo of boarding:

Boarding isn't a *fastlane* action, but a standalone utility that goes hand-in-hand with Pilot. In short, boarding is a **Heroku** (https://www.heroku.com/) deployment with a few parameters and tweaks, allowing you to create an onboarding site that is hosted on Heroku for free. The purpose of the onboarding website is to ask potential testers to enter their details, including their names and email addresses, and it will create test accounts for them and associate these with your application. Refer to the following screenshot:

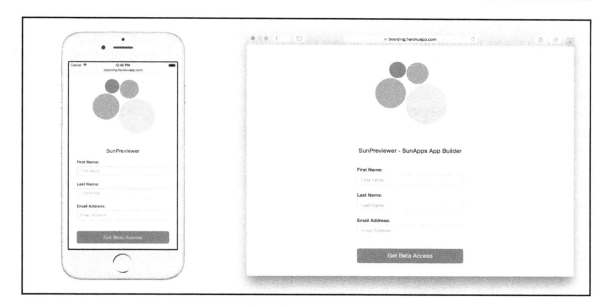

Under the hood, it is essentially an HTML-facing website that is running Pilot, but it makes it easier for you to solicit new testers and provide some onboarding information. To leverage boarding, you will need to sign up on Heroku (`https://www.heroku.com/`) and then go to `https://www.heroku.com/deploy?template=https://github.com/fastlane/boarding`.

You will need to enter your iTunes Connect credentials, as well as the bundle information of your app, and the outcome will be a new Heroku instance of your own, with your credentials. Take a look at the following screenshot:

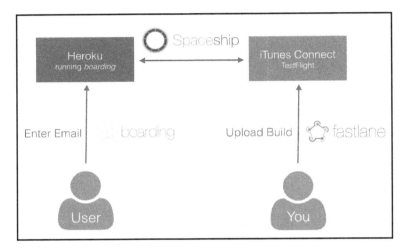

There is also a docker equivalent (emcniece/docker-boarding) where you can host on a server of your own choosing, such as Amazon's EC2.

Updating our Fastfile

Going back to our Fastfile, we will add the following to our lane :beta to upload a new binary to TestFlight, for testing:

```
...
testflight(
        username: "your4;email.com",
        app_identifier: "com.doronkatz.firefox",
        itc_provider: "abcde12345" # pass a specific value to the
iTMSTransporter -itc_provider option
        )
```

You can also use Pilot in lieu of TestFlight in the preceding code.

Next, we will amend the preceding code and add a bit more information to our TestFlight action:

```
testflight(
        username: "your@email.com",
```

```
        app_identifier: "com.doronkatz.firefox",
        beta_app_description: "This is a new build and should be dynamic,
from prompt",
        beta_app_feedback_email: "feedback@firefoxapp.com",
        itc_provider: "abcde12345"
    # pass a specific value to the iTMSTransporter -itc_provider
option
        )
```

Note that for the beta app description, it would probably make more sense in the Command Prompt to prompt the user to enter a message which would then be stored as a variable within this parameter, as each test build would have different descriptive requirements.

Crashlytics and *fastlane*

Finally, before we end this chapter, as promised, I will show you how to integrate Crashlytics into our Fastfile. Normally, you would choose to either have one or the other testing distribution, but for the sake of this chapter, we will opt to have both within the same Fastfile. We will create a new lane, just for Crashlytics. Enter the following:

```
lane: crashlytics do
    crashlytics(
        crashlytics_path: "./Pods/Crashlytics/", # path to your Crashlytics
submit binary.
        api_token: "xxx",
        build_secret: "xxx",
        ipa_path: "./app.ipa"
    )
end
```

Summary

In this chapter, you mastered distributing your app to testers using TestFlight and Crashlytics. You first learned how to distribute a new build manually on TestFlight via the developer portal, as well as how to manage your testers manually, before leveraging *fastlane* to automate and make this process a lot easier.

You were also introduced to boarding, along with Pilot, to help onboard and add new TestFlight users effortlessly. You finally added a Crashlytics lane to your Fastfile, to be able to distribute to Crashlytics.

In the next chapter, we will take a look at one of fastlane's newest actions, precheck (`https://docs.fastlane.tools/actions/precheck/`). It is quite specialized, as it will go through your project before you submit to the App Store and verify your metadata, and it does not break Apple's compliance policies for common issues like using trademark names.

10
Review Your App Metadata with precheck

A new addition to the *fastlane* family, **precheck** (`https://docs.fastlane.tools/actions/precheck`) is a nifty utility that helps developers avoid having to deal with the pain of having their apps rejected by Apple during their submission reviews. Through an ever-adapting set of community-driven App Store rules, precheck checks app metadata and iTunes Connect app descriptions for blacklisted words, such as profanity, trademarks, or copyrighted keywords, giving developers a second pair of eyes prior to going through the gauntlet of the app review process.

By the end of this chapter, you will have learned how to add precheck to your workflow to process through your app metadata and verify that there are no keywords that will break Apple's App Store compliance policies, including:

- Product bug mentions
- Profanity
- Broken URL links
- Placeholder text, future features mentioning
- Copyright date errors
- Customizable word list checking

We will be working with precheck through the command line to:

- Run precheck to verify metadata compliance
- Integrate the lane into our project Fastfile

An overview of App Store rules

Before we dive into the meat of the chapter (on implementing precheck), let's take a moment to go through the app review guidelines, as it will help you understand some of the things that you should normally look out for during the preparation of your app for submission to the App Store. Understanding Apple's guidelines, as well as many of the common pitfalls developers face when submitting their apps for review, will serve you well as an iOS developer in order to avoid many of those issues.

While precheck can and should be leveraged when trying to ensure metadata compliance, this tool should be used in conjunction with, rather than in lieu of, your own common sense and the knowledge this section will outline.

App Store Review Guidelines

The umbrella guidelines that Apple advocate, as part of the **App Store Review Guidelines** (`https://developer.apple.com/app-store/review/guidelines/`), are broken down into a few categories:

- Performance related issues
- Security and privacy related issues
- Payment related issues
- Design related issues
- Legal related issues

This section will go through the various categories that make up the App Store Review Guidelines, organized by the topics of non-compliance content.

Safety

This category focuses on content that is considered offensive, insensitive, defamatory towards religion, race, sexual orientation, gender, or which targets a specific group. This category is broken down into five subcategories: objectionable content, user-generated content, child related categories, physical harm, and developer information.

Objectionable content

Objectionable content is content that is explicit, whether sexual, defamatory, violent, inflammatory (that is, towards a religion) or misleading.

User-generated content

This refers to a platform that is driven by users (with regard to content), such as your own social media app, which opens up its own set of challenges, from bullying to intellectual property. By creating and hosting your own user-generated content, you will need to provide mechanisms for regulating, reporting, and filtering abusive content, and for blocking abusive users.

Child content

Within the App Store, there is a category marked specifically for children, where apps are specifically age-appropriate for children and should not include links out of the app where content cannot be controlled or which allow purchasing opportunities. You can refer to the **Parental Gates** (`https://developer.apple.com/app-store/parental-gates/`) for more information on specific compliance guidelines for children.

Physical harm

This refers to any content that is likely to encourage physical harm to oneself or others, and while there is obvious content that falls into this category, even content such as medical apps that provide inaccurate data that could be used for diagnosing or treating patients would gain extra scrutiny from Apple.

Any content that encourages the use of illicit drugs, excessive amounts of alcohol, and so forth, are also prohibited on the App Store.

Developer information

The developer needs to advertise how he or she can be reached with questions and support issues. The absence of accurate and up-to-date contact information, including URLs, could violate local laws in certain countries.

For a complete list of the guidelines for this section, please refer to `https://developer.apple.com/app-store/review/guidelines/#safety`.

Performance related issues

Performance related issues include app completeness, which requires that all descriptions and metadata are fully working and up-to-date for each version (not placeholders or demo/beta), that the application itself isn't crashing, and that the test accounts for the reviewers are also working completely; this includes screenshots and that the hardware specifications truly match what is needed for the app to work optimally. API-wise, Apple will also look to ensure that no private Apple APIs are being used, networking and additional hardware (GPS, background tasks, and so on) are being used appropriately as needed, and that you are basically being a good hardware citizen.

For a complete list of the guidelines for this section, please refer to `https://developer.apple.com/app-store/review/guidelines/#performance`.

Business related issues

This section refers to payments, in-app purchases, and other monetary processes within your app that may be in breach of compliance, and it is quite a broad section. In relation to app ratings, Apple prohibits any form of payment-incentivizing in order to manipulate reviews or solicit fake reviews, which is common sense. As far as in-app purchasing is concerned, Apple is looking for apps that do not utilize a mode of payment soliciting for the right type of functionality, such as using in-app payments for virtual currencies and subscriptions, whereas Apple Pay or other SDKs can be used for payments for physical goods.

For subscriptions, Apple requires that you follow specific guidelines on how autorenewal works, and, most importantly, any form of payment needs to be obvious and not misleading in any way, as it will be a surefire way for Apple to reject your app. Two good guidelines for Apple Pay include Apple Pay Identity Guidelines (`https://developer.apple.com/apple-pay/Apple-Pay-Identity-Guidelines.pdf`) and the Human User Interface Guidelines (`https://developer.apple.com/ios/human-interface-guidelines/technologies/apple-pay/`).

For a complete list of the guidelines for this section, please refer to `https://developer.apple.com/app-store/review/guidelines/#business`.

Design related issues

From a visual perspective, Apple also has a list of guidelines that they expect developers to adhere to, chief of which is intellectual property. Apple expects that developers do not infringe on the intellectual property of other developers or apps, and by doing so, even if Apple do not sanction it, the developers may open up the possibility for the victims of the intellectual theft to litigate.

From a quality perspective, Apple expects that developer apps are visually rich and functional and have an app-like user experience, and that they are not a living catalog or a non-functioning song or video, but an actual app, as obvious as it sounds. Finally, Apple also doesn't take kindly to spamming the store, such as when developers create multiple Apple IDs for the same app and publish to the App Store.

For a complete list of the guidelines for this section, please refer to `https://developer.apple.com/app-store/review/guidelines/#design`.

Legal related issues

Legal issues are just as critical as the others and developers need to heed them, whether they are matters of privacy (that is, protecting user information through data collection and storage practices, or the Children's Online Privacy Protection Act). The use of location services that are constantly on and reporting user locations for no functional reason and without consent is also another breach of this guideline subsection.

For a complete list of the guidelines for this section, please refer to `https://developer.apple.com/app-store/review/guidelines/#legal`.

Common app rejections

Apple also has a dedicated page that covers many of the common pitfalls developers go through that cause apps to be rejected, as learning from others can help preempt your fate; the page is located at `https://developer.apple.com/app-store/review/rejections/`. Refer to the following screenshot:

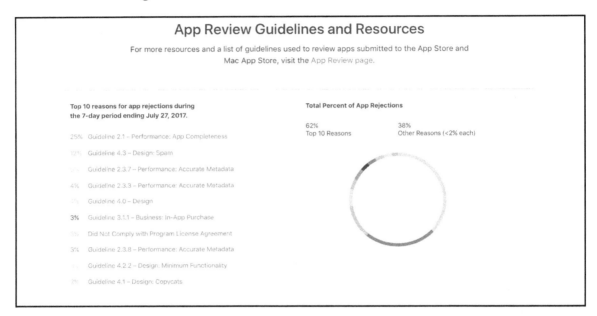

Apple summarizes the most common generic rejection issues as follows:

- **Crashes/Bugs**: Apps that are not ready for production and are quite buggy.
- **Broken Links**: Apps that provide placeholders or non-functioning links.
- **Incomplete Information**: Apps that don't include demo accounts with enough information for testers to review an entire spectrum of content and functionality. Apps that require a specific environment and that are hard to replicate need to be detailed even further, with videos to demo the hardware.
- **Inaccurate Descriptions**: Apps that mislead users, promising certain features or benefits that they won't or cannot deliver.
- **Poor UX**: Apps that provide a poor user experience and interface will get rejected.

- **Advertisements**: Apps that use an **Advertising Identifier** (**IDFA**) to track user information but don't actually display ads themselves will pose a concern for Apple reviewers.
- **Aggregated Information**: Apps that serve as shells for web apps, with content that is not mobile-friendly, present a poor user experience and may get rejected by Apple.
- **Not Enough Value**: Apps that don't provide sufficient value or content, or are enterprise apps that should be in the enterprise channel rather than the consumer-facing App Store.

Refer to `https://developer.apple.com/app-store/review/rejections/` for a complete, up-to-date list of the most common app rejections, updated for the current month.

Handy guideline references

The following links are a great resource guide for you to have on hand each time you publish your app for review, ensuring that you meet compliance across content, intellectual property, as well as UX:

- `https://developer.apple.com/app-store/review/guidelines/`
- `https://developer.apple.com/app-store/review/`
- `https://www.apple.com/legal/intellectual-property/guidelinesfor3rdparties.html`
- `https://developer.apple.com/design/tips/`

We have gone through an overview (although not an exhaustive) list of common developer pitfalls that may lead to app reviewers rejecting apps, as well as a list of common guidelines for what apps should and shouldn't do. Please consult the preceding links and verify by hand that your app complies with all of the guidelines set forth. Having said that, we are going to next introduce you to precheck (`https://docs.fastlane.tools/actions/precheck`), fastlane's newest addition that serves as a secondary means of checking your app metadata for many of the preceding issues. The operative phrase is secondary means, so this should serve in addition to your own checking and validation.

Introducing precheck

precheck is a great, nifty tool that fits well into the publishing *fastlane* workflow, and it aids developers in pre-checking apps for metadata, looking for many of the common causes of app rejections. You can either use the keywork `precheck` or the alias `check_app_store_metadata`. The following is the logo for precheck:

Precheck scours the app metadata, verifying, against a list of keywords and reference sources, that the app does not include:

- Product bug mentions
- Profanity
- Broken URL links
- Placeholder text, future features mentioning
- Copyright date errors
- Customizable word list checking

Running a precheck

The best way to see how this app works is to run it, by entering:

```
fastlane precheck
```

You should see the following results:

```
+--------------------+----------------------+
|         Summary for precheck 2.49.0       |
+--------------------+----------------------+
| app_identifier     | com.doronkatz.firefox |
| username           | dktz@mac.com         |
| default_rule_level | error                |
+--------------------+----------------------+
...
[16:41:10]: Successfully logged in
[16:41:10]: Checking app for precheck rule violations
[16:41:14]:  ✓   Passed: No negative  🍎  sentiment
[16:41:14]:  ✓   Passed: No placeholder text
```

```
[16:41:14]:  ✅  Passed: No mentioning  競  competitors
[16:41:14]:  ✅  Passed: No future functionality promises
[16:41:14]:  ✅  Passed: No words indicating test content
[16:41:14]:  ✅  Passed: No curse words
...
[16:41:14]:  😵  Failed: Incorrect, or missing copyright date-> using a
copyright date that is any different from this current year, or missing a
date
[16:41:14]:  😵  Failed: No broken urls-> unreachable URLs in app metadata
+----------------------------+----------------+
|           Potential problems                |
+----------------------------+----------------+
| Field                      | Failure reason |
+----------------------------+----------------+
| copyright                  | missing text   |
| support URL: (en-US)       | empty url      |
+----------------------------+----------------+

[!] precheck found one or more potential problems that must be addressed
before submitting to review
```

As you can see from our first run, it did discover some potential problems related to copyright and support URLs, so you can resolve those prior to verifying again. Sometimes, you may want to create a specific configuration file with specific parameters that you want to set each time you run precheck, either manually or automatically. You can do so through the creation of a `precheckfile` configuration file.

Precheckfile configuration

To create and initialize a new `precheckfile`, simply enter:

```
fastlane precheck init
[16:51:58]: For more information, check out
https://docs.fastlane.tools/getting-started/ios/setup/#use-a-gemfile
[16:52:01]: Successfully created './fastlane/Precheckfile'. Open the file
using a code editor.
```

As the last line states, within your *fastlane* folder, there is a new `precheckfile` generated with a whole lot of commented-out lines, along with options you can enable that will be called automatically each time you do a precheck. For more information about this configuration, visit `https://docs.fastlane.tools/actions/precheck`.

In general, you can use the available options by entering the following command:

```
fastlane precheck --help
```

You have three possible values for each rule option:

- :skip: Indicates that your metadata will not be checked against this rule
- :warn: When triggered, this rule will warn you of a potential problem

- :fail: When triggered, this rule will cause an error to be displayed, and it will prevent any further *fastlane* commands from running after the precheck finishes

Refer to the following examples:

- negative_apple_sentiment(level: :skip)

- curse_words(level: :warn)

- future_functionality(level: :error)

- other_platforms(level: :error)

- placeholder_text(level: :error)

- test_words(level: :error)

- unreachable_urls(level: :error)

- custom_text(data: ["fabric"], level: :warn)

This level of calibration allows you to focus, enforce, or skip certain tests that you are confident are not needed in your development scenario, or set various warning/error levels to determine what constitutes a failure. It is never a black and white situation when looking at metadata for noncompliant issues, and that is why, as a developer, you will need to assess what level of pre-checking is appropriate for your app.

Updating our Fastfile

Let's go back to our Fastfile once again and integrate precheck into it. In our case, we don't need this for our beta lane, and so we will add this action to our `lane :release` that will allow us to precheck prior to sending our app for review. Add our precheck action above the produce action:

```
...
lane :release do
    # by default deliver will call precheck and warn you of any problems
    # if you want precheck to halt submitting to app review, you can pass
    # precheck_default_rule_level: :error
    deliver(precheck_default_rule_level: :error)

    produce(
      username: 'dktz@mac.com',
      app_identifier: 'com.doronkatz.firefox',
      app_name: 'Firefox for iOS',
      language: 'English',
      app_version: '1.0',
      team_name: 'Doron Katz' # only necessary when in multiple teams
    )
  end
```

We wrapped the precheck action within the deliver action (https://docs.fastlane.tools/actions/deliver/), which we will discuss in a future chapter, but for now, all you need to know is that it is used for uploading screenshots, metadata, and binaries to iTunes Connect, so it makes sense that these two actions are interrelated.

Summary

While we haven't worked with any of the submission actions yet, we took a peek at one of the more advanced processes, and that's precheck. You learned about some of the app rejection pitfalls and things to look out for, as well as how precheck can make your life easier so that you are ready to deliver your app to Apple to review prior to release.

In subsequent chapters, we will look at more of the release actions that *fastlane* provides, from delivering to utilities that take specifically localized screenshots, and more.

11
Taking Localized Screenshots with snapshot

Over the course of the next three chapters, we are going to focus on screenshots, starting with generating screenshots using snapshot (`https://docs.fastlane.tools/actions/snapshot`), followed by framing the screenshots using frameit (`https://docs.fastlane.tools/actions/frameit`) in the next chapter, then finally uploading the screenshots and metadata using deliver (`https://docs.fastlane.tools/actions/deliver`).

snapshot (`https://docs.fastlane.tools/actions/snapshot/`), as its name implies, automates the process of taking localized screenshots across different devices and languages. Whereas you would have to manually utilize Xcode's iOS simulator and explicitly take shots across portrait and landscape times all of your supported languages and device variants (for instance, iPhone 7 Plus, 6, and iPad Pro), snapshot (`https://docs.fastlane.tools/actions/snapshot`) makes the process of taking clear and beautiful screenshots a breeze. In this chapter, we will also dedicate a bit of time to exploring Android's equivalent, screengrab (`https://docs.fastlane.tools/actions/screengrab`).

By the end of this chapter, you will learn how to do the following:

- Add snapshot (`https://github.com/fastlane/fastlane/tree/master/snapshot`) or screengrab (`https://github.com/fastlane/fastlane/tree/master/screengrab`) to your workflow process
- Automate the process of taking screenshots for the devices and languages you support

We will be working with snapshot, through the command line, to do the following:

- Generate localized multidevice and orientation screenshots
- Integrate the lane into our workflow

An overview of capturing screenshots on iOS simulator

The iOS simulator, which, as a developer, you are familiar with as part of the Xcode suite of tools, allows you to simulate running your app across various devices, such as iPhone, iPad, Apple Watch, and Apple TV, interacting with the simulator as you would with a real device. While running through your app and going through the various screens, you are able to manually take a screenshot and copy the current visual state to your Mac Clipboard. Take a look at the following screenshot:

To take a screenshot of a running app in Simulator, select **Edit** | **Copy Screen** to copy to the clipboard, or **File** | **Save Screen Shot** to save the screenshot to your Mac's desktop.

You are also able to take a screenshot (or even record a video) using the command line. With Simulator running, and Terminal open, to take a screenshot you would enter `xcrun simctl io booted screenshot file name.png`.

The last parameter specifies the filename to store the screenshot as. To record a video, you would enter `xcrun simctl io booted recordVideo <filename>.<extension>`.

You stop the recording by entering Terminal's termination command, *Ctrl + C*. Screenshots should show the app in use and not merely the title art, login page, or splash screen. They may also include text overlays and show extended functionality on the device, such as the Touch Bar.

 For more information, refer to the Apple Review Guidelines (`https://developer.apple.com/app-store/review/guidelines/`).

An overview of UI testing

Next up, we will dive into UI testing, the reason being that snapshot (`https://github.com/fastlane/fastlane/tree/master/snapshot`) leverages UI testing, and in particular UI testing scripts, in order to automate grabbing screenshots. While you won't be required to be an expert in this area, having an understanding of how snapshot works under the hood could be useful when you work with more advanced and customizable problems.

UI testing (`https://developer.apple.com/library/content/documentation/DeveloperTools/Conceptual/testing_with_xcode/chapters/09-ui_testing.html`), or user-interface testing, is an Xcode tool that enables developers to automate the testing of the user interface in order to assert and validate the properties and states of the UI elements. This is accomplished via the use of UI recording, which, when run while Simulator is running your app, generates code based on the elements and sequences selected through Simulator.

With the code generated, you can then enhance and expand upon the code in order to create more comprehensive UI tests and test cases that can test various state elements, such as asserting that a button was selected prior to entering a state, or that an element was actually removed after the swipe right-to-left was automated.

The UI testing framework relies on two core technologies: XCTest (`https://developer.apple.com/documentation/xctest`) and Accessibility.

XCTest framework

XCTest is the base framework for UI testing, allowing you to create unit tests. You first create a UI test target in Xcode, then you create UI test classes and methods that will form part of your UI testing methodology.

To create a test case (`https://developer.apple.com/documentation/xctest/defining_test_cases_and_test_methods`), subclass `XCTestCase` (`https://developer.apple.com/documentation/xctest/xctestcase`) within the test case target you have just created, and add test methods and assertions within the methods. As mentioned previously, you would also use UI recording to create the initial script within the method before adding the assertions. In the following code, you create a class with methods that take no parameters, and are always prefixed with the name `test`:

```
class TableValidationTests: XCTestCase {
    /// Tests that a new table instance has zero rows and columns.
    func testEmptyTableRowAndColumnCount() {
        let table = Table()
        XCTAssertEqual(table.rowCount, 0, "Row count was not zero.")
        XCTAssertEqual(table.columnCount, 0, "Column count was not zero.")
    }
}
```

The assertions in the preceding code will create an empty table and assert the row and column count of the table.

UI tests

Within the XCTest framework, the three classes of importance are as follows:

- `XCUIApplication` (`https://developer.apple.com/documentation/xctest/xcuiapplication`)
- `XCUIElement` (`https://developer.apple.com/documentation/xctest/xcuielement`)
- `XCUIElementQuery` (`https://developer.apple.com/documentation/xctest/xcuielementquery#see-also`)

XCUIApplication

XCUIApplication is the proxy class that is used to launch and terminate an application, as well as determine the state (https://developer.apple.com/documentation/xctest/xcuiapplication/2877401-state) of the application. When this is run, it is run in a different process thread to the main application process, for testing purposes.

XCUIElement

Through the aforementioned proxy, you have an interface for the in-app UI elements—which could be labels, buttons, and more—via the XCUIElement (https://developer.apple.com/documentation/xctest/xcuielement), which gives you a pointer to the elements of interest, allowing you to then access a subset of properties, such as UIButton like the state (tapped, not tapped), allowing you to interact with and simulate a tap.

XCUIElementQuery

Elements are also nested hierarchically within a tree, so an application would have various branches for the UI Navigation bar, views, elements, and more, allowing you to cascade downwards as you would in HTML with DOM trees, as well as access. The root element is XCUIApplication(). XCUIElementQuery (https://developer.apple.com/documentation/xctest/xcuielementquery#see-also) is used for the actual queries, working with the element nodes, their children, and more, and besides identifying the UI element type, it also accesses the accessibility identifier or queries via an NSPredicate. This is also made easier through the other core component of UI testing, Accessibility.

Accessibility

The other core technology of UI testing is Accessibility, which is known for providing the ability to enable the same rich experience to disabled users, exposing semantic data on the UI that guides users through the app. Leveraging accessibility that is integrated into UIKit via an API, it allows for UI-testing methods to identify objects and elements uniquely, and cascade and navigate nodes.

UI testing in and of itself is a huge topic and outside the scope of this book; however, the following links will provide a great starting point for you to learn more about UI testing. Some familiarity with the concepts and how to run a UI test will help give you a greater understanding of how to work with this chapter's *fastlane* action.

Introducing snapshot

snapshot (`https://github.com/fastlane/fastlane/tree/master/snapshot`) takes the laborious task of generating localized screenshots across your iOS devices, different languages, devices, and orientation modes and automates it. Coupled with the fact that you would generally take multiple screenshots for each device variant and have to repeat this process for each update you release, this action is certainly going to save you from this painstaking process:

This action takes advantage of UI testing in Simulator to automate the process of taking screenshots, and, once configured, can take screenshots across one or multiple simulators running concurrently to expedite the process.

The final output is a set of screenshots that you can access through an elegant web page, organized across variant devices and languages, to help you organize and set which screenshots to upload for your next build. We will demonstrate all of these next with snapshot.

Setting up snapshot in your project

Unlike the previous *fastlane* actions we have introduced thus far, this will need a bit more of a setup as the tool will actually leverage the iOS simulator. But with some patience, once it is set up, you will reap the rewards of this automation and save yourself a lot of time. So, with that in mind, we are going to need to do the following:

1. Create a new UI test target in our project.
2. Run the *fastlane* command, `fastlane snapshot init`.
3. Include the `./SnapshotHelper.swift` header file to the UI target of our project.
4. Take snapshots on demand.

Let's go through each of these steps one by one and generate screenshots for our Firefox app.

Creating the UI Test Target

As we outlined previously, the first step is creating the new UI Test Target in Xcode. Within Xcode, go to **File** | **New** | **Target...**, as shown in the following screenshot:

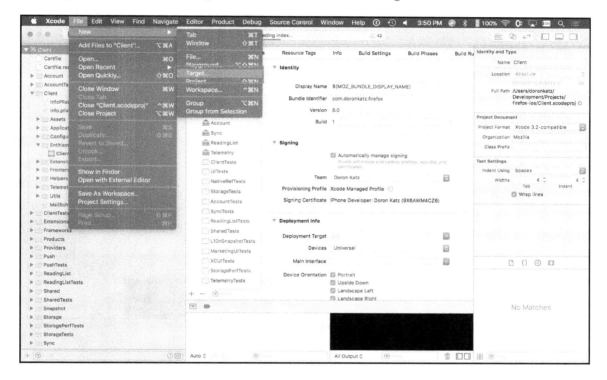

From the file menu, please select New > Target to create a new target

Then, name the test target appropriately, say `FirefoxUITests`:

You will notice that Xcode now generates a new target, as well as a `FirefoxUITests.swift` file, ready for you to create UI test scripts.

Initializing snapshot

Next, we will initialize snapshot by entering in Terminal the following command:

```
fastlane snapshot init
```

You should get back the following:

```
✅    Successfully created SnapshotHelper.swift
'./fastlane/SnapshotHelper.swift'
✅    Successfully created new Snapfile at './fastlane/Snapfile'
------------------------------------------------------
Open your Xcode project and make sure to do the following:
1) Add a new UI Test target to your project
```

```
2) Add the ./fastlane/SnapshotHelper.swift to your UI Test target
   You can move the file anywhere you want
3) Call `setupSnapshot(app)` when launching your app

   let app = XCUIApplication()
   setupSnapshot(app)
   app.launch()

4) Add `snapshot("0Launch")` to wherever you want to create the screenshots

More information on GitHub:
https://github.com/fastlane/fastlane/tree/master/snapshot
```

As we have done step one already, we move to step two, adding the
`SnapshotHelper.swift` file to our target.

Adding SnapshotHelper.swift to the target

The `SnapshotHelper.swift` file was already automatically added to Xcode as a result of
the previous command, so all that's left to do is select the file in Xcode Navigator, and, on
the right-hand pane, ensure that the file is part of your new `FireFoxUITests` target:

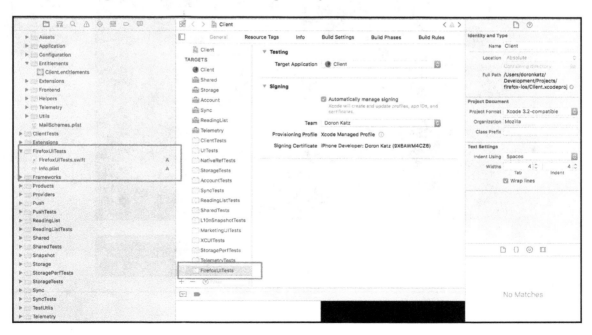

Take note of the FireFoxUITests project files (on the left) as well as the target

Recording your app interactions

Next comes the interactive aspect of this chapter—actually recording and taking snapshots on demand. Earlier on in the chapter, we discussed the theory behind working with UI tests and recording screenshots, so lets put our theory into practice.

In Xcode, open up the `FirefoxUITests.swift` file. Within the `setup()` method, add the following code, replacing all default content:

```
let app = XCUIApplication()
setupSnapshot(app)
app.launch()
```

Next, focus your cursor on the sample function `func TestExample()`, and that should enable the Record button. Select the Record button to start recording, as shown in the following screenshot:

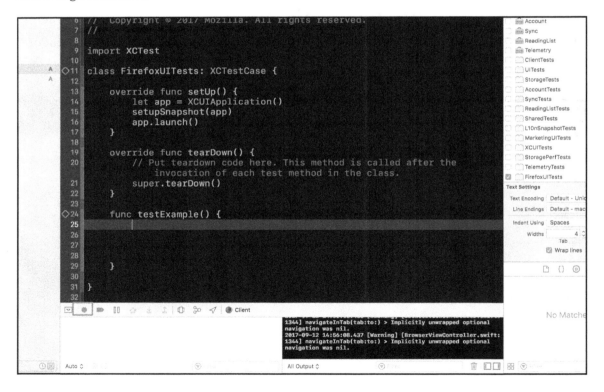

This should launch Simulator, allowing you to interact with the app and start recording the UI steps. For now, go ahead and navigate through the app, selecting buttons and a couple of screens, and when you are done, select the Record button again to stop recording. You should end up with some UI test code automatically added to your `testExample()` method, as follows:

```
21      super.tearDown()
22    }
23
24    func testExample() {
25
26        let app = app2
27        let organizeElement =
              app.scrollViews["IntroViewController.scrollView"]
              .otherElements.containing(.image, identifier:"organize").
              element
28        organizeElement.swipeLeft()
29        organizeElement.swipeLeft()
30        organizeElement.swipeLeft()
31        organizeElement.swipeLeft()
32        app.buttons["IntroViewController.startBrowsingButton"].tap()
33        app.textFields["url"].tap()
34        app.textFields["address"].typeText("cnn.com")
35        app.typeText("\r")
36
37        let app2 = app
38        app2.buttons["TabToolbar.menuButton"].tap()
39        app2.collectionViews.collectionViews.cells["twitter"].tap()
40
41
42
43
44    }
45
46  }
47
```

```
1344] navigateInTab(tab:to:) > Implicitly unwrapped optional
navigation was nil.
2017-09-12 14:56:08.437 [Warning] [BrowserViewController.swift:
1344] navigateInTab(tab:to:) > Implicitly unwrapped optional
navigation was nil.
```

We now have a recording that we can use as a script for testing, and that sets the framework for us to start adding snapshot requests, which we will do by inserting the syntax, `snapshot("0XScreenName")`. Let's start by adding a couple of commands in the method strategically so that we capture the initial onboarding screen of our app, as well as the home screen. Our method should now resemble something similar to the following screenshot:

```
func testExample() {

    snapshot("01HomeScreen")
    let app = XCUIApplication()
    app.buttons["IntroViewController.startBrowsingButton"].tap()
    app.collectionViews.collectionViews.cells["twitter"].tap()
    snapshot("02Twitter")
    app.buttons["TabToolbar.menuButton"].tap()
    app.collectionViews.cells["NewTabMenuItem"].tap()
    snapshot("03NewTab")

}
```

Generating snapshots

With our UI test scripts in place and some snapshot requests, let's trigger our automated snapshots. From Terminal, enter the following:

```
fastlane snapshot
```

You will start observing snapshots triggering across various Simulators, and you should get an output in the Terminal console similar to the following:

```
+------------------------+---------------------+
| Detected Values from './fastlane/Snapfile'   |
+------------------------+---------------------+
| devices                | ["iPhone 7 Plus"]   |
| languages              | ["en-US", "de-DE"]  |
| scheme                 | FirefoxUITests      |
| stop_after_first_error | true                |
| concurrent_simulators  | false               |
+------------------------+---------------------+
 . . .


+------------------------+-----------------------------------------
-------------------+
|
|                                 Summary for snapshot 2.56.0
|
|
```

```
+------------------------------+-------------------------------------------------
------------------+
| devices                      | ["iPhone 7 Plus"]
|
| languages                    | ["en-US", "de-DE"]
|
| scheme                       | FirefoxUITests
|
| stop_after_first_error       | true
|
| concurrent_simulators        | false
|
| project                      | ./Client.xcodeproj
|
| output_directory             |
/Users/doronkatz/Development/Projects/firefox-ios/fastlane/s  |
|                              | creenshots
|
| launch_arguments             | [""]
|
| output_simulator_logs        | false
|
| skip_open_summary            | false
|
| skip_helper_version_check    | false
|
| clear_previous_screenshots   | false
|
| reinstall_app                | false
|
| erase_simulator              | false
|
| localize_simulator           | false
|
| app_identifier               | com.doronkatz.firefox
|
| buildlog_path                | ~/Library/Logs/snapshot
|
| clean                        | false
|
| number_of_retries            | 1
|
| xcode_path                   | /Applications/Xcode.app
|
+------------------------------+-------------------------------------------------
------------------+

[09:44:58]: Building and running project - this might take some time...
```

```
[09:44:58]: snapshot run 1 of 2

. . .
[09:51:31]: > FirefoxUITests
[09:51:31]: > ✓ testExample (25.849 seconds)
[09:51:31]: >      Executed 1 test, with 0 failures (0 unexpected) in
25.849 (25.850) seconds
[09:51:31]: >
[09:51:31]: Collecting screenshots...
[09:51:31]: Found 3 screenshots...
[09:51:31]: Copying '/Users/doronkatz/Development/Projects/firefox-
ios/fastlane/screenshots/de-DE/iPhone7Plus-01HomeScreen-
d41d8cd98f00b204e9800998ecf8427e.png'...
[09:51:31]: Copying '/Users/doronkatz/Development/Projects/firefox-
ios/fastlane/screenshots/de-DE/iPhone7Plus-02Twitter-
d41d8cd98f00b204e9800998ecf8427e.png'...
[09:51:31]: Copying '/Users/doronkatz/Development/Projects/firefox-
ios/fastlane/screenshots/de-DE/iPhone7Plus-03NewTab-
d41d8cd98f00b204e9800998ecf8427e.png'...


+----------------+-------+-------+
|       snapshot results         |
+----------------+-------+-------+
| Device         | en-US | de-DE |
+----------------+-------+-------+
| iPhone 7 Plus  |   ♥   |   ♥   |
+----------------+-------+-------+

[09:51:31]: Generating HTML Report
[09:51:31]: Successfully created HTML file with an overview of all the
screenshots: '/Users/doronkatz/Development/Projects/firefox-
ios/fastlane/screenshots/screenshots.html'
```

Confirming the screenshots

When snapshot has completed its series of snapshots successfully, it should automatically bring up a web page in your default browser with all your screenshots categorized by device variant:

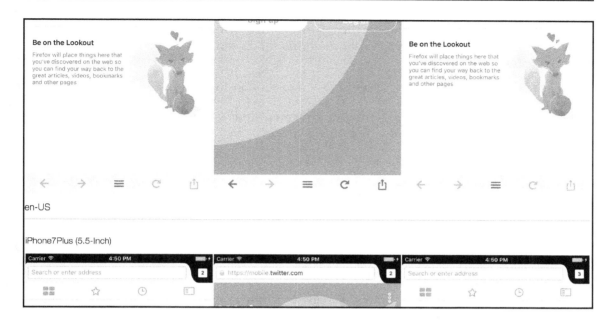

The list of files generated by our snapfile is as follows:

```
fastlane/screenshots/
├── de-DE
│   ├── iPhone7Plus-01HomeScreen-d41d8cd98f00b204e9800998ecf8427e.png
│   ├── iPhone7Plus-02Twitter-d41d8cd98f00b204e9800998ecf8427e.png
│   └── iPhone7Plus-03NewTab-d41d8cd98f00b204e9800998ecf8427e.png
├── en-US
│   ├── iPhone7Plus-01HomeScreen-d41d8cd98f00b204e9800998ecf8427e.png
│   ├── iPhone7Plus-02Twitter-d41d8cd98f00b204e9800998ecf8427e.png
│   └── iPhone7Plus-03NewTab-d41d8cd98f00b204e9800998ecf8427e.png
└── screenshots.html
```

Other snapshot options

Besides the most obvious command path, snapshot supports other optional parameters and flags, starting with a flag that will stop interacting with Simulator after the first error is encountered. The default behavior of snapshot is that if it fails with one device, it will continue on to the next device. You can change that default behavior and terminate immediately by adding the following flag:

```
fastlane snapshot —stop_after_first_error
```

As we saw in our example, at the conclusion of the snapshot-capturing process, it automatically opens up a web page with the results. You can also suppress that action by adding the following flag:

```
fastlane snapshot --stop_after_first_error --skip_open_summary
```

From time to time, you will need to update your snapshot helper file or reset/clear all simulators, and you can do those actions respectively as follows:

```
fastlane snapshot update
fastlane snapshot reset_simulators
```

Besides the options we mentioned in the preceding section, there are dozens of other options you can add to your snapshot as flags, from selecting the scheme automatically, to choosing which devices to focus on:

```
fastlane snapshot --scheme "UITests" --configuration "Release" --sdk
"iphonesimulator"
```

Of course, rather than append numerous flags each time you run this, a more convenient approach is to work with snapfiles, which we will do next. For a list of all screenshot commands, as with other *fastlane* actions, enter the following in Terminal:

```
fastlane snapshot --help
```

Working with snapfiles

In the previous section, we showed you how to trigger your first snapshot, as well as some options you can employ. As with many of the previous actions in this chapter, snapshot provided a convenience configuration file for you to store and easily call, called a snapfile.

We already generated a Snapfile when we initialized snapshot for the first time, earlier on. Go ahead and open it up, and you will see a lot of commented-out lines:

```
# Uncomment the lines below you want to change by removing the # in the
beginning

# A list of devices you want to take the screenshots from
# devices([
#   "iPhone 6",
#   "iPhone 6 Plus",
#   "iPhone 5",
#   "iPad Pro (12.9-inch)",
#   "iPad Pro (9.7-inch)",
#   "Apple TV 1080p"
```

```
#  ])

languages([
  "en-US",
  "de-DE",
  "it-IT",
  ["pt", "pt_BR"] # Portuguese with Brazilian locale
])

# The name of the scheme which contains the UI tests
# scheme "SchemeName"

# Where should the resulting screenshots be stored?
# output_directory "./screenshots"

# clear_previous_screenshots true # remove the '#' to clear all previously
generated screenshots before creating new ones

# Choose which project/workspace to use
# project "./Project.xcodeproj"
# workspace "./Project.xcworkspace"

# Arguments to pass to the app on launch. See
https://github.com/fastlane/fastlane/tree/master/snapshot#launch-arguments
# launch_arguments(["-favColor red"])

# For more information about all available options run
# fastlane snapshot --help
```

As you can see, the comments in the file are self-guiding, articulating how you can tweak the configuration file to set the granularity of the snapshots automation. You can set the target/default scheme, device type, language/localization, output directories, and more.

Running Xcode simulators concurrently

As of Xcode 9, you are able to run multiple simulators at the same time, the net result being that you have the ability to capture screenshots more rapidly. Of course, this will increase resource usage on your computer, and you can choose to disable this default behavior by entering the following:

```
`fastlane snapshot —concurrent_simulators
```

This is the default behavior of Xcode 9, configured so that it can take your screenshots as quickly as possible. This can be toggled to instead run on each device separately, in sequence rather than concurrently, by setting the `:concurrent_simulators` option to `false`.

 While running snapshot with Xcode 9, the simulators will not be visibly spawned. So, while you won't see the simulators running your tests, they will, in fact, be taking your screenshots.

Updating our Fastfile

Let's go back to our Fastfile once again and integrate snapshot into it. We are going to add this to our release lane, and by working with our previous Snapfile convenience file, we don't need to provide any parameters here:

```
...
lane :release do
    # by default deliver will call precheck and warn you of any problems
    # if you want precheck to halt submitting to app review, you can pass
    # precheck_default_rule_level: :error
    deliver(precheck_default_rule_level: :error)
    snapshot
    produce(
      username: 'dktz@mac.com',
      app_identifier: 'com.doronkatz.firefox',
      app_name: 'Firefox for iOS',
      language: 'English',
      app_version: '1.0',
      team_name: 'Doron Katz' # only necessary when in multiple teams
    )
  end
```

An introduction to screengrab

Before concluding this chapter, for the Android developers, it is worth noting that *fastlane* has an equivalent *fastlane* action, called **screengrab** (https://github.com/fastlane/fastlane/tree/master/screengrab#readme). The following is the logo of screengrab:

Just like snapshot, screengrab also automates the process of grabbing screenshots for different variants of Android, in preparation for the Google Play Store. The easiest way to install screengrab is to add it as a Gradle dependency and include the permissions in the `AndroidManifest.xml` file:

```
androidTestCompile 'tools.fastlane:screengrab:x.x.x'

<!-- Allows unlocking your device and activating its screen so UI tests can
succeed -->
<uses-permission android:name="android.permission.DISABLE_KEYGUARD"/>
<uses-permission android:name="android.permission.WAKE_LOCK"/>

<!-- Allows for storing and retrieving screenshots -->
<uses-permission android:name="android.permission.WRITE_EXTERNAL_STORAGE"
/>
<uses-permission android:name="android.permission.READ_EXTERNAL_STORAGE" />

<!-- Allows changing locales -->
<uses-permission android:name="android.permission.CHANGE_CONFIGURATION" />
```

 For instructions on how to configure the JUnit UI tests for screenshots and trigger the generation of screenshots, refer to the GitHub repository (`https://github.com/fastlane/fastlane/tree/master/screengrab#installation`).

Summary

This chapter has been as complex as it has been educational, and you've learned to appreciate the convenience and time gained leveraging this *fastlane* action. Snapshot is a very powerful tool, and as you will discover over the next few chapters, we will be combining Snapshot with other actions, such as frameit, to create beautiful device frames to wrap around your screenshots, as well as automate the uploading of your screenshots along with other metadata up to iTunes Connect to populate your app listing for the App Store.

12
Put Our Screenshots Inside Frames with frameit

In the previous chapter, you learned how to generate localized screenshots using snapshot (`https://docs.fastlane.tools/actions/capture_ios_screenshots/`). In this chapter, we are now going to focus on a related *fastlane* action, frameit (`https://docs.fastlane.tools/actions/frame_screenshots/`), which, as its name suggests, adds device frames around your app screenshots in preparation for your submission to the App Store to give your users a more visual context about how the app looks and feels on a device.

Through a simple *fastlane* action, you can customize your screenshot frames for the various disparate devices you support, such as the iPhone and the iPad (in all screen size variations), as well as in both portrait and landscape modes.

By the end of this chapter, you will learn how to add frameit (`https://github.com/fastlane/fastlane/tree/master/frameit`) to your workflow process, which will do the following:

- Add multiple device frames to the screenshots
- Customize the frame colors

You will be working with frameit from the command line to do the following:

- Run frameit to generate device frames for your existing screenshots, generated in the previous chapter
- Integrate the lane into our project Fastfile

An overview of how to design your App Store product page screenshots

Before embarking on how to integrate frameit to automate the process of beautifying our screenshots, we will first demonstrate the mainstream approach to edited screenshots. In this section, we will demonstrate one approach, which involves the use of one of the most popular contemporary designing tools, Sketch, to crop and frame screenshots around devices to create a more realistic and contextual visual impression. You could substitute the techniques with Adobe Photoshop or any other comparable graphic-authoring tool.

We have already learned how to generate screenshots in the previous chapter, both through snapshot, as well as manually via Xcode Simulator, and thus we assume you already have a set of screenshots to work with in this section.

Beautifying screenshots

Uploading your screenshots directly from the iOS Simulator can seem quite bland, and thus garnishing them with additional visuals, such as device frames, provides greater context in appreciating your app's user experience, promoting your app across the various device platforms, and providing a nonfunctioning, visual prototype of your app, as the final gateway to your users eventually committing to purchasing your app.
Traditionally, developers have relied on designers to visually beautify app screenshots, using industry-popular tools, such as Photoshop or Sketch, by Bohemian Software (`https:/ /www.sketchapp.com/`).

Understanding Photoshop or Sketch beyond demonstrating briefly how to add device frame layers to wrap the screenshots is beyond the scope of this book. For the purposes of this chapter, we are going to demonstrate how to create frames using Sketch.

Sketch is available to buy, but you can also download a trial version if you are interested in following the rest of this section. We will also make use of Sketch App Resources (`https:// www.sketchappsources.com/`), which is a resourceful third-party website that provides free designer resources, including device frames that you can leverage to beautify your app.

We will use the screenshots we generated in the previous chapter, manually beautify them through Sketch, and overlay a frame from the third-party template site we mentioned. This chapter is not a comprehensive tutorial in working with Sketch, and so we advise that you consult the user guide for information on steps you are not familiar with.

Downloading the template files

Before we start on our own canvas, we are going to download an appropriate template that we can use as a frame for our screenshots. For the purpose of this tutorial, we are going to be working with a specific Sketch resource from the third-party site we mentioned earlier, so go to `https://www.sketchappsources.com/free-source/1155-iphone-app-store-assets-sketch-freebie-resouce.html` and select **Download Resources**:

The third-party Sketch resource template we are going to use.

You are more than welcome to use another template and follow the rest of the steps in this section loosely. When the download has completed, open the `sketch` file by double-clicking on it:

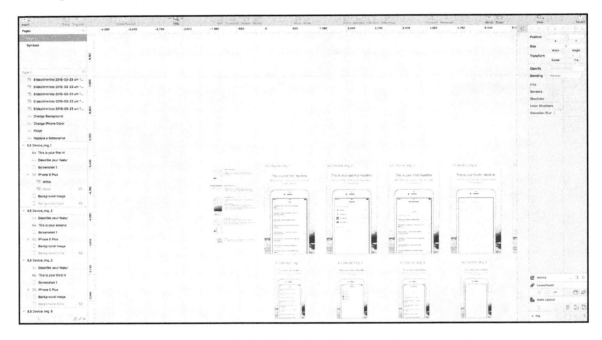

A screenshot of our Sketch template ready for us to customize.

Adding your own screenshots

This particular template has some great instructions on how to replace the placeholder screenshot with your own. Following the instructions on the first slide, select the first screenshot (**img_1**), making sure that you select the actual screenshot, and then on the right-hand side, select the Fill button, as shown in the following screenshot:

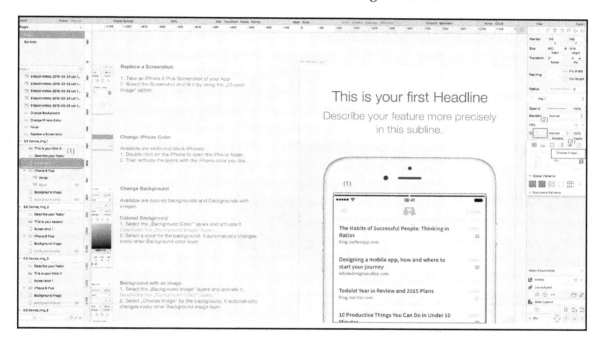

Modifying a screen in Sketch by replacing the Screenshot_1 placeholder image.

Next, select the **Choose Image** option, and select the screenshots you generated in the previous chapter. The first screenshot should now be placed within the confines of the template, as shown in the following screenshot:

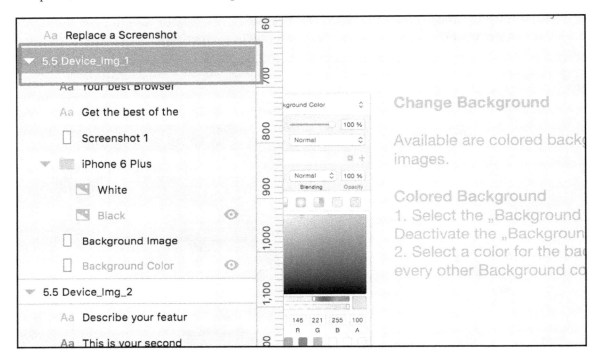

You can see that the Firefox browser is now placed properly and is masked within the iPhone device. You can also go ahead and change the heading and description text by double-clicking it. When you are done, you are ready to export the image in preparation for uploading it to the App Store.

Exporting the screenshots

To export the screenshot image (img1) we just worked on, on the left-hand side, select the art-board layer (**5.5 Device_img_1**):

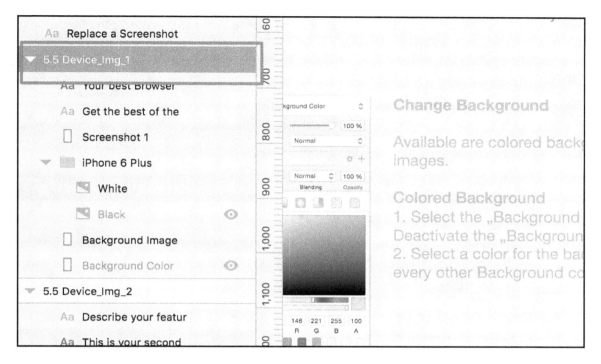

Next, select the right-hand side **Export 5.5 Device_img_1**, and save the exported image in an appropriate location. And that's it—we have saved our first screenshot manually using Sketch.

Dealing with device variants for screenshots

As you can see, it does take a bit of effort and knowledge to work with screenshots and beautify them, especially considering that this is an exercise that needs to be done each time you update your app to ensure the screenshots are kept relevant and accurate. This is especially cumbersome if you don't have any Sketch or Photoshop skills and have to rely on another skilled resource to complete this task.

When you either create a new app or update an existing app, in iTunes Connect, along with uploading your new app binary when you create a new app version, you will be presented with the opportunity to upload new screenshots or update the existing screenshots from the previous upload.

Either way, you upload `.png` or `.jpg` files without transparent areas, and upload images for each device type you are supporting, such as iPhone and iPad. Also worth noting is the fact that screenshots can only be changed each time you upload a new binary app version to the App Store.

Prior to iOS 10, Apple required developers submitting new apps or updates to their apps to submit separate sets of screenshots for each device family (that is, iPhone, iPad, and so on), but now, Apple is accepting one set of screenshots and one app preview per device family, and they will be used across the different device sizes and localizations.

The following are the device variants and their associated resolutions that you have to consider when taking screenshots:

- 4-Inch Phones (that is iPhone 5): 640 x 1136 pixels
- 4.7-Inch Phones (that is iPhone 6/7): 750 x 1134 pixels
- 5.5-Inch Phones (that is iPhone 6 Plus/Plus): 1242 x 2208 pixels
- 7.9-Inch iPads (and 9.7-Inch): 2048 x 1536 pixels
- 12.9-Inch IPad Pros: 2732 x 2048 pixels
- 42-mm Apple Watch: 312 x 390 pixels
- 38-mm Apple Watch: 272 x 340 pixels

As you can see, aside from the necessity of having to be proficient with designer tools such as Sketch or Photoshop to beautify your app screenshots, the process of catering for each screen size and uploading the screenshots is still quite laborious. Although the template has made our lives a bit easier, we still have to do this for all of our screenshots, across all languages, and all device variants.

Next, we will introduce you to the first of three screenshot-related actions, frameit, and demonstrate how it will not only automate the process but remove the need to rely on using design tools such as Sketch.

Introducing frameit

frameit (`https://docs.fastlane.tools/actions/frame_screenshots/`), as introduced at the start of the chapter, wraps device frames around your generated screenshots to give you a polished and perfect set of screenshots that provide visual context and reference for your potential users on the App Store, and may also be used on your websites, emails, or other promotional marketing material. The following is the logo of frameit:

The full list of devices frameit supports can be found at `https://github.com/fastlane/`
`frameit-frames/tree/gh-pages/latest`, and this list gets updated quite frequently.

Running a basic frameit command

Before running frameit, you will need to install a prerequisite helper utility called
ImageMagick by running the following commands first:

```
brew update && brew install imagemagick
```

Now we are ready to see how frameit works by simply entering the following:

```
fastlane frameIt
```

We get a response that shows that *fastlane* is downloading the appropriate frames, as shown
in the following code:

```
...
[19:51:58]: Using device frames version 'latest'
[19:51:58]: --------------------------------
[19:51:58]: --- Device frames disclaimer ---
[19:51:58]: --------------------------------
[19:51:58]: All used device frames are available via Facebook Design:
http://facebook.design/devices
[19:51:58]: -----------------------------------------
[19:51:58]: While Facebook has redrawn and shares these assets for the
benefit
[19:51:58]: of the design community, Facebook does not own any of the
underlying
[19:51:58]: product or user interface designs.
[19:51:58]: By accessing these assets, you agree to obtain all necessary
permissions
[19:51:58]: from the underlying rights holders and/or adhere to any
applicable brand
[19:51:58]: use guidelines before using them.
[19:51:58]: Facebook disclaims all express or implied warranties with
respect to these assets, including
[19:51:58]: non-infringement of intellectual property rights.
```

```
[19:51:58]: ----------------------------------------
[19:51:58]: Downloading device frames to
'/Users/doronkatz/.fastlane/frameIt/latest'
[19:51:58]: Downloading file from
'https://fastlane.github.io/frameIt-frames/latest/version.txt' ...
[19:51:58]: Using frame version '1478730760', you can optionally lock that
version in your Framefile.json using `device_frame_version`
[19:51:58]: Downloading file from
'https://fastlane.github.io/frameIt-frames/latest/files.json' ...
[19:51:58]: Downloading 1 of 41 files from
'https://fastlane.github.io/frameIt-frames/latest/Apple%20iPhone%205c%20Blu
e.png' ...
[19:51:58]: Downloading 2 of 41 files from
'https://fastlane.github.io/frameIt-frames/latest/Apple%20iPhone%205c%20Gre
en.png' ...
[19:51:58]: Downloading 3 of 41 files from
'https://fastlane.github.io/frameIt-frames/latest/Apple%20iPhone%205c%20Red
.png' ...
[19:51:59]: Downloading 4 of 41 files from
'https://fastlane.github.io/frameIt-frames/latest/Apple%20iPhone%205c%20Whi
te.png' ...
[19:51:59]: Downloading 5 of 41 files from
'https://fastlane.github.io/frameIt-frames/latest/Apple%20iPhone%205c%20Yel
low.png' ...
[19:51:59]: Downloading 6 of 41 files from
'https://fastlane.github.io/frameIt-frames/latest/Apple%20iPhone%205s%20Gol
d.png' ...
[19:52:00]: Downloading 7 of 41 files from
'https://fastlane.github.io/frameIt-frames/latest/Apple%20iPhone%205s%20Sil
ver.png' ...
[19:52:00]: Downloading 8 of 41 files from
'https://fastlane.github.io/frameIt-frames/latest/Apple%20iPhone%205s%20Spa
ce%20Gray.png' ...
[19:52:00]: Downloading 9 of 41 files from
'https://fastlane.github.io/frameIt-frames/latest/Apple%20iPhone%206s%20Gol
d.png' ...
[19:52:01]: Downloading 10 of 41 files from
'https://fastlane.github.io/frameIt-frames/latest/Apple%20iPhone%206s%20Ros
e%20Gold.png' ...
[19:52:01]: Downloading 11 of 41 files from
'https://fastlane.github.io/frameIt-frames/latest/Apple%20iPhone%206s%20Sil
ver.png' ...
[19:52:02]: Downloading 12 of 41 files from
'https://fastlane.github.io/frameIt-frames/latest/Apple%20iPhone%206s%20Spa
ce%20Gray.png' ...
[19:52:02]: Downloading 13 of 41 files from
'https://fastlane.github.io/frameIt-frames/latest/Apple%20iPhone%206s%20Plu
s%20Gold.png' ...
```

```
[19:52:04]: Downloading 14 of 41 files from
'https://fastlane.github.io/frameIt-frames/latest/Apple%20iPhone%206s%20Plu
s%20Rose%20Gold.png' ...
[19:52:06]: Downloading 15 of 41 files from
'https://fastlane.github.io/frameIt-frames/latest/Apple%20iPhone%206s%20Plu
s%20Silver.png' ...
[19:52:07]: Downloading 16 of 41 files from
'https://fastlane.github.io/frameIt-frames/latest/Apple%20iPhone%206s%20Plu
s%20Space%20Gray.png' ...
[19:52:08]: Downloading 17 of 41 files from
'https://fastlane.github.io/frameIt-frames/latest/Apple%20iPhone%207%20Gold
.png' ...
[19:52:08]: Downloading 18 of 41 files from
'https://fastlane.github.io/frameIt-frames/latest/Apple%20iPhone%207%20Jet%
20Black.png' ...
[19:52:08]: Downloading 19 of 41 files from
'https://fastlane.github.io/frameIt-frames/latest/Apple%20iPhone%207%20Matt
e%20Black.png' ...
...
[19:53:02]: Added frame: '/Users/doronkatz/Development/Projects/firefox-
ios/ThirdParty/SWTableViewCell/Default-568h@2x_framed.png'
[19:53:02]: Framing screenshot './ThirdParty/SWTableViewCell/check@2x.png'
...
```

And as simple as that, you can go back to your `screenshots` subfolder within the *fastlane* folder of your project, alongside the screenshots generated in the last chapter. You also get a framed version of your screenshots:

```
fastlane/screenshots/
├── de-DE
│   ├── iPhone7Plus-01HomeScreen-d41d8cd98f00b204e9800998ecf8427e.png
│   ├── iPhone7Plus-01HomeScreen-
d41d8cd98f00b204e9800998ecf8427e_framed.png
│   ├── iPhone7Plus-02Twitter-d41d8cd98f00b204e9800998ecf8427e.png
│   ├── iPhone7Plus-02Twitter-d41d8cd98f00b204e9800998ecf8427e_framed.png
│   ├── iPhone7Plus-03NewTab-d41d8cd98f00b204e9800998ecf8427e.png
│   └── iPhone7Plus-03NewTab-d41d8cd98f00b204e9800998ecf8427e_framed.png
├── en-US
│   ├── iPhone7Plus-01HomeScreen-d41d8cd98f00b204e9800998ecf8427e.png
│   ├── iPhone7Plus-01HomeScreen-
d41d8cd98f00b204e9800998ecf8427e_framed.png
│   ├── iPhone7Plus-02Twitter-d41d8cd98f00b204e9800998ecf8427e.png
│   ├── iPhone7Plus-02Twitter-d41d8cd98f00b204e9800998ecf8427e_framed.png
│   ├── iPhone7Plus-03NewTab-d41d8cd98f00b204e9800998ecf8427e.png
│   └── iPhone7Plus-03NewTab-d41d8cd98f00b204e9800998ecf8427e_framed.png
└── screenshots.html
```

Your framed screenshot should resemble the following:

The initial command was extremely straightforward, but you can, of course, customize your output through various parameters and options (as we have with every other *fastlane* action), starting with generating silver frames (Space Gray iPhone):

```
fastlane frameIt silver
```

Our frames now resemble what our command intended:

Making our frames App Store compliant

The preceding screenshots have been generated in full resolution, which is great for adding them to marketing material. However, they are not in the dimensions that we need for the App Store. To make the screenshots App Store compliant, we will need to add a title and, optionally, a background, which, let's face it, will make our screenshots look less bland and textbook-like. To do that, we will create a `Framefile.json` file and set the appropriate properties.

Within the `screenshots` subfolder, create a new file named `Framefile.json`:

```json
{
  "device_frame_version": "latest",
  "default": {
    "keyword": {
      "font": "./fonts/MyFont-Rg.otf"
    },
    "title": {
                "color": "#545454"
    },
    "background": "background.jpg",
    "padding": 50,
    "show_complete_frame": false,
    "stack_title" : false,
    "title_below_image": true
  },

  "data": [
    {
      "filter": "Browse the World",
      "keyword": {
        "color": "#d21559"
      }
    },
    {
      "filter": "Clean Interface",
      "keyword": {
        "color": "#feb909"
      }
    }
  ]
}
```

In the preceding JSON file, we made reference to a background image. Feel free to choose any background image you want, or follow our example where we downloaded a stock background image from `https://static.pexels.com/photos/8395/lights-night-unsharp-blured.jpg`. Ensure that you save the image as `background.jpg` in the appropriate location.

We will test our Framefile shortly, after updating our Fastfile with our newest action, and we will see it in action shortly.

Updating our Fastfile

Finally, let's add to our previous Fastfile entry by ensuring that each time we generate a screenshot, we wrap it around a frame. We are going to create a new lane called `:screenshots`:

```
...
lane :gen_screenshots do
        capture_screenshots
        frame_screenshots(white: true, path: './fastlane/screenshots')
end
        ...
```

Before we wrap up this chapter, give this new lane a try by running the following:

```
fastlane gen_screenshots
```

Summary

Now you've mastered beautification of your bland screenshots with frames, and added titles and a background, rounding off our two-chapter exercise on generating App Store-compliant screenshots.

In the next chapter, we will go through the process of uploading the screenshots and metadata to iTunes Connect, leveraging another action, called deliver (`https://docs.fastlane.tools/actions/upload_to_app_store/`).

13
Upload Screenshots and Metadata with deliver

The two previous chapters helped us nicely set up where we want to be, generating screenshots and beautifying them. By the end of this chapter, we are going to finally deliver (`https://docs.fastlane.tools/actions/upload_to_app_store/`) our screenshots, along with our metadata and binaries, to iTunes Connect. This critical action will allow us to automate the process of uploading our build, nicely packaged with all the required assets and descriptions, in preparation for submitting our app to Apple's review team.

This chapter promises to be a pivotal one in the goal of creating your ultimate fastlane workflow.

By the end of this chapter, you will have learned how to add deliver to your workflow process, which will:

- Upload the generated screenshots
- Upload the final IPA file directly
- Manage, preview, and upload app metadata seamlessly

We will be working with deliver through the command line to:

- Run deliver to upload screenshots, metadata, and a binary IPA file to iTunes Connect
- Integrate the lane into our project Fastfile

How to manually upload a new build to iTunes Connect

To appreciate the sheer amount of work deliver (https://github.com/fastlane/fastlane/tree/master/deliver) does for you under the hood, we are going start off by running through the motions of uploading a new build to iTunes Connect manually, complete with all the screenshots and metadata, as well as uploading our binary via Xcode.

In the early chapters, we went through creating an iTunes Connect record of our app, and it is assumed that you have already accomplished that ahead of this chapter. It is also assumed that you have an iTunes Connect role of either admin, technical, app manager, or developer.

Before we enter our metadata and upload our screenshots, the manual sequence is to first use Xcode to upload a new build to iTunes Connect, which will create a new prerelease version of your app. You can also opt to use **Application Loader** (http://help.apple.com/itc/apploader/) instead of Xcode, which we will cover in the next section.

Uploading using Xcode

From within Xcode, associating your iTunes Connect account allows your app to immediately associate itself with the metadata available in the iTunes Connect record you have created. To begin the process of uploading our binary, we will start by:

1. Updating our build number.
2. Creating an archive of our app.
3. Uploading our archive to iTunes Connect.

In previous chapters, we worked on provisioning profiles and certificates, and so we should now be confident that we have our provisioning profiles in order.

Updating version and build number

When we create a new version of our app, we need to update our version number. However, we update the build number prior to uploading a new build of our app to iTunes Connect. The latter increments each time you upload a new build number (of the same version).

If you haven't worked with version numbers previously, they are essentially set in the following number format: `major.minor.maintenance`. That is, the first set of digits represents the major revision, followed by the minor revision, and, finally, a maintenance version, if needed. It should resemble something like 1.2.0. Within Xcode, go to the project navigator, and select your project (**Client**). Then select **General,** and you should see your version and build numbers.

Archiving

Next, we need to archive your app into a mode that Xcode can distribute, regardless of whether the final destination is the App Store or an Enterprise Distribution channel. To generate an archive, perform the following in Xcode:

1. Select a generic device from the **Scheme** toolbar, or your own device, making sure you don't have a simulator device selected.
2. Next, select **Product** | **Archives** from the menu to bring up the Archive Organizer, as shown in the following screenshot:

Next, select **Upload to App Store...** to upload the app to iTunes Connect. The Archive Organizer will prompt you to choose an iTunes Connect team, and then prompt you to review and confirm the app, as well as the provisioning profile and entitlements. Then, select **Upload** to upload the archive to iTunes Connect. iTunes Connect will ensure your archive is valid by running a quick diagnostic, and report a warning if there are any issues. Presuming you haven't had any troubles with the upload, you will subsequently be able to verify your new version and build in iTunes Connect by going to **Activity** | **Build Number** | **Build Settings,** as shown in the following screenshot:

Uploading using Application Loader

A standalone app separate from Xcode, **Application Loader** (`http://help.apple.com/itc/apploader/#/apdATD1E927-D1E1A1303-D1E927A1126`) can be accessed from Xcode by going to **Xcode** | **Open Developer Tool** | **Application Loader**, which will then prompt you to sign in using your iTunes Connect account. Application Loader is a simplified tool, so to upload it, all you need to do is, from the **Template Chooser,** choose **Deliver Your App**. From there, select your binary/archive. It will extrapolate the metadata from iTunes Connect and ask you to confirm your app metadata. Select **Next** to proceed with uploading the binary to iTunes Connect:

Entering your app metadata

Within iTunes Connect, you have the ability to add metadata prior to submission, including marketing information, keywords, and a description of your app. Take a look at the following screenshot:

iOS App 1.0
Prepare for Submission

Submit for Review

Promotional Text   ?

Keywords   ?

Support URL   ?

Description   ?

Marketing URL   ?

In the **App Information** page, you will need to opt into the primary and secondary categories your app belongs to:

For more information on the types of metadata iTunes Connect supports, refer to **iTunes Connect Properties** (`https://developer.apple.com/library/content/documentation/LanguagesUtilities/Conceptual/iTunesConnect_Guide/Chapters/Properties.html#//apple_ref/doc/uid/TP40011225-CH26-SW1`).

Submitting your app to be reviewed

For any single version of your app, you are able to upload any number of builds; however, only one candidate is selected to be submitted for App Review, and, subsequently, the App Store version. Apple refers to the candidate build as the current build. As we only have one build in our current chapter (unless you've uploaded multiple builds), select the nominated version by going to iTunes Connect under **App Store | Build section** and selecting the version of your choice:

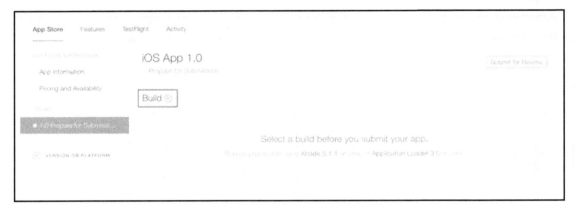

Select the Build (+) button from the App Store screen to allow you to choose which build version to put forward for submission to the App Store

You will then get a modal popup asking you to select the build that will be the current build selected for submission:

Selecting **Done** displays the build number in the **Build** section, along with the date of the upload. After setting the current build, we are now ready to finally submit our app for App Review. Back in the **App Store** tab, select the **Submit for Review** button on the top-right:

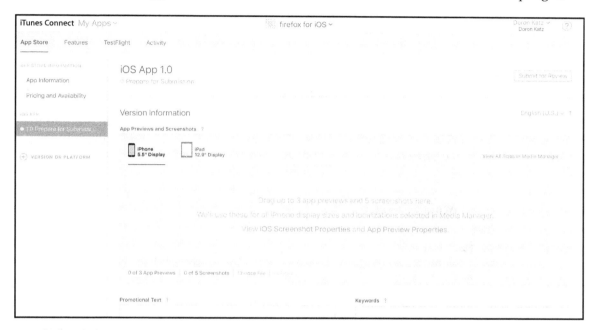

You will then be asked questions that relate to Export Compliance, as well as other legal questions (including Privacy Compliance), before you are able to select **Submit** and finally submit your app. These are the steps involved in uploading a new build for submission to the App Review team. While it's not complicated on its own, it does involve quite a few steps, and you can quite clearly see that this is something that should be automated, and it is. We will look at how deliver improves our submitting process quite significantly.

Introducing deliver

deliver (https://docs.fastlane.tools/actions/deliver/) automates all of the cumbersome and laborious steps we did earlier and uploads existing metadata directly to iTunes Connect, providing a much more manageable approach to updating your app's metadata. You can either use the keyword `deliver`, or the alias `upload_to_app_store`.

The following is the logo of deliver:

Generating your deliverfile metadata

Before running deliver, we will first need to extract the existing metadata from our app that may be available on iTunes Connect, which we will do by entering the following into the Terminal; ensure you enter your iTunes Connect credentials when asked:

```
fastlane deliver init
```

You will get the following console result:

```
. . .
[18:38:44]: Writing to
'./fastlane/metadata/review_information/email_address.txt'
[18:38:44]: Writing to
'./fastlane/metadata/review_information/demo_user.txt'
[18:38:44]: Writing to
'./fastlane/metadata/review_information/demo_password.txt'
[18:38:44]: Writing to './fastlane/metadata/review_information/notes.txt'
[18:38:44]: Successfully created new configuration files.
[18:38:44]: Downloading all existing screenshots...
[18:38:45]: Successfully downloaded all existing screenshots
[18:38:45]: Successfully created new Deliverfile at path
'./fastlane/Deliverfile'
. . .
```

You will have also observed that it created a `Deliverfile` in your `fastlane` directory, as well as the following metadata:

```
fastlane/metadata/
├── copyright.txt
├── en-US
│   ├── description.txt
│   ├── keywords.txt
│   ├── marketing_url.txt
│   ├── name.txt
│   ├── privacy_url.txt
│   ├── promotional_text.txt
│   ├── release_notes.txt
```

```
|       ├──── subtitle.txt
|       └──── support_url.txt
├──── primary_category.txt
├──── primary_first_sub_category.txt
├──── primary_second_sub_category.txt
├──── review_information
|       ├──── demo_password.txt
|       ├──── demo_user.txt
|       ├──── email_address.txt
|       ├──── first_name.txt
|       ├──── last_name.txt
|       ├──── notes.txt
|       └──── phone_number.txt
├──── secondary_category.txt
├──── secondary_first_sub_category.txt
├──── secondary_second_sub_category.txt
└──── trade_representative_contact_information
        ├──── address_line1.txt
        ├──── city_name.txt
        ├──── country.txt
        ├──── is_displayed_on_app_store.txt
        ├──── postal_code.txt
        ├──── state.txt
        └──── trade_name.txt
```

Open up the metadata folder, and take a look at all the metadata files. We will use this folder as our central location for updating our metadata, so take the liberty of maintaining whatever you need here. deliver also uses your screenshots folder to upload the latest screenshots that you might have generated (which we did in the previous chapters).

We will also purposefully commit our changes to the metadata folder each time we make changes, as this is the best-practice recommendation.

Uploading our metadata

Once we've made all of our necessary changes and generated the screenshots we want to have uploaded to iTunes Connect, we are finally ready to upload our metadata. The simplest command is to use the following:

```
fastlane deliver
```

It will confirm that it has successfully uploaded the metadata by returning the following:

```
. . .
+----------------------------------------+---------------------------+
|                 deliver 2.61.0 Summary                             |
+----------------------------------------+---------------------------+
| app_identifier                         | com.doronkatz.firefox     |
| username                               | dktz@mac.com              |
| screenshots_path                       | ./fastlane/screenshots    |
| metadata_path                          | ./fastlane/metadata       |
| edit_live                              | false                     |
| platform                               | ios                       |
| skip_binary_upload                     | false                     |
| skip_screenshots                       | false                     |
| skip_metadata                          | false                     |
| skip_app_version_update                | false                     |
| force                                  | false                     |
| submit_for_review                      | false                     |
| automatic_release                      | false                     |
| dev_portal_team_id                     | UL9R22xWB5                |
| overwrite_screenshots                  | false                     |
| run_precheck_before_submit             | true                      |
| precheck_default_rule_level            | warn                      |
| ignore_language_directory_validation   | false                     |
+----------------------------------------+---------------------------+
. . .
[22:18:41]: Verifying the upload via the HTML file can be disabled by
either adding
[22:18:41]: `force true` to your Deliverfile or using `fastlane deliver --
force`
[22:18:41]: Does the Preview on path './Preview.html' look okay for you?
(y/n)
y
[22:19:49]: HTML file confirmed...

[22:19:50]: Activating language en-US...
[22:19:51]: Uploading metadata to iTunes Connect
[22:19:52]: Successfully uploaded set of metadata to iTunes Connect
[22:19:53]: Starting with the upload of screenshots...
[22:19:53]: Activating language en-US...
[22:19:55]: Uploading 1 screenshots for language en-US
[22:19:55]: Uploading './fastlane/screenshots
. . .


+----------------------------+---------------------+
|          Summary for precheck 2.61.0            |
+----------------------------+---------------------+
| default_rule_level         | warn                |
```

```
| app_identifier         | com.doronkatz.firefox |
| username               | dktz@mac.com          |
| include_in_app_purchases | true                |
+------------------------+-----------------------+
```

```
. . .
[22:20:11]: ☑  Passed: No negative  sentiment
[22:20:11]: ☑  Passed: No placeholder text
[22:20:11]: ☑  Passed: No mentioning  competitors
[22:20:11]: ☑   Passed: No future functionality promises
[22:20:11]: ☑  Passed: No words indicating test content
[22:20:11]: ☑  Passed: No curse words
[22:20:11]: ☑  Passed: No words indicating your IAP is free
[22:20:11]: ☑  Passed: Incorrect, or missing copyright date
[22:20:17]: ☑  Passed: No broken urls
[22:20:17]: precheck 🕵 🕵  finished without detecting any potential
problems 📖
```

```
. . .
```

You will be prompted, with an auto-generated HTML file, to confirm your metadata prior to the upload, as follows:

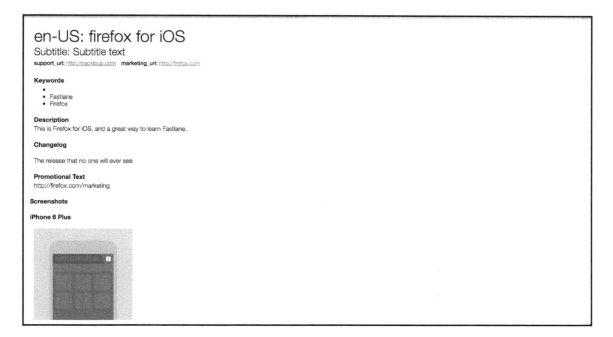

Verifying on our iTunes Connect, we can see that our listing, along with the updated metadata changes we've made, has successfully been uploaded. Refer to the following screenshot:

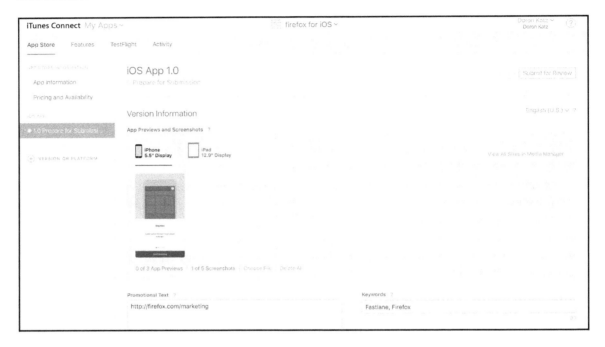

Other deliver options

You can download the latest screenshots, in addition to the metadata we downloaded earlier, into the `screenshots` folder by entering the following:

```
fastlane deliver download_screenshots
```

If you want to immediately mark the upload for review by Apple Review, add the following parameter:

```
fastlane deliver --ipa "App.ipa" --submit_for_review
```

To explicitly set the `pkg` (macOS) file, include the following:

```
fastlane deliver —pkg "App.pkg"
```

For an exhaustive list of parameters available to you, visit the deliver fastlane docs (`https:/`
`/docs.fastlane.tools/actions/deliver/`).

Updating our Fastfile

Finally, let's add to our previous `:release` lane by adding the deliver action right after
produce, as follows:

```
...
lane :release do
    # by default deliver will call precheck and warn you of any problems
    # if you want precheck to halt submitting to app review, you can pass
    # precheck_default_rule_level: :error
    deliver(precheck_default_rule_level: :error)
    snapshot
    produce(
      username: 'dktz@mac.com',
      app_identifier: 'com.doronkatz.firefox',
      app_name: 'Firefox for iOS',
      language: 'English',
      app_version: '1.0',
      team_name: 'Doron Katz' # only necessary when in multiple teams
    )
    deliver(
      submit_for_review: true
      metadata_path: "./metadata"
    )
  end    ...
```

Now our Fastfile will generate the screenshots and then deliver the metadata back to iTunes
Connect, each time we call this lane (fastlane release). In our parameters, we are forcing
submit for review.

Summary

This concludes our chapter on uploading our metadata to iTunes Connect, completing our
cycle from building, to adding App Store information, to upload and review. deliver is a
powerful action, allowing us to gracefully maintain our metadata locally, rather than
remotely, to provide a versioned approach to working with your assets and metadata.

14

Automate Unit Tests with scan

So far, we have accomplished a lot with fastlane, automating our workflow from registering to building our apps to publishing them to the app store, along with screenshots and metadata. As you pasue to appreciate how much easier our workflow is, be assured that we aren't done yet; there is still a lot more to offer, and we will continue to press on with our next action, scan (`https://docs.fastlane.tools/actions/run_tests/`).

scan fits into our fastlane workflow seamlessly, allowing us to conduct automated testing, either adhoc or as part of our Fastfile, making it easier to create specific configurations to output tests in either HTML, JSON, Unit reports, or through sending the outcome straight to Slack. This action is certainly an important one that should be a part of your lane right before you publish to the App Store, or for beta-testing, to ensure the unit and regression integrity is maintained.

Before we dive deep into what fastlane offers us, we will give you a quick introduction to how to conduct unit testing in iOS 11, which will serve as an excellent segue into the rest of this chapter. We will also be using our project to explore existing unit tests.

By the end of this chapter, you will have learned how to add scan to your workflow process, which will:

- Create a test script
- Run a test script
- Create a test script report

We will be working with scan through the command line to:

- Create and run test scripts
- Integrate the lane into our project Fastfile

An introduction to testing in iOS 11 and Swift 4

This section won't cover everything with unit testing, and there are really interesting sub-topics with testing that you should get familiar with at your own leisure. For some great unit-testing resources, refer to **What's New in Testing** (WWDC 2017) (`https://developer.apple.com/videos/play/wwdc2017/409/`) and **Testing with Xcode** (`https://developer.apple.com/library/content/documentation/DeveloperTools/Conceptual/testing_with_xcode/chapters/03-testing_basics.html`).

Unit testing can be defined as a function that tests an aspect of your app. A good testing strategy takes into account testing any new components that are created or changed, from the core functionality boundary testing, to testing bug fixes. Testing also needs to be repeatable and self-validating, or, in other words, you should be able to assert the same results each time you run the test, and the tests should be a clear pass or fail. Furthermore, good tests also need to be independent and decoupled, and should not require any dependencies, setup, or tear-down prior to the commencement of the next testing method.

With that in mind, we are going to start by creating a skeleton unit test class and then explore some of the existing and complete unit test cases to get an idea of the construct of unit testing.

Create a test target

In Xcode, with our project open, we are going to work off the one specific navigator tab, the Test Navigator, which we will familiarize ourselves with as we leverage for running and viewing the results of our tests. In the first screenshot, you can see that we already have a few test targets from the project's contributors, as well as the `FirefoxUITests` UI testing class we created in the previous chapter. Take a look at the following screenshot:

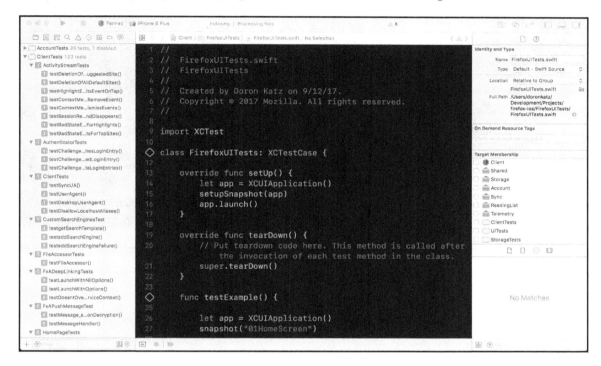

Pre-existing project test targets

In the bottom left-hand side, select the plus (+) button, and then select **New Unit Test Target...** to create our new test target. You could also create a UI Test Target similarly, to test and assert visual elements, which we did indirectly back in Chapter 11, *Taking Localized Screenshots with snapshot*, as part of grabbing screenshots. You can use the name FirefoxFastlaneTests for the target. Take a look at the following screenshot:

Creating our own UI Test Target

You should subsequently see the following template:

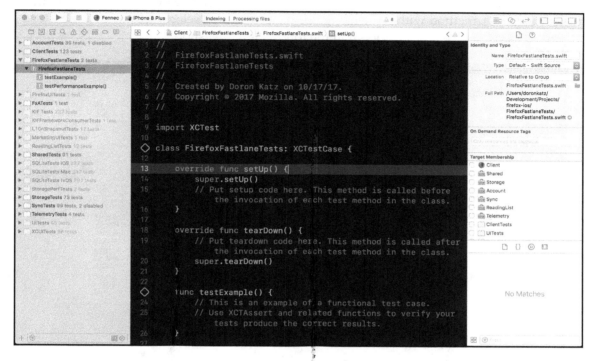

The generated test target template created for you

The default template comes with three methods: setup(), tearDown(), and testExample(). The first method is for any preliminary changes that need to be made prior to all the test cases being called, such as initializing an object or setting a specific state. Conversely, the tearDown() method resets the state to what it was prior to the setup() method, to ensure repeatability.

Go ahead and run the sample template with the `testExample()` method that won't produce anything (as it's empty), either by entering *command+U* or by right-clicking on the `testExample()` method within the navigator pane, and then selecting `Run "FireFoxFastlaneTests"`, as shown in the following screenshot:

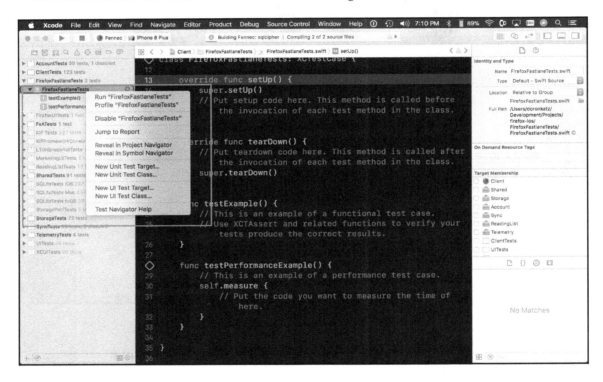

Using the left pane and selecting our test target to run our tests

The way we just demonstrated would run all the unit tests in the class, of which we only have one. Another way to run just one specific test case is to either select the `testExample()` node from the left-side navigation and right-click, instead of selecting the entire class, or, within the code, right-clicking on the diamond associated with that method. Refer to the following screenshot:

The testExample() method within the FirefoxFastlaneTests test target

Adding a simple unit test

To actually see some results, let's add a simple assertion that will automatically fail. In the `testExample()` method, add `XCTAssert(false)`.

Test this method, and you should get a failure, as shown next:

As clear as day, Xcode alerts us to a failed test, pointing at the assertion that failed, along with an (**x**) on the navigation pane, as well as within the code. Looking at the console, we can get even more granular knowledge as to what went wrong, as well as a summary of all the tests that passed and failed.

Examining other test cases

As we are fortunate to have a lot of existing completed test suites and test cases in our open source project, let's go ahead and open up `ClientTests` from the navigation pane and select the Play button, as shown in the following screenshot, to kick off all the tests in this suite:

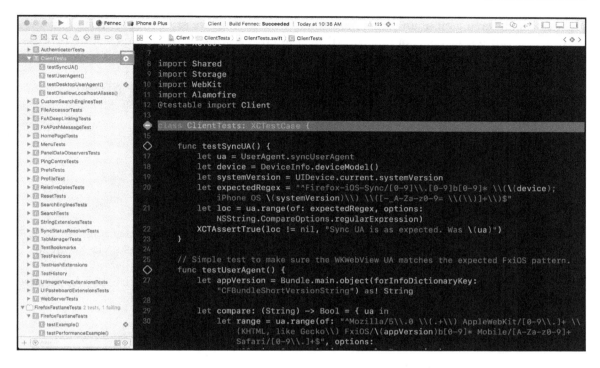

Hopefully, they should all pass, and you will get a series of ticks in the pane, as well as in the code, instead of x's. Take some time to examine this test class/suite, and you will see a lot of interesting test cases. Let's examine the test case `testDesktopUserAgent()`:

```
func testDesktopUserAgent() {
        let compare: (String) -> Bool = { ua in
            let range = ua.range(of: "^Mozilla/5\\.0 \\(Macintosh; Intel
Mac OS X [0-9_]+\\) AppleWebKit/[0-9\\.]+ \\(KHTML, like Gecko\\)
Safari/[0-9\\.]+$", options: NSString.CompareOptions.regularExpression)
            return range != nil
        }

        XCTAssertTrue(compare(UserAgent.desktopUserAgent()), "Desktop user
agent computes correctly.")
    }
```

This simple comparison test case asserts two sets of strings, the desktop user agent against a specific string range, asserting true, otherwise failing the test. There are certainly all types of assertions and tests you can do beyond testing for positive or negative, and they are certainly worth exploring more.

Now that you have a bit of an understanding of unit testing, we are going to start automating our tests as part of our workflow, thereby creating a continuous testing process as part of our continuous delivery mechanism.

"Continuous testing is the process of executing automated tests as part of the software delivery pipeline to obtain immediate feedback on the business risks associated with a software release candidate."

—Wikipedia

Introducing scan

scan, alias for the run_tests action (`https://docs.fastlane.tools/actions/run_tests/`) automates the process of running tests, and while you can certainly run tests via Xcode, as we have demonstrated in the preceding section, it isn't something you will want to do manually, especially as you take note of all the many test suites we have already. Apple also provides a command-line way of running test scripts, using `xcodebuild`:

```
xcodebuild \
  -workspace MyApp.xcworkspace \
  -scheme "MyApp" \
  -sdk iphonesimulator \
  -destination 'platform=iOS Simulator,name=iPhone 6,OS=8.1' \
  test
```

With scan, we can conduct our testing using one command, `fastlane scan`, which wraps the previous command into a pretty-formatted output of the results when run via the command line, as well as outputting the results in HTML and JUnit formats. The major benefit of leveraging scan as part of fastlane is that we can integrate it into our existing lane workflow, as well as Jenkins, which we will demonstrate in the later chapters of the book. The following is the logo of scan:

Running a simple scan

Before we get into all the different options scan provides us, let's run the simplest of paths by entering the following in the Terminal:

```
fastlane scan
```

The console will prompt you for which scheme to select, so select 2. Fennec. After successfully running the tests, the console will return:

```
. . .
[11:15:08]: > Test Suite SharedTests.xctest started
[11:15:08]: > ArrayExtensionTests
[11:15:08]: >  testUnion (0.003 seconds)
[11:15:08]: > ✓ testUnique (0.001 seconds)
[11:15:08]: > AsyncReducerTests
[11:15:08]: > ✓ testAccumulation (0.002 seconds)
[11:15:08]: > ✓ testFailingAppend (0.102 seconds)
[11:15:08]: > ✓ testFailingCombine (0.001 seconds)
[11:15:08]: > ✓ testSimpleBehaviour (0.001 seconds)
[11:15:08]: > ✓ testWaitingFillerAppendingBehaviour (0.530 seconds)
[11:15:09]: > ✓ testWaitingFillerBehaviour (0.514 seconds)
[11:15:09]: > ✓ AuthenticationKeychainInfoTests
[11:15:09]: > ✓ testEncodingAndDecoding (0.007 seconds)
[11:15:09]: > ✓ testNilIntervalsArentZero (0.007 seconds)
[11:15:09]: > DeferredTests
[11:15:09]: > ✓ testDeferred (0.001 seconds)
[11:15:09]: > ✓ testFailAccumulate (0.001 seconds)
[11:15:09]: > ✓ testMultipleUponBlocks (0.001 seconds)
[11:15:09]: > ✓ testOperators (0.001 seconds)
[11:15:09]: > ✓ testPassAccumulate (0.001 seconds)
[11:15:09]: > FeatureSwitchTests
[11:15:09]: > ✓ test0Percent (0.100 seconds)
[11:15:09]: > ✓ test100Percent (0.097 seconds)
[11:15:09]: > ✓ test30Percent (0.090 seconds)
[11:15:09]: > ✓ test50Percent (0.091 seconds)
[11:15:09]: > ✓ testAppConstantsWin (0.001 seconds)
[11:15:09]: > ✓ testConsistentWhenChangingPercentage (0.002 seconds)
[11:15:09]: > ✓ testForceDisabled (0.001 seconds)
[11:15:12]: > 🕐   testPerformance measured (0.005 seconds)
[11:15:12]: > ✓ testPerformance (2.598 seconds)
[11:15:12]: > ✓ testPersistent (0.001 seconds)
[11:15:12]: > ✓ testUserEnabled (0.001 seconds)
[11:15:12]: > HexExtensionsTests
[11:15:12]: > ✓ testHexDecodedData (0.002 seconds)
[11:15:12]: > ✓ testHexDecodedDataWithInvalidInput (0.001 seconds)
```

```
[11:15:12]: > ✓ testHexEncodedString (0.001 seconds)
[11:15:12]: > NSMutableAttributedStringExtensionsTests
[11:15:12]: > ✓ testColorsSubstring (0.001 seconds)
[11:15:12]: > ✓ testDoesNothingWhenSubstringNotFound (0.001 seconds)
[11:15:12]: > ✓ testDoesNothingWithEmptySubstring (0.001 seconds)
[11:15:12]: > NSURLExtensionsTests
[11:15:12]: > ✓ testBaseDomainForExceptionDomain (0.001 seconds)
[11:15:12]: > ✓ testBaseDomainForExceptionDomainWithAdditionalSubdomain
(0.001 seconds)
[11:15:12]: > ✓ testBaseDomainForWildcardDomain (0.001 seconds)
[11:15:12]: > ✓ testBaseDomainForWildcardDomainWithAdditionalSubdomain
(0.001 seconds)
[11:15:12]: > ✓ testBugzillaURLDomain (0.001 seconds)
[11:15:12]: > ✓ testCanadaComputers (0.001 seconds)
[11:15:12]: > ✓ testdecodeReaderModeURL (0.003 seconds)
[11:15:12]: > ✓ testdisplayURL (0.001 seconds)
[11:15:12]: > ✓ testdomainURL (0.002 seconds)
[11:15:12]: > ✓ testencodeReaderModeURL (0.001 seconds)
[11:15:12]: > ✓ testExceptionDomain (0.001 seconds)
[11:15:12]: > ✓ testgetQuery (0.001 seconds)
[11:15:12]: > ✓ testhavingRemovedAuthorisationComponents (0.001 seconds)
[11:15:12]: > ✓ testhostPort (0.001 seconds)
[11:15:12]: > ✓ testhostSLD (0.001 seconds)
[11:15:12]: > ✓ testIPv6Domain (0.001 seconds)
[11:15:12]: > ✓ testisAboutHomeURL (0.001 seconds)
[11:15:12]: > ✓ testisAboutURL (0.001 seconds)
[11:15:12]: > ✓ testisErrorPage (0.001 seconds)
[11:15:12]: > ✓ testisLocal (0.001 seconds)
[11:15:12]: > ✓ testisReaderModeURL (0.001 seconds)
[11:15:12]: > ✓ testisWebPage (0.001 seconds)
[11:15:12]: > ✓ testKeepsAboutSchemeInURL (0.001 seconds)
[11:15:12]: > ✓ testKeepsHTTPSAndRemovesTrailingSlashInURL (0.001 seconds)
[11:15:12]: > ✓ testKeepsHTTPSAndTrailingSlashInURL (0.000 seconds)
[11:15:12]: > ✓ testKeepsHTTPSInURL (0.001 seconds)
[11:15:12]: > ✓ testMultipleSuffixesInsideURL (0.001 seconds)
[11:15:12]: > ✓ testNormalBaseDomainWithManySubdomains (0.001 seconds)
[11:15:12]: > ✓ testNormalBaseDomainWithSingleSubdomain (0.001 seconds)
[11:15:12]: > ✓ testNormalBaseSubdomain (0.001 seconds)
[11:15:12]: > ✓ testNormalBaseSubdomainWithAdditionalSubdomain (0.005
seconds)
[11:15:12]: > ✓ testnormalizedHostAndPath (0.001 seconds)
[11:15:12]: > ✓ testorigin (0.001 seconds)
[11:15:12]: > ✓ testoriginalURLFromErrorURL (0.001 seconds)
[11:15:12]: > ✓ testRemovesHTTPAndTrailingSlashFromURL (0.001 seconds)
[11:15:12]: > ✓ testRemovesHTTPButNotTrailingSlashFromURL (0.001 seconds)
```

```
[11:15:12]: > ✓ testRemovesHTTPFromURL (0.001 seconds)
[11:15:12]: > ✓ testschemeIsValid (0.001 seconds)
[11:15:12]: > ✓ testWildCardDomainWithManySubdomains (0.001 seconds)
[11:15:12]: > ✓ testWildCardDomainWithSingleSubdomain (0.000 seconds)
[11:15:12]: > ✓ testWithQueryParam (0.001 seconds)
[11:15:12]: > ✓ testwithQueryParams (0.001 seconds)
[11:15:12]: > PhoneNumberFormatterTests
[11:15:12]: > ✓ testFallsBackToSpecifiedLocaleForGuessingCountryCode (0.003
seconds)
[11:15:12]: > ✓ testFormatsNumber (0.001 seconds)
[11:15:12]: > ✓ testReturnsInputStringWhenFormattingFails (0.001 seconds)
[11:15:12]: > ✓ testReturnsInputStringWhenParsingFails (0.001 seconds)
[11:15:12]: > ✓ testReturnsInputStringWhenValidatingFails (0.001 seconds)
[11:15:12]: > ✓ testSelectsInternationalFormatWithCountryCode (0.001
seconds)
[11:15:12]: > ✓ testSelectsNationalFormatWithoutCountryCode (0.001 seconds)
[11:15:12]: > ✓ testUsesCarrierForGuessingCountryCode (0.001 seconds)
[11:15:12]: > ResultTests
[11:15:12]: > ✓ testResult (0.001 seconds)
[11:15:12]: > RollingFileLoggerTests
[11:15:12]: > ✓ testNewLogCreatesLogFileWithTimestamp (0.009 seconds)
[11:15:12]: > ✓ testNewLogDeletesOldestLogFileToMakeRoomForNewFile (0.034
seconds)
[11:15:12]: > ✓ testNewLogDeletesPreviousLogIfItsTooLarge (0.014 seconds)
[11:15:12]: > SupportUtilsTests
[11:15:12]: > ✓ testURLForTopic (0.001 seconds)
[11:15:12]: > UtilsTests
[11:15:12]: > ✓ testChunk (0.002 seconds)
[11:15:12]: > ✓ testMapUtils (0.001 seconds)
[11:15:12]: > ✓ testOptArrayEqual (0.001 seconds)
[11:15:12]: > ✓ testOptFilter (0.001 seconds)
[11:15:12]: > ✓ testParseTimestamps (0.001 seconds)
[11:15:12]: >     Executed 91 tests, with 0 failures (0 unexpected) in
4.271 (4.351) seconds
[11:15:12]: >
[11:15:14]: > All tests
[11:15:14]: > Test Suite FxATests.xctest started
[11:15:14]: > FxATests
[11:15:14]: > 🕐 testPerformanceExample measured (0.000 seconds)
[11:15:14]: > ✓ testPerformanceExample (0.272 seconds)
[11:15:14]: >     Executed 1 test, with 0 failures (0 unexpected) in 0.272
(0.275) seconds
[11:15:14]: >
[11:15:24]: > All tests
[11:15:24]: > Test Suite TelemetryTests.xctest started
[11:15:24]: > EventTests
```

```
[11:15:24]: > ✓ testEventValidation (0.006 seconds)
[11:15:24]: > ✓ testIdentifierStringValidation (0.001 seconds)
[11:15:24]: > ✓ testPickling (0.001 seconds)
[11:15:24]: > ✓ testUnpickling (0.002 seconds)
[11:15:24]: >     Executed 4 tests, with 0 failures (0 unexpected) in
0.010 (0.014) seconds
[11:15:24]: >
[11:15:34]: > Selected tests
[11:15:34]: > Test Suite AccountTests.xctest started
[11:15:34]: > FirefoxAccountTests
[11:15:34]: > ✓ testSerialization (0.027 seconds)
[11:15:34]: > FxAClient10Tests
[11:15:34]: > ✓ testClientState (0.003 seconds)
[11:15:34]: > ✓ testErrorOutput (0.006 seconds)
[11:15:34]: > ✓ testKeysSuccess (0.005 seconds)
[11:15:34]: > ✓ testLoginFailure (0.003 seconds)
[11:15:34]: > ✓ testLoginSuccess (0.002 seconds)
[11:15:34]: > ✓ testSignSuccess (0.002 seconds)
[11:15:34]: > ✓ testUnwrapKey (0.001 seconds)
[11:15:34]: > FxALoginStateMachineTests
[11:15:34]: > ✓ testAdvanceFromCohabitingAfterVerifiedDuringOutage (0.046
seconds)
[11:15:34]: > ✓ testAdvanceFromCohabitingAfterVerifiedWithoutNetwork
(0.009 seconds)
[11:15:34]: > ✓ testAdvanceFromEngagedAfterVerified (0.062 seconds)
[11:15:34]: > ✓ testAdvanceFromEngagedAfterVerifiedWithoutNetwork (0.003
seconds)
[11:15:34]: > ✓ testAdvanceFromEngagedBeforeVerified (0.002 seconds)
[11:15:34]: > ✓ testAdvanceFromMarried (0.007 seconds)
[11:15:34]: > ✓ testAdvanceFromMarriedAfterPasswordChange (0.032 seconds)
[11:15:34]: > ✓ testAdvanceFromMarriedWithExpiredCertificate (0.018
seconds)
[11:15:34]: > ✓ testAdvanceFromMarriedWithExpiredKeyPair (0.009 seconds)
[11:15:34]: > ✓ testAdvanceWhenInteractionRequired (0.002 seconds)
[11:15:34]: > FxAStateTests
[11:15:34]: > ✓ testSerialization (0.047 seconds)
[11:15:34]: > HawkHelperTests
[11:15:34]: > ✓ testGetBaseContentType (0.001 seconds)
[11:15:34]: > ✓ testSpecRequestString (0.008 seconds)
[11:15:34]: > ✓ testSpecSignatureExample (0.001 seconds)
[11:15:34]: > ✓ testSpecWithoutPayloadExample (0.001 seconds)
[11:15:34]: > ✓ testSpecWithPayloadExample (0.001 seconds)
[11:15:34]: > LivePushClientTests
[11:15:37]: > ✓ testClientRegistration (3.170 seconds)
[11:15:38]: > ✓ testClientUpdate (0.783 seconds)
```

```
[11:15:38]: > PushCryptoTests
[11:15:38]: > ✔ testDecrypt_aes128gcm (0.005 seconds)
[11:15:38]: > ✔ testDecrypt_aesgcm (0.003 seconds)
[11:15:38]: > ✔ testFail_aes128gcm (0.001 seconds)
[11:15:38]: > ✔ testFail_aesgcm (0.001 seconds)
[11:15:38]: > ✔ testKeyGeneration (0.001 seconds)
[11:15:38]: > ✔ testRoundTrip_aes128gcm (0.002 seconds)
[11:15:38]: > ✔ testRoundtrip_base64urlSafe (0.001 seconds)
[11:15:38]: > ✔ testRoundtrip_base64urlSafe_withSpecialChars (0.001
seconds)
[11:15:38]: > TokenServerClientTests
[11:15:38]: > ✔ testAudienceForEndpoint (0.001 seconds)
[11:15:38]: > ✔ testErrorOutput (0.001 seconds)
[11:15:38]: > ✔ testTokenFailure (0.002 seconds)
[11:15:38]: > ✔ testTokenSuccess (0.002 seconds)
[11:15:38]: >        Executed 38 tests, with 0 failures (0 unexpected) in
4.272 (4.318) seconds
...
** TEST FAILED **
[11:15:57]: Exit status: 65
+--------------------+-----+
|      Test Results  |     |
+--------------------+-----+
| Number of tests    | 432 |
| Number of failures | 1   |
+--------------------+-----+
...
```

As you can see, scan ran all of our test suites, and we got one failure, which is expected because we had intentionally written our method to fail. Go ahead and comment out the XCTAssert(false) line we inserted previously, or remove it so that we don't hit that failure again in future test runs.

Viewing the output results

Besides the console results, you can also view your results in HTML and XML/JUnit format, and you will find the new files within your fastlane/test_output folder:

```
fastlane/test_output/
├── report.html
└── report.junit
```

Opening the `report.html` file in your browser, you should get a beautifully laid-out report:

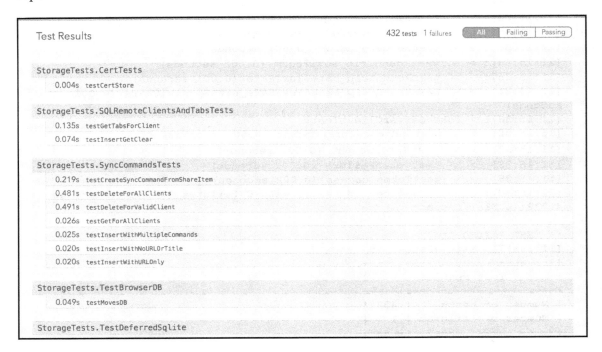

Running a specific scan

Like our other fastlane actions, scan (`https://docs.fastlane.tools/actions/scan/`) also provides you with the ability to pass in parameters to be more specific in your scan/testing. Enter the following to conduct the same tests, but automatically specify our project and scheme, as well as constrain tests to iPhone 7:

```
fastlane scan --project "Client.xcodeproj" --scheme "Fennec" --device
"iPhone 7" --clean
```

For an exhaustive list of parameters the action accepts, enter `fastlane action scan`.

Generating a Scanfile

Like many of our other fastlane actions, scan also has its very own Scanfile, which provides you with the conveniences of storing your specific environment parameters, rather than having you include all those parameters each time you manually run a test. Create a new Scanfile by entering:

```
fastlane scan init
```

In the newly created file, fastlane/Scanfile, add the following:

```
scheme "Fennec"
devices ["iPhone 7s", "iPhone 7"]
project "Client.xcodeproj"
clean true
open_report true

output_types "html"
```

If you run scan again, all you need to do is enter:

```
fastlane scan
```

After it finishes compiling and running the tests, it will automatically open up the testing report in your browser, courtesy of open_report true.

Updating our Fastfile

To round off this chapter, we are going to continue to build onto our fastlane workflow by adding a new lane, as follows:

```
...
  desc "Runs all the tests"
  lane :test do
    run_tests
  end
```

We could also add the scan action to other lanes, such as our beta lane, right after the gym action, and before testflight, so that we maintain our continuous testing ambitions.

Summary

You will find that scan will become a really integral part of your workflow in many different lanes, as you look toward code quality being part of your continuous delivery process. This will be further emphasized in our next chapter, as we demonstrate how to integrate Jenkins CI into our workflow.

15
Integrating Git into the fastlane Workflow

Up until now, we have been using Git to access the sample code repository of this project. We have also more recently incorporated Git with Jenkins CI Jenkins CI (`https://jenkins.io/`) as part of our fastlane workflow, listening for new branch commits. In fact, even within our sample project, Carthage leverages Git as part of its dependency management to download all the dependency libraries.

Our focus has been on working with the more common actions that correlate to specific tasks, from provisioning to generating screenshots, and from building to publishing, with the primary objective of making our lives as developers significantly more convenient through a systematic continuous delivery workflow. In this chapter, we are going to actually integrate Git into our fastlane more intimately.

In this chapter, you will learn how to integrate various Git actions into your existing fastlane lanes to further enrich the developer processes and experiences. You will also learn how to include shell scripts for when there is no corresponding fastlane action for a specific Git action.

The following skills will be learned in this chapter:

- Introducing the various Git actions and commands
- Calling Bash commands using fastlane
- Integrating Git actions into our fastlane workflow

Introducing the various Git actions and commands

Git is the quintessential developer tool, a must for when developers collaborate with a team to ensure the appropriate collaboration and perseverance of code throughout the software project life. Up until now, we have used Git as an auxiliary to our other processes, such as fastlane, where we update the Fastfile, make any other code changes, and then commit using Git, separately. Here, we are going to learn how to incorporate Git into our fastlane workflow, embedding various Git actions into our lanes to further automate our Git interactions.

Fastlane supports a plethora of Git actions as part of its library, which we are going to cover in this section. We will then discuss how to work with the sh action to call shell commands directly for when you want a specifically customized git (or other) action that is not part of the library.

In the next chapter, we are going to cover how to create your own plugins and actions.

ensure_git_status_clean

The first Git action we will look at is ensure_git_status_clean (https://docs. fastlane.tools/actions/ensure_git_status_clean/#ensure_git_status_clean), with the sole purpose of ensuring, prior to running whatever other fastlane action you intend to run, that the current local Git state is clean. What this means is that you don't have any uncommitted or nonmerged changes locally, whereby running a git commit through an action would break anything.

Running this with the optional parameter show_uncommitted_changes will output any uncommitted change back to the console, but, either way, it will purposely fail the lane call and prevent any other commands from running.

ensure_git_branch

ensure_git_branch (https://docs.fastlane.tools/actions/ensure_git_branch/ #ensure_git_branch) is used to assert that the action is being run from within a specific Git branch, and is used by teams to enforce specific development branching models, such as the **Gitflow workflow** (https://www.atlassian.com/git/tutorials/comparing-workflows/ gitflow-workflow), and raise an exception and stop lane execution if the developer isn't working from a specific branch. You will need to pass a mandatory parameter branch to specify what branch the code repository needs to be in, as shown in the following code:

```
lane :testing do
    ..
        ensure_git_branch(branch:"stage")
    ..
```

create_pull_request

Specifically for processes such as the aforementioned Gitflow workflow, create_pull_request (https://docs.fastlane.tools/actions/create_pull_request/ #create_pull_request) automatically initiates a new pull request from the specific branch and is specific to GitHub. The outcome of this will include a console success message that states the pull request number, as well as the URL of the pull request. There are quite a few mandatory and optional parameters you can pass with this action. The following list shows the mandatory arguments:

- api_token: The GitHub pull request API token that you would need to obtain and add as an argument. You can get the token by navigating to https:// github.com/settings/tokens.
- repo: The name of the GitHub repository you will be submitting the pull request to.
- title: The title of the pull request, as it will be filed within GitHub.

For the list of all the optional arguments, refer to the specific action file for create_pull_request. We will cover how to read as well as create new custom actions in the next chapter.

git_pull

As its namesake indicates, `git_pull` (https://docs.fastlane.tools/actions/git_pull/#git_pull) executes a Git pull and pulls the latest from the repository, and, with the addition of the optional argument, `only_tags` will only pull the tags rather than any new commits.

git_commit

`git_commit` (https://docs.fastlane.tools/actions/git_commit/#git_commit) provides *fastlane* users with the ability to commit the current changes automatically, saving developers having to automatically commit. More succinctly, this action is best leveraged towards the end of your lane execution, say after you have completed various unit testing in addition to the building. `git_commit` simply adds a new commit, with the parameter's path and message, `commit_version_bump` (https://docs.fastlane.tools/actions/commit_version_bump/#commit_version_bump) to set which files are to be included as part of the commit (optionally) and the specific commit message to include, respectively.

push_to_git_remote

After you've called the `git_commit` action, you will then logically call the `push_to_git_remote` (https://docs.fastlane.tools/actions/push_to_git_remote/#push_to_git_remote) action to push your changes back to the server. This action provides for quite a few optional arguments, including setting which local branch to push from, the remote branch to push to, whether to do a force push, and whether to push tags to the remote.

git_tag_exists

Moving from commits to tags, the first of the three prominent `git_tag` actions is `git_tag_exists` (https://docs.fastlane.tools/actions/git_tag_exists/#git_tag_exists), which is used to verify whether a tag with a specific name already exists prior to pushing it, to ensure that it is passing the mandatory tag parameter to check against, and will simply respond with a boolean value and message back to the console. This action is intended to be used in conjunction with other actions in order for it to work:

```
'if git_tag_exists(tag: "staging/0.1.1")
    UI.message("Found it 🚀 ")
```

```
else
        add_git_tag(grouping: "staging", build_number: "0.1.1"
  end'
```

add_git_tag

We just showed you a simple example in the previous action, but add_git_tag (https://
docs.fastlane.tools/actions/add_git_tag/#add_git_tag) is quite powerful in and of
itself. In its simplest usage, you can add a new tag, as follows:

```
add_git_tag(
        tag: "v0.1.1"
)'
```

This action, however, enables you to more granularly add a groping (that is, /staging/) to
organize your tag, a prefix (that is, v) to your version number, and the specific build
number, which it takes from the increment_build_number from your Xcode project
automatically rather than you having to specify an explicit tag version number. The rest of
the optional arguments include:

- message: The tag message to be included as part of the tag commit
- force: This forces the tag to be added
- sign: Enable a GPG-signed tag

For the list of all the optional arguments, refer to the specific action file add_git_tag
(https://docs.fastlane.tools/actions/add_git_tag/#add_git_tag). We will cover how
to read as well as create new custom actions in the next chapter.

push_git_tags

Finally, as with Git pushes preceding Git commits, the same holds true for tags, and `push_git_tags` (`https://docs.fastlane.tools/actions/push_git_tags/#push_git_tags`) pushes all the new tags you have committed, either by using the previous action or through manually adding a new tag. This action comes with two optional arguments—a force that forces the push to remote, and a remote to specify a nondefault remote location to push to. There are always new actions added regularly, as well as vendor-specific ones, so it is recommended that you regularly consult the `actions` repository (`https://docs.fastlane.tools/actions/#fastlane-actions`) as well as ensure that you always update your fastlane installation. We will next look at how to call custom bash shell commands using fastlane.

Calling bash commands using fastlane

If for some reason you need to call a specific command that is not available in the current fastlane library, you have two options. Ideally, if what you need to do would be useful for the general public, create your own action/plugin, as long as it's appealing and generic enough for other developers. If it's a very specific action, fastlane lets you run specific shell `sh` commands as if you were in the Command Prompt yourself.

Running a shell command is as simple as adding it to your lane, with an action similar to the following:

```
...
sh("git add ./screenshots")
...
sh("git commit -m:'Specific update text'")
..
sh "bash ./script.sh"
```

It's quite versatile. As you can see, you are able to interact with your bash shell directly from within fastlane, calling specific shell scripts that you've created, as part of your workflow. In subsequent chapters, we are going to add even more advanced actions, as well as our own crafted action plugin, but, as for what we've learned so far, we are going to put that into practice and update our Fastfile, accordingly.

Improving and optimizing our fastlane workflow

Let's put our theory into practice and improve our Fastfile by including purposeful Git actions, starting with a lane that you may have noticed previously, but that we haven't covered yet, namely the prebuilt `before_all *` lane. This lane gets called before any fastlane lane is called, and is a great place to put any actions and commands that would commonly apply across all of the lanes—for instance, when running any preparation or cleanup scripts prior to calling a build or test.

Working with the before_all lane

We are going to start off by calling the `carthage` (https://docs.fastlane.tools/actions/carthage/#carthage) action to ensure we have the most up-to-date dependencies. Using the `bootstrap` command argument, we can optimize this call so that it only downloads the necessary dependencies as required:

```
platform :ios do
  before_all do
    carthage(
      command: options[:update] ? "update" : "bootstrap",
      platform: "iOS",
      use_binaries: false
    )
  end
```

Looking at our existing Fastfile, it would also make sense for us to move our `match` command to the `before_all` lane as well, so that we can ensure that we have the latest provisioning profiles and certificates, ahead of any of our subsequent fastlane calls, so let's go ahead and move our `match` call so that it's only called once, at the start:

```
before_all do
  carthage(
    command: "bootstrap",
    platform: "iOS",
    use_binaries: false
  )
  match(git_url: "git@bitbucket.org:xxxx/my-fastlane-keys.git",
    type: "development",
    app_identifier: "com.yourid.firefox")
end
```

Ensuring our fastlane is always the latest

Finally, as is good practice, we can ensure our fastlane version is always up to date by including the `update_fastlane` (`https://docs.fastlane.tools/actions/update_fastlane/#update_fastlane`) preceding the `carthage` action.

Optimizing our beta distribution workflow

Next, we are going to optimize our beta distribution workflow so that we will encompass everything we need in this lane. Our strategy for submitting new builds to TestFlight would be as follows:

1. Ensure that we have the latest code from the repository so that we are in fact merging and integrating our changes with any other changes so that users can test the latest changes.
2. After we successfully build our app with no errors, we will want to run some unit tests.
3. Get a list of all the commits to put as part of our change log that we pass to TestFlight as our build description.
4. Bump our project version, commit, and push our changes to Git.
5. Create a new beta tag in Git, and push to our repository.
6. Upload our binary file to TestFlight to distribute to our users.

If you have been following the exercises thus far, then our lane should currently resemble something similar to the following:

```
lane :beta do
  register_devices(devices_file: "devices.txt")
    gym(scheme: "Fennec",
      output_name:"firefox.ipa",
      silent: false,
      output_directory: "./Export"
    )
    scan
    testflight(
      username: "your@email.com",
      app_identifier: "com.doronkatz.firefox",
      beta_app_description: "This is a new build and should be dynamic,
from prompt",
      beta_app_feedback_email: "feedback@firefoxapp.com",
      itc_provider: "abcde12345" # pass a specific value to the
iTMSTransporter -itc_provider option
```

```
)
```

Getting the latest code and ensuring a clean Git status

First up, we will add the following two actions to the start of our beta lane to ensure our Git environment is clean:

```
lane :beta do
    ensure_git_status_clean
    git_pull
        ...
```

It is important that we ensure we have a clean local Git environment (no changes) before doing a Git pull.

Building our app and running tests

We have already done this over the course of this book, as shown by the gym and scan actions in our lane.

Getting a list of commits to form the changelog

We will want to be able to dynamically add notes when we call TestFlight (or any test distribution action) as part of our changelog. One approach is to leverage the last set of commits as part of our changelog, and changelog_from_git_commits (https://github.com/fastlane/fastlane/blob/master/fastlane/lib/fastlane/actions/changelog_from_git_commits.rb) is the perfect action for that. Refer to the action documentation (https://github.com/fastlane/fastlane/blob/master/fastlane/lib/fastlane/actions/changelog_from_git_commits.rb) for a list of the various arguments you can pass so that you can craft the perfect set of notes and the number of commits to go back and so forth, but, for the sake of this example, we are going to simply pass in a pretty argument to format the commit messages more cleanly.

We will update our testflight action in the same lane, passing in the changelog variable that we assign to get the commit messages as a parameter:

```
    ...
    scan
    changelog = changelog_from_git_commits(pretty: '%h %s')
    testflight(
        username: "your@email.com",
        app_identifier: "com.doronkatz.firefox",
```

```
        beta_app_description: changelog,
        beta_app_feedback_email: "feedback@firefoxapp.com",
        itc_provider: "abcde12345" # pass a specific value to the
iTMSTransporter -itc_provider option
    )
            . . .
```

Bumping our project version, committing, and pushing our changes to Git

After successfully building our app and running the tests, we can confidently bump our Git commit and project versions, and push the changes back to our repository. Let's start with bumping our Git commit version first. To do that, you would simply add the commit_version_bump (https://docs.fastlane.tools/actions/commit_version_bump/#commit_version_bump) action right after the testflight action:

```
. . .
commit_version_bump(
        message: 'Build Version Bump by fastlane',
        xcodeproj: "Client.xcodeproj",
        force: true
)
```

To increment our project build number, add the increment_build_number (https://github.com/fastlane/fastlane/blob/master/fastlane/lib/fastlane/actions/increment_build_number.rb) action right before the commit_version call:

```
increment_build_number(xcodeproj: "Client.xcodeproj")
commit_version_bump(
        message: 'Build Version Bump by fastlane',
        xcodeproj: "Client.xcodeproj",
        force: true
)
```

Next, we will create a new tag to signify that a new build is ready for testing, leveraging add_git_tag (https://github.com/fastlane/fastlane/blob/master/fastlane/lib/fastlane/actions/add_git_tag.rb):

```
. . .
commit_version_bump(
        message: 'Build Version Bump by fastlane',
        xcodeproj: "Client.xcodeproj",
        force: true
)
```

```
add_git_tag(grouping: "testing")
```

Finally, we will push our changes back to our repository, including our tags:

```
push_to_git_remote
push_git_tags
```

Summary

This chapter was all about optimization, and, for us, being able to optimize our workflow by integrating various Git commands to automatically pull and commit, as well as push out new tags. In our coding exercises, we also learned how to bump our version number, as well as how to use a few new actions to help us create a dynamic changelog for our TestFlight distribution. While we very briefly looked at some of the action plugins, we are going to dive deeper into understanding how to read fastlane action code, as well as creating our own plugins.

In the next chapter, we will dive deeper into plugins, the third-party plugin community, and creating our own action plugin.

16
Creating and Using fastlane Action Plugins

In the chapters leading up to this one, we have explored numerous fastlane actions that have helped us automate our continuous delivery workflow significantly, cherry-picking various actions to integrate from Git to building, testing, and publishing our apps. fastlane is an open platform, and as such, if you cannot find a specific action, you can always create one.

fastlane encourages third-party developers to contribute to the creation of plugins that benefit the community, but even if it doesn't benefit a broader user base, you can always create your own actions for your own project and team's benefit. In this chapter, we are going to first explore the existing plugin ecosystem before learning how to add an existing plugin into our existing app, then learn how to create our own simple plugin.

The objective of this chapter is to learn the basics of how plugins work and how to implement, as well as author and submit, new plugins.

In this chapter, you will learn the following skills:

- Discovering fastlane plugins
- Implementing a fastlane plugin
- Creating your own fastlane plugin
- Publishing a fastlane plugin

Discovering new action plugins

fastlane actions should be second-nature to you now, as we have leveraged many useful plugins that have made our lives a lot easier as developers, whether by interacting with testing platforms such as TestFlight and Hockey or incrementing our project build numbers and pushing new git commits, as we demonstrated in the last chapter. There are, in fact, two forms of action plugins that fastlane provides: built-in actions (`https://docs.fastlane.tools/actions/#fastlane-actions`) and third-party actions (`https://docs.fastlane.tools/plugins/available-plugins/`), with the difference being that for the latter, you will need to install explicitly in order to utilize.

build-in plugins

The plugins that come with fastlane and can be leveraged right out of the box can be found at `https://github.com/fastlane/fastlane/tree/master/fastlane/lib/fastlane/actions`. You can go ahead and browse through all the various actions, and you will notice a few of them are already familiar to you from the previous chapter; for instance, the `add_git_tag` (`https://docs.fastlane.tools/actions/add_git_tag/`) action:

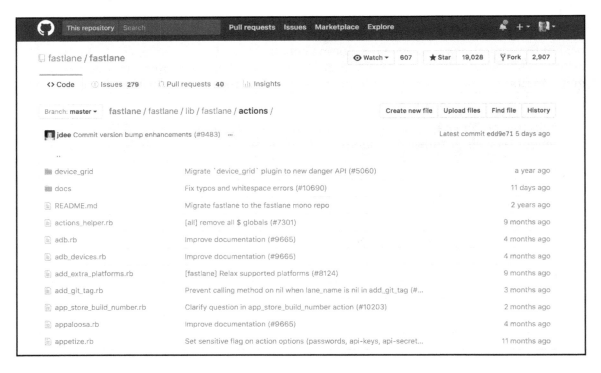

We will look at the inner workings of a plugin in the next section of this chapter.

Third-party plugins

Beyond the plugins that come pre-baked with fastlane, you have access to a growing and vibrant community of third-party plugins (`https://docs.fastlane.tools/plugins/available-plugins/`) that can further enrich your continuous delivery workflows. Beyond the obvious iOS actions, interestingly, you will also find not only Android-specific plugins, but even Xamarin and Cordova web development plugins, which shows that fastlane is quickly moving beyond the domain of being just an iOS-dominated toolchain. Take a look at the following screenshot:

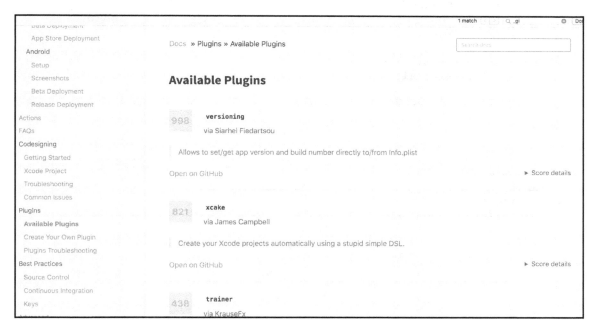

For instance, there is a translation plugin by Jakob Jensen (`https://github.com/trifork/fastlane-plugin-translation`) that can pull boilerplate translations from a Google sheet (`https://www.google.com/sheets/about/`) document. Refer to the following screenshot:

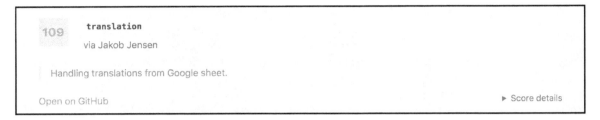

To browse the ever-growing list of third-party plugins, make sure to regularly revisit `https://docs.fastlane.tools/plugins/available-plugins/`, or enter in Command Prompt:

```
$ fastlane search_plugins
[08:42:01]: Listing all available fastlane plugins


+-----------------------------------+-----------------------------------
+-----------+
|                                   Available fastlane plugins
|
+-----------------------------------+-----------------------------------
+-----------+
| Name                              | Description                       |
Downloads  |
+-----------------------------------+-----------------------------------
+-----------+
| versioning                        | Allows to set/get app version and |
191516     |
|                                   | build number directly to/from     |
|
|                                   | Info.plist                        |
|
| update_project_codesigning        | Updates the Xcode 8 Automatic     |
73506      |
|                                   | Codesigning Flag                  |
|
| trainer                           | Convert xcodebuild plist files to |
47870      |
|                                   | JUnit reports                     |
|
| aws_s3                            | Upload IPA and APK to S3          |
43270      |
```

bugsnag 28463		Uploads dSYM files to Bugsnag
update_provisioning_profile_speci 28185		Update the provisioning profile
fier		in the Xcode Project file for a
		specified target
changelog 25493		Automate changes to your project
		CHANGELOG.md
tpa 25201		TPA gives you advanced user
		behaviour analytics, app
		distribution, crash analytics and
		more
appicon 23630		Generate required icon sizes and
		iconset from a master application
		icon.
increment_version_code 23421		Increment the version code of
		your android project.
carthage_cache 21899		A Fastlane plugin that allows to
		cache Carthage/Build folder in
		Amazon S3.
gs_deliver 21422		Gradoservice plugin to rule apps
		releases
automated_test_emulator_run 21206		Starts n AVDs based on JSON file
		config. AVDs are created and
		configured according to user
		liking before instrumentation

		test process (started either via
		shell command or gradle) and
		killed/deleted after test process
		finishes.
sentry 19344		Upload symbols to Sentry
polidea 16390		Polidea's fastlane action
aws_device_farm 16377		Run UI Tests on AWS Devicefarm
gs_project_flow_ios 14547		Plugin contains project flow code
		for code sharing between projects
prepare_build_resources 13949		Prepares certificates and
		provisioning profiles for
		building and removes them
		afterwards.
sharethemeal 13610		ShareTheMeal
commit_android_version_bump 11741		This Android plugins allow you to
		commit every modification done in
		your build.gradle file during the
		execution of a lane. In fast, it
		do the same as the
		commit_version_bump action, but
		for Android
badge 11197		Add a badge overlay to your app
		icon
synx 11076		Organise your Xcode project

	folder to match your Xcode
	groups.
review_time 10929	Fetches live iOS and macOS review
	times from appreviewtimes.com
localization 10011	Export/import app localizations
	with help of xcodebuild
	-exportLocalizations/-importLocal
	izations tool
xcake 9741	Create your Xcode projects
	automatically using a stupid
	simple DSL.
get_version_name 9727	Get the version name of an
	Android project.
ruby 9685	Useful fastlane actions for Ruby
	projects
applivery 9427	Upload new build to Applivery
pretty_junit 9156	Pretty JUnit test results for
	your Android projects.
onesky 8791	Helps to update the translations
	of your app using the OneSky
	service.
clubmate 8043	Print the Club Mate logo in your
	build output
deploy_file_provider 8027	Prepares metadata files with

```
|                                     | structure ready for AppStore,       |
|                                     |                                     |
|                                     | PlayStore deploy                    |
|                                     |                                     |
| get_version_code                    | Get the version code of anAndroid   |
7843        |                                                                |
|                                     | project. This action will return    |
|                                     |                                     |
|                                     | the version code of your project    |
|                                     |                                     |
|                                     | according to the one set in your    |
|                                     |                                     |
|                                     | build.gradle file                   |
|                                     |                                     |
| yarn                                | Execute Yarn commands from your     |
7362        |                                                                |
|                                     | Fastfile                            |
|                                     |                                     |
| setup_fragile_tests_for_rescan      | Suppress stabile tests so that      |
6565        |                                                                |
|                                     | 'scan' can run the fragile tests    |
|                                     |                                     |
|                                     | again                               |
|
. . .
```

You can also add a specific name to search for at the end of the command line. Next, we will examine the architecture of a simple plugin, how it is structured, and how to call the plugin.

Implementing a fastlane plugin

Before we look at third-party action plugins, we will quickly examine the structure of a built-in plugin; in fact, one we have already implemented previously, add_git_tag (https://github.com/fastlane/fastlane/blob/master/fastlane/lib/fastlane/actions/add_git_tag.rb). While we used it in the previous chapter, it helps to understand the inner workings of the plugin, as well as the available mandatory and optional parameters/arguments.

You can view documentation for a specific built-in plugin/action by calling `fastlane action action_name`; for instance:

```
$ fastlane action add_git_tag
```

This would return to Command Prompt:

```
Loading documentation for add_git_tag:


+----------------------------------------------------------------------
----------------------------------------+
|                                                       add_git_tag
|
+----------------------------------------------------------------------
----------------------------------------+
| This will add an annotated git tag to the current branch
|
|
|
| This will automatically tag your build with the following format:
`<grouping>/<lane>/<prefix><build_number>`,    |
| where: - `grouping` is just to keep your tags organised under one
'folder', defaults to 'builds' - `lane` is    |
| the name of the current fastlane lane - `prefix` is anything you want to
stick in front of the version number,    |
| e.g. 'v' - `build_number` is the build number, which defaults to the
value emitted by the                        |
| `increment_build_number` action  For example for build 1234 in the
'appstore' lane it will tag the commit with    |
| `builds/appstore/1234`
|
|
|
| Created by lmirosevic, maschall
|
+----------------------------------------------------------------------
----------------------------------------+


+---------------+---------------------------+------------------------+-------
---+
|                                        add_git_tag Options
|
+---------------+---------------------------+------------------------+-------
---+
| Key           | Description               | Env Var                |
Default |
+---------------+---------------------------+------------------------+-------
---+
```

```
---+
| tag          | Define your own tag   | FL_GIT_TAG_TAG         |
|              |                       |                        |
|              | text. This will replace |                      |
|              |                       |                        |
|              | all other parameters  |                        |
|              |                       |                        |
| grouping     | Is used to keep your  | FL_GIT_TAG_GROUPING    |
builds  |      |                       |                        |
|              | tags organised under  |                        |
|              |                       |                        |
|              | one 'folder'. Defaults |                       |
|              |                       |                        |
|              | to 'builds'           |                        |
|              |                       |                        |
| prefix       | Anything you want to  | FL_GIT_TAG_PREFIX      |
|              |                       |                        |
|              | put in front of the   |                        |
|              |                       |                        |
|              | version number (e.g.  |                        |
|              |                       |                        |
|              | 'v')                  |                        |
|              |                       |                        |
| build_number | The build number.     | FL_GIT_TAG_BUILD_NUMBER |
|              |                       |                        |
|              | Defaults to the result |                       |
|              |                       |                        |
|              | of                    |                        |
|              |                       |                        |
|              | increment_build_number |                       |
|              |                       |                        |
|              | if you're using it    |                        |
|              |                       |                        |
| message      | The tag message.      | FL_GIT_TAG_MESSAGE     |
|              |                       |                        |
|              | Defaults to the tag's |                        |
|              |                       |                        |
|              | name                  |                        |
|              |                       |                        |
| commit       | The commit or object  | FL_GIT_TAG_COMMIT      |
|              |                       |                        |
|              | where the tag will be |                        |
|              |                       |                        |
|              | set. Defaults to the  |                        |
|              |                       |                        |
|              | current HEAD          |                        |
|              |                       |                        |
| force        | Force adding the tag  | FL_GIT_TAG_FORCE       | false
```

```
|
| sign            | Make a GPG-signed tag,   | FL_GIT_TAG_SIGN         | false
|
|                 | using the default        |                         |
|
|                 | e-mail address's key     |                         |
|
+-------------+------------------------+-------------------------+------
---+
```

You can see from the preceding results that, in addition to the description of the purpose of the plugin, it provides a clear, itemized list of parameters the plugin accepts. Using the notes above, you could, for instance, call the action in your Fastfile, as follows:

```
add_git_tag(
        tag:"0.1",
        grouping: "release",
        prefix: "v")
```

Another way of examining the plugin's arguments, as well as the inner workings of the action, is to actually view the plugin code itself from the list of built-in plugins (https:// docs.fastlane.tools/actions/#fastlane-actions). In this case, select the add_git_tag.rb (https://docs.fastlane.tools/actions/add_git_tag/) file. The structure may look a bit overwhelming at first, but we will break it down into the sections that you should concentrate on. You can visually segment the anatomy of the plugin as follows:

```
module Fastlane # 1
  module Actions # 2
            class AddGitTagAction < Action # 3
                  def self.run(options) # 4
                  ...
                  def self.description # 5
                  ...
                  def self.details # 6
                  ...
                  def self.available_options # 7
                  ...
                  def self.example_code # 8
                  ...
                  def self.category # 9
                  ...
                  def self.authors # 10
                  ...
                  def self.is_supported?(platform) # 11
```

You will have the `Fastlane` (1) module, as well as its sub-module, `Actions` (2). Within the sub-module, you declare a class that will correspond to the plugin's intent, (3) `AddGitTagAction`. Within the class, we define eight methods/functions:

- `self.run`
- `self.description`
- `self.details`
- `self.available_options`
- `selfexamplecode`
- `self.category`
- `self.authors`
- `self.is_supported`

self.run

The `self.run` method is the first, as well as the most important, function/method in the plugin. It details the actual commands that this plugin will execute:

1. You have the option of adding a lane context (which lane to call this within) or running without context, as shown in the following.
2. The method then assigns, to the variable tag from the options dictionary, the value of the key `:tag`, as well as `:grouping` and `:prefix`. We will discuss the options dictionary shortly.
3. The message variable is assigned the `:message` key value; if there isn't one, assign it the value of the `:tag` key we constructed in the previous step.
4. Using `cmd`, we construct our shell commands, calling the `git` tag command adding the various properties we assigned to our tag and message variables.
5. Finally, we output to Command Prompt a `UI.message` letting the client know we are adding a `git` tag and executing the `cmd` shell variable using `Actions.sh`:

```
def self.run(options)
        # lane name in lane_context could be nil because you can just call
$fastlane add_git_tag which has no context
        lane_name =
Actions.lane_context[Actions::SharedValues::LANE_NAME].to_s.delete(' ') #
no spaces allowed

        tag = options[:tag] ||
"#{options[:grouping]}/#{lane_name}/#{options[:prefix]}#{options[:build_num
```

```
ber]}"
        message = options[:message] || "#{tag} (fastlane)"

        cmd = ['git tag']

        cmd << ["-am #{message.shellescape}"]
        cmd << '--force' if options[:force]
        cmd << '-s' if options[:sign]
        cmd << "'#{tag}'"
        cmd << options[:commit].to_s if options[:commit]

        UI.message "Adding git tag '#{tag}' 🎉."
        Actions.sh(cmd.join(' '))
      end
```

self.description

This function describes the purpose of this plugin action:

```
def self.description
        "This will add an annotated git tag to the current branch"
    end
```

self.details

The details function will go into further detail, articulating how to use this action, explaining the format and the purpose of the various options/parameters:

```
def self.details
        [
            "This will automatically tag your build with the following
format: `<grouping>/<lane>/<prefix><build_number>`, where:",
            "- `grouping` is just to keep your tags organised under one
'folder', defaults to 'builds'",
            "- `lane` is the name of the current fastlane lane",
            "- `prefix` is anything you want to stick in front of the version
number, e.g. 'v'",
            "- `build_number` is the build number, which defaults to the
value emitted by the `increment_build_number` action",
            "",
            "For example for build 1234 in the 'appstore' lane it will tag
the commit with `builds/appstore/1234`"
        ].join("\n")
    end
```

self.available_options

This function details all the available parameters that the user is able to include in his/her call to this action, wrapped within a `FastlaneCore:: ConfigItem.new()` comma-separated block. As you can see from the following block of code, each argument item is broken up into the following:

- `key`: The unique key/name of the argument (that is, tag)
- `env_name`: The environment name
- `description`: Description of what the argument does
- `default_value` (optional): The default value it will use if none is passed in by the client
- `optional` (optional): States whether this argument is mandatory or not

Refer to the following code:

```
def self.available_options
        [
            FastlaneCore::ConfigItem.new(key: :tag,
                                         env_name: "FL_GIT_TAG_TAG",
                                         description: "Define your own tag
text. This will replace all other parameters",
                                         optional: true),
            FastlaneCore::ConfigItem.new(key: :grouping,
                                         env_name: "FL_GIT_TAG_GROUPING",
                                         description: "Is used to keep your
tags organised under one 'folder'. Defaults to 'builds'",
                                         default_value: 'builds'),
            FastlaneCore::ConfigItem.new(key: :force,
                                         env_name: "FL_GIT_TAG_FORCE",
                                         description: "Force adding the tag",
                                         optional: true,
                                         is_string: false,
                                         default_value: false)

        ...
```

self.example_code

This function optionally illustrates to the user how to use this action with an example code. This is a good opportunity for you to put in the sample code in an appropriately structured format, such as:

```
def self.example_code
[
    heroku(name:"newapptest")
]
end
```

self.category

This function sets which category this action belongs to, for organizational reasons; for instance:

```
def self.category
    :misc
end
```

self.authors

This function states whom the authors of this action/plugin is/are:

```
def self.authors
    ["Doron Katz"]
end
```

Now that we understand the anatomy of a plugin, we can start looking at how we would go about implementing our own plugin, which we will do next.

Creating your own fastlane plugin

The knowledge gained from the previous section will now help us design our own third-party plugin. In this section, we are going to first go over the types of plugins that the community normally accepts, as well as those that might not be approved. We will then go through the process of creating a new skeleton plugin, before embarking on our own plugin, which will be a `Heroku` plugin for creating a new Heroku project via CLI.

"Heroku is a cloud platform as a service *(PaaS), supporting several* programming languages, *that is used as a web application deployment model. Applications that are run on Heroku typically have a unique domain (typically* applicationname.herokuapp.com*) used to route HTTP requests to the correct dyno. Each of the application containers, or dynos, is spread across a "dyno grid," which consists of several servers. Heroku's [Git]*(https://en.m.wikipedia.org/wiki/Git_ (software)*) server handles application repository pushes from permitted users."* —Wikipedia)

While you may not always want to publish your new plugin out to the community, if you do decide to do so, you will need to justify why it is needed, essentially by discussing your plugin's broad appeal. The rule of thumb that the *fastlane* website states is that it should generally aim to solve developer pain points, along with good documentation and test coverage. Cases in which the community may not accept a new action include if the action does not have any broad appeal or is complex and hard to maintain.

Creating our new plugin

Let's get started on creating our new Heroku plugin. The easiest way to create a plugin in fastlane is to enter the following in a Terminal:

```
$ fastlane new_plugin
```

fastlane will then guide you through the various steps interactively to set up your plugin, including creating a Pluginfile and installing all the required dependencies your plugin will need. The three files that will be generated (and should be version controlled) include:

1. Gemfile
2. Gemfile.lock
3. fastlane/Pluginfile

Following the interactive prompts, you should get something similar to the following:

```
[09:00:04]: What would you like to be the name of your plugin?
heroku
[09:01:05]: Please enter a short summary of this fastlane plugin:
This plugin will allow you to manage your heroku apps, from creating a new
app, to listing users.
generate a new heroku project for you, leveraging the heroku CLI command-
line.
[09:02:42]: Please enter a detailed description of this fastlane plugin:
This heroku plugin leverages the *heroku cli* to manage your heroku apps
```

and users, as well as processes.

Your plugin was successfully generated at fastlane-plugin-heroku_new_project/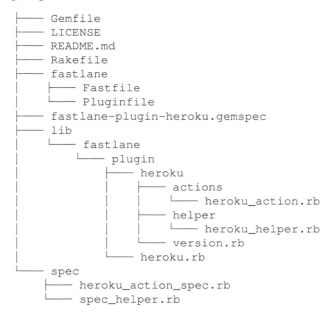

To get started with using this plugin, run

    fastlane add_plugin heroku_new_project

from a fastlane-enabled app project directory and provide the following as the path:

    /Users/doronkatz/Development/Projects/fastlane-plugin-heroku_new_project

fastlane will subsequently create a new folder for you, with the file structure you need to get going. You should version control the entire folder structure:

```
├──── Gemfile
├──── LICENSE
├──── README.md
├──── Rakefile
├──── fastlane
│      ├──── Fastfile
│      └──── Pluginfile
├──── fastlane-plugin-heroku.gemspec
├──── lib
│      └──── fastlane
│             └──── plugin
│                    ├──── heroku
│                    │      ├──── actions
│                    │      │      └──── heroku_action.rb
│                    │      ├──── helper
│                    │      │      └──── heroku_helper.rb
│                    │      └──── version.rb
│                    └──── heroku.rb
└──── spec
       ├──── heroku_action_spec.rb
       └──── spec_helper.rb
```

Creating our first Action

The primary location we will be working through will be in the `/lib/fastlane/plugin/heroku/actions` subfolder, where we can create as many actions as we need as part of our plugin. Using your favorite code editor, open up this entire folder, and then open the file `/fastlane-plugin-heroku/lib/fastlane/plugin/heroku/actions/heroku_action.rb`.

This is akin to the `https://github.com/fastlane/fastlane/tree/master/fastlane/lib/fastlane/actions` folder structure we talked about earlier, going through the pre-built plugins.

The interactive wizard we just initiated helped fill out a lot of the properties of this file, but let's go ahead and fill out the `self.run` and `self.availableoptions` functions first. For the first function, `self.run`, we are adding the (options) parameter so that we can accept parameters from the available options section. Go ahead and fill out the function as follows:

```ruby
module Fastlane
  module Actions
    class HerokuAction < Action
      def self.run(options)
        if options[:name]
          app_name = options[:name]
          cmd = "heroku apps:create \"#{app_name}\""
          UI.message "Creating heroku app '#{app_name}' 🌀."
          Actions.sh(cmd)
        else
          UI.user_error!("You need a name for your heroku app")
        end
      end
```

What this function does is:

1. Assign the value of the options parameter name to the `app_name` variable.
2. Create a `cmd` variable that calls the Heroku `cli` command to create a new app, taking the `app_name` parameter as the name of the app:

   ```
   heroku apps:create \"#{app_name}\"
   ```

3. We then output a message to our console confirming that we have created a new Heroku app.
4. We finally call the `cmd` command using the shell command `Actions.sh`.

Next, we establish the single parameter our action accepts, with the function `self.available_options`:

```
def self.available_options
    [
        FastlaneCore::ConfigItem.new(key: :name,
                            env_name: "HEROKU_NAME",
                         description: "The name of your app",
                            optional: false,
                                type: String)
    ]
end
```

Open up the file `/fastlane/Fastfile`, so we can add our new action into the test lane:

```
lane :test do
  heroku(name:"newapptest")
end
```

Testing our plugin

Now we are ready to test our simple plugin. In order to run the test, you will need to make sure you have a Heroku account. Go to heroku.com (https://www.heroku.com/) and sign up for an account. Next, to install the Heroku `cli`, run the following in your Terminal:

brew install heroku/brew/heroku

Still within the Terminal, go to the root folder of your *fastlane* plugin project and install our plugin by entering:

fastlane action heroku

Your console will output the following, confirming our plugin installed successfully:

```
[09:30:46]: Installing Ruby gem 'fastlane-plugin-heroku'...
. .
[09:31:03]: Successfully installed 'fastlane-plugin-heroku'
+-------------------------------+----------+--------+
|                 Used plugins                     |
+-------------------------------+----------+--------+
| Plugin                        | Version  | Action |
+-------------------------------+----------+--------+
| fastlane-plugin-heroku        | 0.1.0    | heroku |
+-------------------------------+----------+--------+

Loading documentation for heroku:
```

```
+-----------------------------------------------------------------
--------------------------------+
|                                              heroku
|
|
+-----------------------------------------------------------------
--------------------------------+
| This plugin will allow you to manage your heroku apps, from creating a
new app, to listing users.         |
|
|
| This heroku plugin leverages the *heroku cli* to manage your heroku apps
and users, as well as processes. |
|
|
| Created by Doron Katz
|
+-----------------------------------------------------------------
--------------------------------+


+------+----------------------+------------+---------+
|                  heroku Options                    |
+------+----------------------+------------+---------+
| Key  | Description          | Env Var    | Default |
+------+----------------------+------------+---------+
| name | The name of your app | HEROKU_NAME |        |
+------+----------------------+------------+---------+


+-------------------------------------------------+
|               heroku Return Value               |
+-------------------------------------------------+
| Confirmation of the app being created in heroku |
+-------------------------------------------------+
```

Now we can test our action using the auto-generated Fastfile, which we had amended to pass in a name for our new project. Run the following in Command Prompt:

```
fastlane test
```

You will get the following result on your console:

```
+------------------------+---------+--------+
|              Used plugins               |
+------------------------+---------+--------+
| Plugin                 | Version | Action |
+------------------------+---------+--------+
| fastlane-plugin-heroku | 0.1.0   | heroku |
+------------------------+---------+--------+
```

```
[09:35:28]: Driving the lane 'test'  🚀
[09:35:28]: --------------------
[09:35:28]: --- Step: heroku ---
[09:35:28]: --------------------
[09:35:28]: Creating heroku app 'mysamplefastlaneapp'  🔍.
[09:35:28]: $ heroku apps:create "mysamplefastlaneapp"
[09:35:32]: > Creating mysamplefastlaneapp... done
[09:35:32]: > https://mysamplefastlaneapp.herokuapp.com/  |
https://git.heroku.com/mysamplefastlaneapp.git


+------+--------+-------------+
|        fastlane summary      |
+------+--------+-------------+
| Step | Action | Time (in s) |
+------+--------+-------------+
| 1    | heroku | 3           |
+------+--------+-------------+


[09:35:32]: fastlane.tools finished successfully  🎉
```

And there you have it; your first action plugin. Of course, this is quite a contrived example, and you will need to do more in order to publish the plugin to the community, as we will discuss next.

Publishing your plugin

Before you publish your plugin, beyond what we had just accomplished, you will also need to:

- Add more defensive code to ensure you cover situations such as the user not having installed the Heroku `cli`, and perhaps also installing the `cli` plugin in that case
- Add test cases to demonstrate you have covered multiple scenarios as part of your coverage, to make your plugin community-ready
- Finally, ensure that you document your plugin comprehensively in the README.md file, similar to the following README of the prominent community plugin fastlane-cosigner: https://github.com/Mindera/fastlane-plugin-cosigner/blob/master/README.md

You have two options for publishing your plugin. The first (and recommended) way is via `https://rubygems.org/`, which entails:

1. Creating an account at `RubyGems.org`.
2. Running the following to generate a new plugin folder structure for you:

```
fastlane add_plugin [name]
```

3. Publishing your plugin to a GitHub repository.
4. Updating the `fastlane-plugin-plugin_name.gemspec` file to point the home page to your GitHub repository.
5. Running the following:

```
$ bundle install
$ rake install
$ rake release
```

The second option, as far as publishing is concerned, is to make your plugin available via GitHub by asking your users to add the following to the Pluginfile:

```
gem "fastlane-plugin-[plugin_name]", git:
"https://github.com/[user]/[plugin_name]"
```

Summary

This chapter guided you through understanding the fastlane third-party plugin community and the anatomy of a plugin, before embarking on creating and publishing your own plugin. More importantly, this chapter further demonstrated how extensible fastlane is as a toolchain platform for fitting in with your specific workflow, showing you how vibrant its community is. While this chapter demonstrated how to work with custom actions, our next chapter will focus on how to customize our integration of Slack to create a more robust communications notification for our continuous delivery workflow.

17
Integrating Slack into the fastlane Workflow

An important component of fastlane is being able to notify the appropriate stakeholders of the various actions and their outcomes, such as when you have received successful or problematic unit test results, when a new commit has just occurred, or when a new distribution is about to be released internally or externally. Either way, fastlane supports a more transparent and collaborative continuous delivery workflow, and in this chapter, we are going to focus on one of the most popular contemporary software collaboration tools, an instant-messaging client, and the platform known as **Slack** (https://slack.com/).

This chapter will focus on how to integrate Slack at appropriate key points of our workflow, to enable our stakeholders to become more informed of the progress of our development and delivery processes. The objective of this chapter is to learn how to integrate various Slack actions into our existing fastlane workflow so that we can further inform our stakeholders through communicating and publishing status updates into our various Slack channels.

In this chapter, you will look at the following topics:

- Introduction to Slack as a developer's communications platform of choice
- Configuring Slack hooks to connect to fastlane
- Adding various Slack actions into our fastlane workflow

Introducing Slack – a developer's communications platform of choice

You may or may not have come across Slack before, but over the past few years, Slack has emerged as the *de facto* communications platform of choice for contemporary software teams, especially startups. An ominous trend over the last few years has been the decline in the use of emails for teams to communicate with, and interestingly enough, this trend is also seen among the younger generation in nonworking environments, opting to leverage social media and text messages in lieu of emails and phone calls:

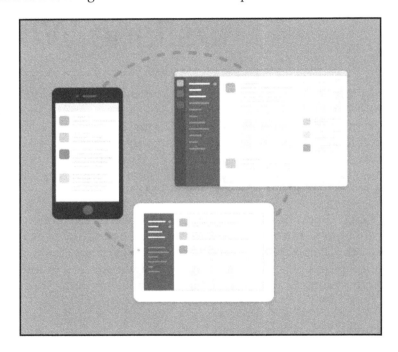

Released in late 2014, Slack emerged as the developer's favorite tool for communication ahead of the likes of the more mature platforms, such as Skype and HipChat, dethroning even Google Chat/Hangouts because of its robust extensibility. That is, in addition to being an elegant and easy to use tool, segmented by public and private channels, as well as direct messaging, Slack is built with the purpose of being able to integrate other platforms as plugins, as well as being able to integrate itself into other platforms.

Inject Slack into this workflow and it will act as an informative conduit bot. In contrast to humans communicating (that is, developer to developer) via the platform, `bots` have emerged as the platform's most innovative and essential agent. Bots can be thought of—as Slack suggests—as virtual team members that you can send a direct message to.

For example, you can have a bot that you can send a direct message to using simple English to schedule a meeting with other team members, and it will create a calendar event and invite the intended attendees. Taking a look at the Slack bot marketplace, you can appreciate how vibrant the third-party community is:

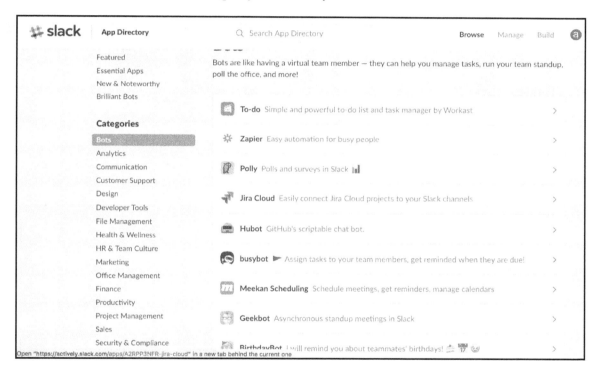

Looking at a typical development environment, teams usually employ the following technology platform stacks:

- **JIRA** (`https://www.atlassian.com/`) by Atlassian for project management, distributing tickets and user stories across the development team
- GitHub/GitLab for source control management
- Various server configurations, from Jenkins for the CI to hosting the team's application backend

Leveraging the **jira bot** (`https://slack.com/apps/A2RPP3NFR-jira-cloud`), rather than emailing users when a ticket's status changes, the bot could inform the specific developer group of status updates and comments right within the appropriate Slack channel. Developers would thereby be able to keep up to date with JIRA and the project without leaving Slack:

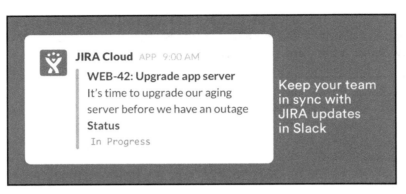

Similarly, taking a look at the `GitHub bot`, developers would be notified of post commits, pull requests, and the essential activities right from within Slack, with issues posted to the nominated channel:

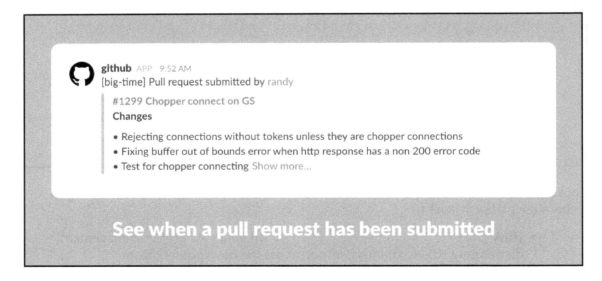

The Jenkins CI, which we covered in earlier chapters, has its own `bot` as well to inform stakeholders of updates to the various continuous integration activities that are triggered regularly.

As you can see, Slack is an invaluable communications tool for development teams, a more modern and robust approach to project communications. Next, we are going to configure Slack so that we can connect to it from fastlane.

Configuring Slack webhooks to connect to fastlane

If you don't already have a Slack account and workspace, go ahead and create one by going to `https://slack.com/`. Once you've created your workspace and added a few channels, you will create an incoming webhook, which will expose a custom token for fastlane to leverage to post messages to specific channels.

Incoming webhooks are a simple way to post messages from external sources into Slack. They make use of normal HTTP requests with JSON payloads, which includes the message and a few other optional details.

From either your Slack desktop app or via the website, once logged in, go to **Custom Integrations** | **Incoming WebHooks** to commence configuring and exposing our Webhook URL.

Following the instructions on the subsequent page, you should get a Webhook URL that you will need to note down, as we will be using it shortly. Feel free to customize the name and icons of your new webhook bot, if you want:

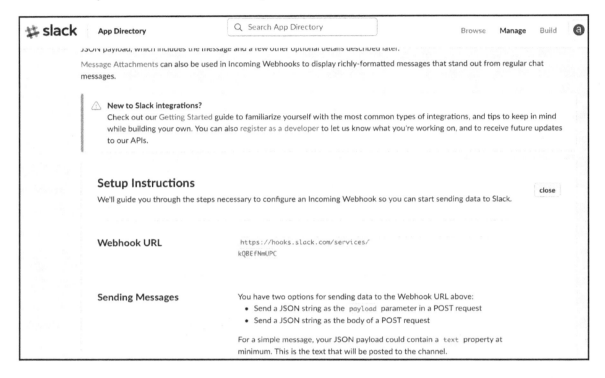

Now we have set up everything we need on Slack, let's move to our fastlane environment, and in particular our Fastfile, in order to start more fully integrating Slack.

Adding Slack actions into our workflow

We will be working with the in-built `slack action` and calling it within our Fastfile, so go ahead and open up the file. The first thing we are going to do is create a private lane, which is a lane that can't be called from the command line (or externally), but only from within another lane. At the bottom of the file, add the following:

```
private_lane :slack do |options|
    message = options[:message]
    success = options[:success]
    payload = options[:payload]
```

```
version     = get_version_number(xcodeproj: "Client.xcodeproj")
build       = get_build_number(xcodeproj: "Client.xcodeproj")
slack(
  message: message + " :" + version + ":" + build,
  slack_url: "https://YOUR_WEBHOOK_URL",
  success: success,
  payload: payload)
end
```

What we are doing here is creating a generic function called slack that we can call by passing arguments depending on the type of Slack message we want to convey. Make sure you replace the slack_url key with the value of your own webhook URL.

You could also place the slack_url in your AppFile if you wanted to separate the specific environment variables from the implementation of the Fastfile.

Now, to call this private lane, we will first create a Slack message posting on our testlane, right after the scan call to let our team know that our test ran successfully. Amend your test lane as follows (note that we are using the action name scan instead of run_tests as scan is an alias of run_tests):

```
desc "Runs all the tests"
  lane :test do
    scan
    slack(message: "Successfuly ran all the unit tests", success: true,
payload: {})

  end
```

Run this lane from the Command Prompt, and you should get the following back:

```
[13:35:25]: -------------------------------------------------
[13:35:25]: --- Step: Verifying required fastlane version ---
[13:35:25]: -------------------------------------------------
[13:35:25]: Your fastlane version 2.64.0 matches the minimum requirement of
2.41.0
[13:35:25]: -------------------------------
[13:35:25]: --- Step: default_platform ---
[13:35:25]: -------------------------------
[13:35:25]: Driving the lane 'ios test' 🚀
[13:35:25]: -------------------------------
[13:35:25]: --- Step: update_fastlane ---
[13:35:25]: -------------------------------
[13:35:25]: Looking for updates for fastlane...
[13:35:28]: Nothing to update ✅
[13:35:28]:
```

```
[13:35:28]: --------------------
[13:35:28]: --- Step: match ---
[13:35:28]: --------------------
...
+-----------------------+-----------------------------------------------------
------+
|                               Summary for scan 2.64.0
|
+-----------------------+-----------------------------------------------------
------+
| scheme                | Fennec
|
| devices               | ["iPhone 7s", "iPhone 7"]
|
| project               | Client.xcodeproj
|
| clean                 | true
|
| open_report           | true
|
| output_types          | html
|
| derived_data_path     |
/Users/doronkatz/Library/Developer/Xcode/DerivedData   |
|                       | /Client-fbzuyxhiifcmtcdzbwjjmexdybae
|
| skip_build            | false
|
| output_directory      | ./fastlane/test_output
|
| buildlog_path         | ~/Library/Logs/scan
|
| include_simulator_logs | false
|
| skip_slack            | false
|
| slack_only_on_failure | false
|
| use_clang_report_name | false
|
| fail_build            | true
|
| xcode_path            | /Applications/Xcode.app
|
+-----------------------+-----------------------------------------------------
------+

[13:35:45]: $ set -o pipefail && env NSUnbufferedIO=YES xcodebuild -scheme
```

```
Fennec -project Client.xcodeproj -destination 'platform=iOS
Simulator,id=FE616E17-4058-4F9A-87C6-DF949A0714F8' -derivedDataPath
'/Users/doronkatz/Library/Developer/Xcode/DerivedData/Client-
fbzuyxhiifcmtcdzbwjjmexdybae' clean build test | tee
'/Users/doronkatz/Library/Logs/scan/Client-Fennec.log' | xcpretty  --report
html --output '/Users/doronkatz/Development/Projects/firefox-
ios/fastlane/test_output/report.html' --report junit --output
'/var/folders/68/946ywfgx3jq3bwhy02std9tc0000gn/T/junit_report20171107-5408
2-19de92a'
[13:35:45]: > Loading...
[13:35:47]: > Check Dependencies
[13:35:47]: > Check Dependencies
[13:35:47]: > Cleaning Client/Shared [Fennec]
[13:35:47]: > Check Dependencies
[13:35:47]: > Check Dependencies
[13:35:47]: > Cleaning Client/Storage [Fennec]
[13:35:47]: > Check Dependencies
[13:35:47]: > Cleaning Client/Telemetry [Fennec]
[13:35:47]: > Check Dependencies
[13:35:47]: > Cleaning Client/Account [Fennec]
[13:35:47]: > Check Dependencies
[13:35:47]: > Cleaning Client/Sync [Fennec]
[13:35:47]: > Check Dependencies
[13:35:47]: > Cleaning Client/ReadingList [Fennec]
[13:35:47]: > Check Dependencies
[13:35:47]: > Cleaning Client/Client [Fennec]
[13:35:47]: > Check Dependencies
[13:35:48]: > Clean Succeeded
[13:35:48]: > Building Client/Shared [Fennec]
[13:35:48]: > Check Dependencies
...
[13:45:09]: > ✓ testInsertWithNoURLOrTitle (0.024 seconds)
[13:45:09]: > ✓ testInsertWithURLOnly (0.022 seconds)
[13:45:09]: > TestBrowserDB
[13:45:09]: > ✓ testMovesDB (0.052 seconds)
[13:45:09]: > TestDeferredSqlite
[13:45:09]: > ✓ testCancelling (0.002 seconds)
[13:45:09]: > TestFaviconsTable
[13:45:09]: > ✓ testFaviconsTable (0.030 seconds)
[13:45:09]: > TestSQLiteBookmarks
[13:45:09]: > ✓ testBookmarks (0.043 seconds)
[13:45:09]: > ✓ testBufferStorage (0.043 seconds)
[13:45:09]: > ✓ testLocalAndMirror (0.076 seconds)
[13:45:09]: > ✓ testRecursiveAndURLDelete (0.075 seconds)
[13:45:09]: > ✓ testTreeBuilding (0.052 seconds)
...
[13:59:55]: --------------------------------
```

```
[13:59:55]: --- Step: get_version_number ---
[13:59:55]: ------------------------------
[13:59:55]: $ cd /Users/doronkatz/Development/Projects/firefox-ios &&
agvtool what-marketing-version -terse
[13:59:56]: > "Client.xcodeproj/../Account/Info.plist"=8.0
[13:59:56]: > "Client.xcodeproj/../AccountTests/Info.plist"=8.0
[13:59:56]: > "Client.xcodeproj/../Client/Info.plist"=8.0
[13:59:56]: > "Client.xcodeproj/../ClientTests/Info.plist"=8.0
[13:59:56]: > "Client.xcodeproj/../FirefoxFastlaneTests/Info.plist"=1.0
[13:59:56]: > "Client.xcodeproj/../FirefoxUITests/Info.plist"=1.0
[13:59:56]: > "Client.xcodeproj/../ReadingList/Info.plist"=8.0
[13:59:56]: > "Client.xcodeproj/../ReadingListTests/Info.plist"=8.0
[13:59:56]: > "Client.xcodeproj/../Shared/Supporting Files/Info.plist"=8.0
[13:59:56]: > "Client.xcodeproj/../SharedTests/Info.plist"=8.0
[13:59:56]: > "Client.xcodeproj/../Storage/Info.plist"=8.0
[13:59:56]: > "Client.xcodeproj/../StoragePerfTests/Info.plist"=8.0
[13:59:56]: > "Client.xcodeproj/../StorageTests/Info.plist"=8.0
[13:59:56]: > "Client.xcodeproj/../Sync/Info.plist"=8.0
[13:59:57]: > "Client.xcodeproj/../SyncTests/Info.plist"=8.0
[13:59:57]: > "Client.xcodeproj/../Telemetry/Info.plist"=1.0
[13:59:57]: > "Client.xcodeproj/../TelemetryTests/Info.plist"=1.0
[13:59:57]: > "Client.xcodeproj/../UITests/Info.plist"=8.0
[13:59:57]: > "Client.xcodeproj/../XCUITests/Info.plist"=8.0
[13:59:57]: ------------------------------
[13:59:57]: --- Step: get_build_number ---
[13:59:57]: ------------------------------
[13:59:57]: $ cd /Users/doronkatz/Development/Projects/firefox-ios &&
agvtool what-version -terse
[13:59:58]: > 2
[13:59:58]: --------------------
[13:59:58]: --- Step: slack ---
[13:59:58]: --------------------
[13:59:59]: Successfully sent Slack notification
[13:59:59]: Cruising back to lane 'ios test' 🚗
```

```
+-------+------------------------------------+-------------+
|                  fastlane summary                        |
+-------+------------------------------------+-------------+
| Step  | Action                             | Time (in s) |
+-------+------------------------------------+-------------+
| 1     | Verifying required fastlane        | 0           |
|       | version                            |             |
| 2     | default_platform                   | 0           |
| 3     | update_fastlane                    | 2           |
| 4     | match                              | 6           |
| 5     | Switch to ios slack lane | 0                      |
| 6     | get_version_number                 | 1           |
```

```
| 7     | get_build_number                    | 0           |
| 8     | slack                               | 1           |
+-------+-------------------------------------+-------------+
```

`[13:59:59]: fastlane.tools finished successfully`

On top of those results, if you have your Slack client open on either your desktop or mobile device, provided your webhook URL was successfully configured, you should get the following message pop up:

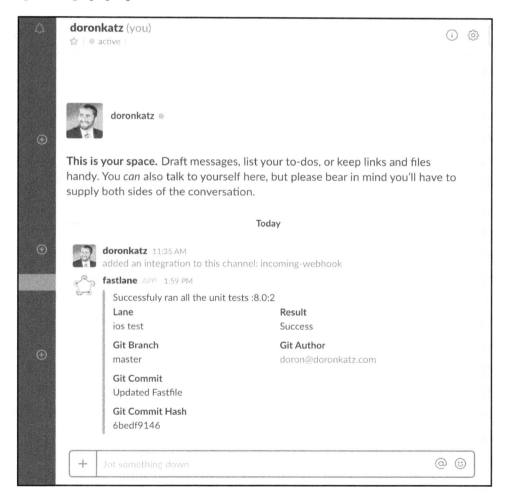

You can see how easy it is to customize our Slack messages, by injecting the version and build numbers right into our message to give greater context to our message. But more importantly, with just a little bit of effort, we were able to successfully post a meaningful notification to our developers automatically via Slack.

Let's add some more Slack messages throughout our Fastfile. Update your action lane as follows to notify our team when a new build was successfully completed:

```
lane :build do
  build_ios_app(scheme: "Fennec",
    output_name:"firefox.ipa",
    silent: false,
    export_method: "ad-hoc",
    output_directory: "./Export"
      )
  slack(message: "Successfuly completed a new build", success: true,
payload: {})

end
```

Finally, let's add to our beta lane to notify users and include the changelog within the message, along with the incremented Git and build versions, as follows (note that we are using the action name `gym` instead of `build_ios_app` to demonstrate that they are interchangeable):

```
lane :beta do
    ensure_git_status_clean
    git_pull
    register_devices(devices_file: "devices.txt")
    gym(scheme: "Fennec",
        output_name:"firefox.ipa",
        export_method: "ad-hoc",
        silent: false,
        output_directory: "./Export"
      )
    scan
    changelog = changelog_from_git_commits(pretty: '%h %s')
    testflight(
      username: "dktz@mac.com",
      app_identifier: "com.doronkatz.firefox",
      beta_app_description: changelog,
      beta_app_feedback_email: "feedback@firefoxapp.com",
      itc_provider: "abcde12345" # pass a specific value to the
iTMSTransporter -itc_provider option
      )
    increment_build_number(xcodeproj: "Client.xcodeproj")
```

```
commit_version_bump(
  message: 'Build Version Bump by fastlane',
  xcodeproj: "Client.xcodeproj",
  force: true
)
add_git_tag(grouping: "testing")
push_to_git_remote
push_git_tags
slack(message: "Distributed a new build to TestFlight.", success: true,
payload: {"changelog": changelog})

end
```

Slack action arguments

Beyond how we just used the slack action, you can also pass in the following parameters:

- message: The message that will appear on the slack posting
- channel: With this, you can either specify a ##channel or @username
- use_webhook_configured_username_and_icon: A true/false value to signify whether to use the webhook's configured username and icon or specify your own
- slack_url: The webhook URL we obtained earlier
- username: The overriding username to use instead of the webhook's default username
- icon_url: The overriding icon URL to use instead of the webhook's default use_webhook_configured_username_and_icon
- payload: This allows you to add additional payload attachments to your message
- default_payloads: This allows you to remove some of the default payloads
- success: You can use this to flag whether the build was successful or not—useful for tests and builds

Summary

In the preceding chapters, we learned about the various aspects of fastlane that help us with our continuous delivery workflow. This chapter was all about communicating the various actions to stakeholders via the popular developer communication platform Slack. We learned how to configure Slack to give us a webhook URL so that we can call the `slack` action within our various lanes.

Ideally, we should look at leveraging Slack for all the critical lane conclusions in our workflow, from successful or failed tests to internal distributions, publishing to the App Store, and even in conjunction with Git-specific actions, such as triggering a Git pull request.

In our final chapter, we take a holistic look at best practices with fastlane to further fine-tune our continuous delivery goals.

18
Continuous Delivery Best Practices

Congratulations on embarking on the challenge of learning a new toolchain, one that will empower you and your development team to automate the process of delivery, or rather continuous delivery. In taking the opportunity to learn about fastlane, you've achieved the ability to automate the process of the following:

- Creating, maintaining, and distributing provisioning and push-notification profiles and certificates
- Creating your iOS app and its associative metadata on iTunes Connect and Apple Developer Portal
- Building, packaging, and distributing your iOS app for testing, as well as the App Store
- Running unit testing as part of your continuous delivery workflow
- Generating, beautifying, and uploading screenshots of your app automatically to iTunes Connect
- Integrating the Jenkins CI as part of your continuous integration strategy
- Integrating Slack and Git, and creating and incorporating your own custom action plugins into your Fastfile

The objective of this chapter is to learn about continuous delivery best practices, specifically how to optimally manage and organize your Fastfile and its associated lanes and actions.

The following skills will be learned in this chapter:

- Organizing your lanes
- Making use of configuration files
- Private lanes and lane contexts

Organizing your lanes

We have constantly been updating our Fastfile throughout this chapter as we learned new concepts. Now is our opportunity to actually put some structure and method to our Fastfile—as it is the backbone of our continuous delivery workflow—by adding some best practices. Evaluating and tweaking your Fastfile should be part of your routine, looking for ways to optimally manage and streamline it, so let's go ahead and do that.

before_all and after_all lanes

The first and last lanes in your Fastfile should be `before_all` and `after_all`, system lanes that are called before any other lane and after any other lane, respectively. That is, if you call a beta testing or building lane, rather than duplicate an action in each of those lanes, you can place it in the `before_all` lane to start before any other lane, or the `after_all` lane for any cleaning up or exiting actions you would need to call.

Based on the types of lanes you have already established for your Fastfile, a few suggested actions for the `before_all` lane would include the following:

- Ensuring your Git status is clean (`ensuregitstatus_clean`)
- Pulling the latest Git changes (`git_pull`)
- Cleaning up and rebuilding `cocoapods/carthage`
- Running unit tests

With that in mind, we will update our Fastfile to add some common actions to our `before_all` lane, so go ahead and add the following to fastlane:

```
platform :ios do
############################ PRE ############################
before_all do

  update_fastlane
    ensure_git_status_clean
```

```
        git_pull
    carthage(

        command: "bootstrap",

        platform: "iOS",

        use_binaries: false

    )

        sync_code_signing(git_url: "git@bitbucket.org:doron_katz/my-fastlane-
    keys.git",

        type: "adhoc",

        app_identifier: "com.doronkatz.firefox")

            test

    end
```

Let's examine what we've just added to this lane:

1. We called `update_fastlane`, which is an action that updates our fastlane instance if there is a newer version.
2. Then we got the latest changes from our Git repository.
3. Next, we called carthage to ensure that our dependencies are updated and integrity-maintained.
4. We called `sync_code_signing`—as we are leveraging the Git-based provisioning management workflow—to ensure our certificates and provisioning profiles are up to date and accessible.
5. Finally, we called `test`, which is in fact a call to our public lane for testing our project.

Turning our attention to the `after_all` lane, we will look at including actions that will either clean up our environment or communicate an outcome. Some good suggestions for actions that would go into this lane include the following:

- A Slack message to let the client know whether fastlane ran successfully
- Clean your project artifacts (`clean_build_artifacts`)

- Delete unnecessary files generated during the built (that is, `ipa`, or `zoo`, `dSYM.zip`)
- Git commit and/or push, as well as `git_tag_push`

```
############################# POST #############################
after_all do |lane|
    # This block is called, only if the executed lane was successful
        changelog = changelog_from_git_commits(pretty: '%h %s')

commit_version_bump(

    message: 'Build Version Bump by fastlane',

    xcodeproj: "Client.xcodeproj",

    force: true

    )

        slack(message: "Successfuly ran fastlane with lane '#(lane).",
success: true, payload: {"lane": lane})
        push_to_git_remote

    push_git_tags

    end
```

Later on in this chapter, we will go through and clean up the rest of the lanes so that they are nicely decoupled and focused.

Managing errors and exceptions

There is another type of built-in lane that you may have noticed if you explored our Fastfile a bit more, and that is the `error` lane. This lane is really useful as it catches a lot of errors and exceptions in a "catch-all" manner if you haven't handled catching any errors from within your other lanes.

When an error or exception does occur, the following lane will be triggered, and this will be a great opportunity for us to notify our users. In our case, we are simply going to notify our users via Slack, so add the following line within the lane:

```
error do |lane, exception|

    slack(message: "fastlane encountered the error '#(exception)' emanating
```

```
from the lane '#(lane)'.", success: false, payload: {"exception": exception,
"lane": lane})


    end
```

Note that the lane exposes two arguments, `lane` and `exception`, which allow us to specify which lane the error came from and what the exception was, respectively.

Managing the rest of our lanes

So far, we've cleaned up our `before_all` and `after_all` lanes and updated our `error` lanes. Let's take this opportunity to also organize the rest of our lanes, optimizing and cleaning up each of them. Amend the rest of our Fastfile as follows:

```
#------------------------ Test ------------------------#
desc "Runs all the tests"
lane :test do
  build
  run-tests
  slack(message: "Successfuly ran all the unit tests", success: true,
payload: {})
end

#------------------------ Screenshots ------------------------#
lane :gen_screenshots do
  capture_ios_screenshots
  frame_screenshots(white: true, path: './fastlane/screenshots')
  slack(message: "Successfuly generated new screenshots", success: true,
payload: {})
end

#------------------------ Build ------------------------#
lane :build do
  build_ios_app(scheme: "Fennec",
    output_name:"firefox.ipa",
    silent: false,
    export_method: "ad-hoc",
    output_directory: "./Export"
      )
  slack(message: "Successfuly completed a new build", success: true,
payload: {})

end
```

```
############################## DISTRIBUTION
##############################

#----------------------- Beta -----------------------#
lane :beta do
  register_devices(devices_file: "devices.txt")
  build_ios_app(scheme: "Fennec",
      output_name:"firefox.ipa",
      export_method: "ad-hoc",
      silent: false,
      output_directory: "./Export"
  )
  testflight(
    username: "dktz@mac.com",
    app_identifier: "com.doronkatz.firefox",
    beta_app_description: changelog,
    beta_app_feedback_email: "feedback@firefoxapp.com",
    itc_provider: "abcde12345" # pass a specific value to the
iTMSTransporter -itc_provider option
  )
  increment_build_number(xcodeproj: "Client.xcodeproj")
  commit_version_bump(
    message: 'Build Version Bump by fastlane',
    xcodeproj: "Client.xcodeproj",
    force: true
  )
  changelog = changelog_from_git_commits(pretty: '%h %s')
  add_git_tag(grouping: "testing")
  slack(message: "Distributed new build to TestFlight.", success: true,
payload: {"changelog": changelog, "build": get_build_number, "version":
get_version_number})
  end

#----------------------- App Store -----------------------#
lane :release do
  # by default deliver will call precheck and warn you of any problems
  # if you want precheck to halt submitting to app review, you can pass
  # precheck_default_rule_level: :error
  upload_to_appstore(precheck_default_rule_level: :error)
  gen_screenshots
  create_app_online(
    username: 'dktz@mac.com',
    app_identifier: 'com.doronkatz.firefox',
    app_name: 'Firefox for iOS',
    language: 'English',
    app_version: '1.0',
    team_name: 'Doron Katz' # only necessary when in multiple teams
  )
```

```
    deliver(
      submit_for_review: true,
      force: true,
      metadata_path: "./metadata"
    )
  end

  ########################### POST ##############################
  after_all do |lane|
    changelog = changelog_from_git_commits(pretty: '%h %s')

    commit_version_bump(
      message: 'Build Version Bump by fastlane',
      xcodeproj: "Client.xcodeproj",
      force: true
    )
    slack(message: "Successfuly ran fastlane with lane '#(lane).", success:
true, payload: {"lane": lane})
    push_to_git_remote
  end

  ############################# EXCEPTION HANDLING
  ###############################
  error do |lane, exception|
    slack(message: "fastlane encountered the error '#(exception)' emanating
from the lane '#(lane)'.", success: false, payload: {"exception": exception,
"lane": lane})
  end
end

############################ PRIVATE LANES ############################
#----------------------- slack -----------------------#
private_lane :slack do |options|
    message = options[:message]
    success = options[:success]
    payload = options[:payload]
    version     = get_version_number(xcodeproj: "Client.xcodeproj")
    build       = get_build_number(xcodeproj: "Client.xcodeproj")
    slack(
      message: message + " :" + version + ":" + build,
      slack_url:
"https://hooks.slack.com/services/T0M12J6PM/B7WFYBEH2/yeXTwXWH1opDNvkQBEfNm
UPC",
      success: success,
      payload: payload)
end
```

Making use of configuration files

Throughout our book, we have covered various convenience configuration files that have made calling our action a bit easier. Some of the configuration files may be familiar to you, having leveraged them to work with the various actions, but we will cover each of the configuration files again, as we look to further optimize our Fastfile setup.

Appfile

Appfile is a convenience configuration file that stores information that you can use across your entire fastlane toolchain. It is commonly used for storing variable properties, such as your Apple ID and application identifier, decoupling the information from your Fastfile. When you initialize a new fastlane project, the toolchain should automatically generate an Appfile for you within your /fastlane folder. Go ahead and open up the file, adding your own application and account credentials, as appropriate:

```
app_identifier "com.youridentifier.firefox" # The bundle identifier of your
app
apple_id "yourappleaccount@mac.com" # Your Apple email address

team_id "YOURTEAMID" # Developer Portal Team ID

# itc_team_name "Company Name"
# itc_team_id "18742801"

...
```

To fetch a credential property from within the Fastfile, you would call it using the following syntax:

```
identifier =
CredentialsManager::AppfileConfig.try_fetch_value(:app_identifier)
team_id = CredentialsManager::AppfileConfig.try_fetch_value(:team_id)
```

Let's try and clean up our Fastfile by replacing any references to our identifier or Apple ID with references to our configuration file. Our updated Fastfile should now reference our credentials, as follows:

```
...
    testflight(
      username:
CredentialsManager::AppfileConfig.try_fetch_value(:apple_id),
      app_identifier:
CredentialsManager::AppfileConfig.try_fetch_value(:app_identifier),
```

```
        beta_app_description: changelog,
        beta_app_feedback_email: "feedback@firefoxapp.com",
        itc_provider: "abcde12345" # pass a specific value to the
iTMSTransporter -itc_provider option
        )
...
```

Deliverfile

We discussed `deliverfile` back in `Chapter 13`, *Upload Screenshots and Metadata with deliver*, as part of the process of delivering and uploading app metadata and builds to iTunes Connect. `deliverfile` can be leveraged in order to set default values for much of your metadata, across multiple languages. For instance, you can set boilerplates for release notes, as follows:

```
release_notes({
    'default' => "a new and interesting app",
    'de-FR' => "une nouvelle application intéressante"
})
description({
        'default' => "Firefox for iOS",
        'de-FR' => "firefox pour ios"
})
support_url({
        'default' => "https://firefox.com"
})
```

Any of the other folders generated by `deliverfile` can be consolidated into the preceding configuration. Consult the `deliver` documentation for more information on how you can customize your configuration file.

Gymfile

While building our app in our Fastfile, when we call our `gym` action we include quite a few parameters:

```
...
build_ios_app(scheme: "Fennec",
        output_name:"firefox.ipa",
        silent: false,
```

```
        export_method: "ad-hoc",
        output_directory: "./Export"
          )
  ...
```

Let's clean up our references to `gym` by creating our Gymfile. Enter the following in the Terminal:

`fastlane gym init`

fastlane will have created a new Gymfile for you to edit, so go ahead and open it up, adding the following to the file:

```
scheme: "Fennec"
output_name:"firefox.ipa"
silent: false
export_method: "ad-hoc"
output_directory: "./Export"
```

Now that we are storing our gym configuration settings here, we can go back into our Fastfile, replacing all our gym calls that have parameters, removing all parameters, as follows:

```
lane :build do
    gym
    slack(message: "Successfuly completed a new build", success: true,
payload: {})
  end
```

Our calls are now a lot cleaner as we don't have to duplicate code when adding to our configuration files. Moreover, if we do need to make a change, we do it once within our GymFile.

Snapfile

For generating screenshots, Snapfile allows you to set the languages and devices that you want `capture_ios_screenshots` to generate for you. Set your Snapfile as follows:

```
# A list of devices you want to take the screenshots from
devices([
"iPhone 6",
"iPhone 6 Plus",
"iPhone 7 Plus"
])
```

```
languages([
  "en-US",
  "de-DE",
  "it-IT",
  ["pt", "pt_BR"] # Portuguese with Brazilian locale
])
app_identifier "com.doronkatz.firefox" # The bundle identifier of your app
scheme "Fennec"
clear_previous_screenshots true # remove the '#' to clear all previously
generated screenshots before creating new ones
project: "./Client.xcodeproj"
number_of_retries 2
reinstall_app true
stop_after_first_error true
```

Using the `capture_ios_screenshots` documentation as your reference, feel free to configure your configuration file properties as appropriate.

Framefile

Following on from `capture_ios_screenshots`, where we generated our screenshots, we "framed" our screenshots using `frame_screenshots` back in Chapter 12, *Put Our Screenshots Inside Frames with frameit*. Within the `/screenshots` folder, we created a `Framefile.json` configuration file that allowed us to set various customizations for our screenshot framers, such as colors, fonts, and template selection:

```json
{
  "device_frame_version": "latest",
  "default": {
    "keyword": {
      "font": "./fonts/MyFont-Rg.otf"
    },
    "title": {
              "color": "#545454"
    },
    "background": "background.jpg",
    "padding": 50,
    "show_complete_frame": false,
    "stack_title" : false,
    "title_below_image": true
  },

  "data": [
    {
      "filter": "Browse the World",
```

```
      "keyword": {
        "color": "#d21559"
      }
    },
    {
      "filter": "Clean Interface",
      "keyword": {
        "color": "#feb909"
      }
    }
  ]
}
```

Matchfile

We took advantage of Matchfile way back in Chapter 5, *Sync Profiles and Certificates with match*, to manage our provisioning and certification profiles via a shared and managed Git repository. Setting our git_url and type (that is, development, ad-hoc, and App Store), calling sync_code_signing allows us to save time by passing those parameters directly within the Fastfile. Our Matchfile, which we previously worked on, should contain the following code:

```
git_url "git@bitbucket.org:yourname/my-keys.git"

type "development" # The default type, can be: appstore, adhoc or
development
```

Scanfile

run-tests was used in Chapter 14, *Automate Unit Tests with scan*, as part of our workflow to run automated tests. Where we called run-tests from within our Fastfile, we created a Scanfile configuration file to consolidate our configuration arguments:

```
scheme "Fennec"
devices ["iPhone 7s", "iPhone 7"]
project "Client.xcodeproj"
clean true
open_report true
output_types "html"
```

As we discussed in Chapter 14, *Automate Unit Tests with scan*, we provided arguments for options, such as targeting specific iOS devices and the type of reports we want to output.

Real-world examples of configuration files

Take a look at some real application examples of the configuration files we've discussed by going to the following URL:

```
https://github.com/fastlane/examples
```

Private lanes and lane contexts

You will have already seen some examples of private lanes in your educational journey through this book, and in fact, we already have a private lane, Slack. While you should already be able to work out what private lanes are, it is worth discussing when and why you would create private lanes.

Private lanes are akin to private functions/methods in modern programming languages, allowing you to protect a specific block of code from being accessed externally. In the case of fastlane, you will want to create private lanes for bits of code that you just want to call within your Fastfile and not from Command Prompt or anywhere else outside. In our case, we put our nominated method as a private lane because we don't want to expose the ability for people to call these methods from the command line, as we simply want to restrict its usability to those predefined lanes that are calling it.

Lane contexts allow you to share values in between lanes, providing you with the so-called context within your current lane. We haven't really discussed lane contexts before. Simply put, you can get access to the following globally-accessible variables from any part of your Fastfile:

```
lane_context[SharedValues::LANE_NAME]                        # The name of the
current lane (stays the same when switching lanes)
lane_context[SharedValues::BUILD_NUMBER]                     # Generated by
`increment_build_number`
lane_context[SharedValues::VERSION_NUMBER]                   # Generated by
`increment_version_number`
lane_context[SharedValues::SNAPSHOT_SCREENSHOTS_PATH]        # Generated by
_snapshot_
lane_context[SharedValues::PRODUCE_APPLE_ID]                 # The Apple ID of
the newly created app
lane_context[SharedValues::IPA_OUTPUT_PATH]                  # Generated by
_gym_
lane_context[SharedValues::DSYM_OUTPUT_PATH]                 # Generated by
_gym_
lane_context[SharedValues::SIGH_PROFILE_PATH]                # Generated by
_sigh_
```

```
lane_context[SharedValues::SIGH_UDID]                      # The UDID of the
generated provisioning profile
lane_context[SharedValues::HOCKEY_DOWNLOAD_LINK]           # Generated by
`hockey`
lane_context[SharedValues::GRADLE_APK_OUTPUT_PATH]         # Generated by
`gradle`
lane_context[SharedValues::GRADLE_ALL_APK_OUTPUT_PATHS]    # Generated by
`gradle`
lane_context[SharedValues::GRADLE_FLAVOR]                  # Generated by
`gradle`
lane_context[SharedValues::GRADLE_BUILD_TYPE]              # Generated by
`gradle`
```

To get information about the available lane variables, run `fastlane action [action_name]`.

Final words

I want to thank you for taking this journey with me, embarking on learning a new toolkit that will hopefully become part of your everyday development process. fastlane is an amazing toolkit, supported by an amazing community, and is something that has no doubt enriched the lives of many developers. I encourage you to explore the fastlane documentation some more at `https://docs.fastlane.tools`, get involved with the community, and hopefully contribute to fastlane's development yourself.

Lastly, if you ever get stuck implementing something with fastlane, don't hesitate to reach out to the community, create a new GitHub issue, and also help others if you see an issue you have encountered and resolved previously. We are certainly excited to see how this toolchain evolves as the Apple and iOS ecosystem evolves, as well as the inspiration that will promote a truly continuous delivery development workflow for developers.

Configurations, Tools, and Resources

What you will learn

The objective of this appendix is to provide additional information on topics not covered in our book in greater detail.

Skills learned

The following skills will be learned in this appendix chapter:

- Working with fastlane and Gemfiles
- Setting up two-factor authentication for your CI

Working with fastlane and Gemfiles

Leveraging a Gemfile to run fastlane lanes and actions will yield a speedier execution of the toolchain. To get started, the first thing you will need to do is install **Bundler** (https://bundler.io/) by entering the following:

```
sudo gem install bundler
```

Bundler provides a consistent environment for Ruby projects by tracking and installing the exact gems and versions that are needed. Bundler is an exit from dependency hell, and it ensures that the gems you need are present in development, staging, and production. Starting work on a project is as simple as bundle install.

(source: bundler.io)

Next, create a Gemfile in the root of your project, adding the following basic template contents:

```
source "https://rubygems.org"
gem "fastlane"
```

What is happening here is that it first tells the bundler to look for gems declared in the specific Gemfile located at https://rubygems.org by default, but you can also request that gems be fetched from a private gem server. We then request any version of fastlane. To tell bundle to actually get the gems, run bundle install:

```
$ bundle install

Using CFPropertyList 2.3.5
Using public_suffix 2.0.5
Using addressable 2.5.2
Using babosa 1.0.2
Using bundler 1.16.0.pre.3
Using claide 1.0.2
Using colored 1.2
Using colored2 3.1.2
Using highline 1.7.8
Using commander-fastlane 4.4.5
Using declarative 0.0.10
Using declarative-option 0.1.0
Using unf_ext 0.0.7.4
Using unf 0.1.4
Using domain_name 0.5.20170404
Using dotenv 2.2.1
Using excon 0.59.0
Using multipart-post 2.0.0
```

```
Using faraday 0.13.1
Using http-cookie 1.0.3
Using faraday-cookie_jar 0.0.6
Using faraday_middleware 0.12.2
Using fastimage 2.1.0
Using gh_inspector 1.0.3
Using jwt 2.1.0
Using little-plugger 1.1.4
Using multi_json 1.12.2
Using logging 2.2.2
Using memoist 0.16.0
Using os 0.9.6
Using signet 0.8.1
Using googleauth 0.6.2
Using httpclient 2.8.3
Using mime-types-data 3.2016.0521
Using mime-types 3.1
Using uber 0.1.0
Using representable 3.0.4
Using retriable 3.1.1
Using google-api-client 0.13.6
Using json 2.1.0
Using mini_magick 4.5.1
Using multi_xml 0.6.0
Using plist 3.3.0
Using rubyzip 1.2.1
Using security 0.1.3
Using slack-notifier 1.5.1
Using terminal-notifier 1.8.0
Using unicode-display_width 1.3.0
Using terminal-table 1.8.0
Using tty-screen 0.5.1
Using word_wrap 1.0.0
Using nanaimo 0.2.3
Using xcodeproj 1.5.3
Using rouge 2.0.7
Using xcpretty 0.2.8
Using xcpretty-travis-formatter 1.0.0
Using fastlane 2.64.0
Bundle complete! 1 Gemfile dependency, 57 gems now installed.
Use `bundle info [gemname]` to see where a bundled gem is installed.
```

To tell bundle to update the dependencies from the Gemfile, run `bundle update`:

```
$ bundle update

Fetching gem metadata from https://rubygems.org/.............
Fetching gem metadata from https://rubygems.org/..
```

```
Resolving dependencies......
Using CFPropertyList 2.3.5
Using public_suffix 2.0.5
Using addressable 2.5.2
Using babosa 1.0.2
Using bundler 1.16.0.pre.3
Using claide 1.0.2
Using colored 1.2
Using colored2 3.1.2
Using highline 1.7.8
Using commander-fastlane 4.4.5
Using declarative 0.0.10
Using declarative-option 0.1.0
Using unf_ext 0.0.7.4
Using unf 0.1.4
Using domain_name 0.5.20170404
Using dotenv 2.2.1
Using excon 0.59.0
Using multipart-post 2.0.0
Using faraday 0.13.1
Using http-cookie 1.0.3
Using faraday-cookie_jar 0.0.6
Using faraday_middleware 0.12.2
Using fastimage 2.1.0
Using gh_inspector 1.0.3
Using jwt 2.1.0
Using little-plugger 1.1.4
Using multi_json 1.12.2
Using logging 2.2.2
Using memoist 0.16.0
Using os 0.9.6
Using signet 0.8.1
Using googleauth 0.6.2
Using httpclient 2.8.3
Using mime-types-data 3.2016.0521
Using mime-types 3.1
Using uber 0.1.0
Using representable 3.0.4
Using retriable 3.1.1
Using google-api-client 0.13.6
Using json 2.1.0
Using mini_magick 4.5.1
Using multi_xml 0.6.0
Using plist 3.3.0
Using rubyzip 1.2.1
Using security 0.1.3
Using slack-notifier 1.5.1
Using terminal-notifier 1.8.0
```

```
Using unicode-display_width 1.3.0
Using terminal-table 1.8.0
Using tty-screen 0.5.1
Using word_wrap 1.0.0
Using nanaimo 0.2.3
Using xcodeproj 1.5.3
Using rouge 2.0.7
Using xcpretty 0.2.8
Using xcpretty-travis-formatter 1.0.0
Using fastlane 2.64.0
Bundle updated!
```

Now, for any fastlane commands, ensure that you run them as follows:

```
bundle exec fastlane [lane]Setting up two-factor authentication for your CI
```

Setting up two-factor authentication for your CI

When uploading your builds to iTunes Connect using your CI platform (Jenkins CI or Bamboo, for instance), you will need to generate an application-specific password from Apple, as you won't be able to handle prompts to enter a dynamic code each time.

To generate an application-specific password, do the following:

1. Go to `appleid.apple.com/account/manage`.
2. Select the **Generate Password** link in the **Security** section.
3. Enter a name for the new application-specific password and note down the password. Refer to the following screenshot:

4. Set the application-specific password using the
   FASTLANE_PASSWORD environment variable.

5. Generate a login session for your CI machine by running the following:

```
fastlane spaceauth -u user@;email.com
```

7. Set the generated token from the previous step to the
   FASTLANE_SESSION environment variable.

Online resources

This book has provided you with a concise but complete journey through fastlane. There are certainly more advanced topics worth exploring beyond this book, and I encourage you to explore the following:

- Using a Gemfile with Fastlane
- How does Bundler work?
- Fastlane FAQs
- Fastlane codesigning troubleshooting
- Fastlane plugin troubleshooting
- Continuous integration best practices with fastlane

Other Books You May Enjoy

If you enjoyed this book, you may be interested in these other books by Packt:

Continuous Delivery with Docker and Jenkins
Rafał Leszko

ISBN: 978-1-78712-523-0

- Get to grips with docker fundamentals and how to dockerize an application for the Continuous Delivery process
- Configure Jenkins and scale it using Docker-based agents
- Understand the principles and the technical aspects of a successful Continuous Delivery pipeline
- Create a complete Continuous Delivery process using modern tools: Docker, Jenkins, and Ansible
- Write acceptance tests using Cucumber and run them in the Docker ecosystem using Jenkins
- Create multi-container applications using Docker Compose
- Managing database changes inside the Continuous Delivery process and understand effective frameworks such as Cucumber and Flyweight
- Build clustering applications with Jenkins using Docker Swarm
- Publish a built Docker image to a Docker Registry and deploy cycles of Jenkins pipelines using community best practices

Learn iOS 11 Programming with Swift 4 - Second Edition
Craig Clayton

ISBN: 978-1-78839-075-0

- Get to grips with Swift 4 and Xcode 9, the building blocks of Apple development
- Get to know the fundamentals of Swift 4, including strings, variables, constants, and control flow
- Discover the distinctive design principles that define the iOS user experience
- Build a responsive UI and add privacy to your custom-rich notifications
- Preserve data and manipulate images with filters and effects
- Bring in SiriKit to create payment requests inside your app
- Collect valuable feedback with TestFlight before you release your apps on the App Store

Leave a review - let other readers know what you think

Please share your thoughts on this book with others by leaving a review on the site that you bought it from. If you purchased the book from Amazon, please leave us an honest review on this book's Amazon page. This is vital so that other potential readers can see and use your unbiased opinion to make purchasing decisions, we can understand what our customers think about our products, and our authors can see your feedback on the title that they have worked with Packt to create. It will only take a few minutes of your time, but is valuable to other potential customers, our authors, and Packt. Thank you!

Index

www.ingramcontent.com/pod-product-compliance
Lightning Source LLC
Chambersburg PA
CBHW080619060326
40690CB00021B/4749